M000206533

Samuel Ringgold Ward

BLACK LIVES

———

Yale University Press's Black Lives series seeks to tell the fullest range of stories about the both notable and overlooked Black figures who profoundly shaped world history. Each book in our series is intended to add a chapter to our larger understanding of the breadth of the experiences of Black people as these have unfolded through time. Using a variety of approaches, the books in this series trace the indelible contributions that individuals of African descent have made to their worlds, and explore how their lives embody and shape the changing conditions of modernity and challenge definitions of race and practices of racism in their societies.

ADVISORY BOARD

David Blight   Henry Louis Gates, Jr.   Jacqueline Goldsby
Yale University   Harvard University   Yale University

Samuel Ringgold Ward

———

A LIFE OF STRUGGLE

———

R. J. M. Blackett

———

Black Lives

Yale University Press | New Haven and London

The Black Lives series is supported with a gift
from the Germanacos Foundation.

Published with assistance from Jonathan W. Leone, Yale '86.

Copyright © 2023 by R. J. M. Blackett.
All rights reserved.
This book may not be reproduced, in whole or in part,
including illustrations, in any form (beyond that copying permitted
by Sections 107 and 108 of the U.S. Copyright Law and except by
reviewers for the public press), without written permission
from the publishers.

Yale University Press books may be purchased in quantity for
educational, business, or promotional use. For information,
please e-mail sales.press@yale.edu (U.S. office) or
sales@yaleup.co.uk (U.K. office).

Set in Freight Text Pro type by Integrated Publishing Solutions.
Printed in the United States of America.

Library of Congress Control Number: 2022938500
ISBN 978-0-300-25494-5 (hardcover : alk. paper)

A catalogue record for this book is available from the British Library.

This paper meets the requirements of ANSI/NISO Z39.48-1992
(Permanence of Paper).

10 9 8 7 6 5 4 3 2 1

To my sisters: Cheryl, Judith, Patricia, Simone, and Joanne.
I'm a lucky man.

CONTENTS

———

PREFACE

LOOKING BACK over his many years in the trenches, fighting against the twin evils of slavery and discrimination, Frederick Douglass remembered a Free Soil Party meeting he attended in Buffalo, New York, with Samuel Ringgold Ward and a number of other African Americans. Ward, he recalled, attracted attention wherever he appeared. "As an orator and thinker, he was vastly superior, I thought, to any of us, and being perfectly black and of unmixed African descent, the splendors of his intellect went directly to the glory of the race. In depth of thought, fluency of speech, readiness of wit, logical exactness, and general intelligence, Samuel R. Ward has left no successor among the colored men amongst us, and it was a sad day for our cause when he was laid low in the soil of a foreign country." There is no better description of Ward and his contributions to the struggle for Black freedom, citizenship, and equality. There is also that sad coda to Douglass's reminiscence: Ward had turned his back on America, ending his life in obscurity in Jamaica. That may explain why Ward, who gave up on America, has escaped the biographer's gaze. Searching for an explanation of Ward's later years, one observer could do no better than call it "remarkable and strange." He could have added "elusive."[1]

Samuel Ringgold Ward was born a slave on the Eastern Shore of Maryland in 1817. He and his parents escaped when he was a mere three months old to rural southern New Jersey, where they settled among other fugitives from slavery in an area dominated by Quakers. Years later, the family moved to the relative safety and anonymity of New York City, where he attended the African Free School whose alumni, including James McCune Smith, Alexander Crummell, and William Howard Day, would play prominent roles in the struggle for equal rights. Ward felt the full force of American racism when a White mob attacked an anti-slavery meeting in 1834. It was, in a way, a baptism of fire and an introduction to the struggle that would come to dominate his life for the next twenty years. He was ordained a Congregationalist minister in 1839. Two years later, he accepted the offer to minister to an all-White congregation in South Butler, New York. For many, it represented a slight crack in the edifice of racism. A couple years later, Ward moved to another all-White and larger congregation in Cortland, New York. It was in this period that he established himself as one of the leading figures in the struggle against slavery and discrimination. He was employed as a lecturer for the American Antislavery Society, and when the society split in 1840, Ward threw in his lot with the new American and Foreign Anti-Slavery Society, believing that the Constitution and involvement in the political process offered the best means of ending slavery. He was a mainstay of the Liberty Party, which would nominate him for a state assembly seat in 1848. Two days later, Ward issued his manifesto. He opposed war with Mexico and the expansion of slavery in any of the territories gained by the United States. He condemned the clause in the Wilmot Proviso that allowed for the return of escaped slaves; called for the abolition of slavery in Washington, DC; opposed the internal slave trade; insisted on the recognition of Haiti; demanded the prohibition of alcohol; and pledged to fight for the full restoration of the right to vote for the state's forty thousand Black citizens. The manifesto tells us much of what we need to know about Ward's commitment to the cause of freedom. The following year, Ward started his first newspaper, the *True American*. He merged it with Stephen Myer's *Northern Star and Freeman's Advocate* soon after to form the *Impartial Citizen*, which would become the major organ of the Liberty Party.

The anti-abolitionist riots in New York City and the constant struggle against racism wore on Ward and his contemporaries in ways that are not always easy to discern. There were moments, such as in 1839, when he considered a future in a place where the pall of racism was not so heavy. He thought seriously about moving to Trinidad following the end of the Apprenticeship Scheme, which officially ended slavery there in 1838, but in the end chose to stay and fight. There were, however, constant reminders of the growing political influence of American slavery. The Supreme Court's decision in the *Prigg* case in 1842 weighed heavily on him. All this coincided with his discovery that he had been born a slave, something his parents had kept from him. He was now no longer a free Black, as he had thought, but a fugitive slave, a man without free papers and vulnerable to capture and return to Maryland—a man, in effect, without a country. He took the passage of the Fugitive Slave Law in 1850 personally, as an existential threat. His public defiance of the law made him even more vulnerable. The day Ward arrived at Syracuse, after a grueling tour of the West, the city was thrown into turmoil with word that Jerry McHenry, a Missouri slave, had been captured and was being held in a local jail pending a rendition hearing. Ward and others visited Jerry in his cell. Minutes later, a crowd stormed the jail, freed Jerry, and sent him to Canada. Fearing arrest, Ward followed Jerry to Canada.

Ward would never return. He did in Canada what he had done in the United States: he became a leading voice in the newly formed

Anti-Slavery Society of Canada, which devoted much of its energy and resources to providing for the rising number of escaped slaves who were entering the country in the wake of the Fugitive Slave Law. He was also one of the founding editors of the *Provincial Freeman,* whose first number appeared in March 1853.

Ward left soon after on a tour of Britain to raise funds for the Anti-Slavery Society, leaving the newspaper in the capable hands of Mary Ann Shadd. He was a rousing success wherever he went, raising a substantial sum of money for the society and promoting the cause of abolition in the United States. He lectured widely on slavery, temperance, peace, and missionary causes. He sometimes found himself at loggerheads with British supporters of the American Antislavery Society but, by and large, he stayed clear of the controversies that continued to beset the movement. Like many other Black Americans who visited Britain, Ward moved in some heady social circles, rubbing elbows with lords and ladies who invited him to social events where he was lionized. They were fascinated by his color and size: a very black man, standing over six feet and weighing, one besotted admirer estimated, "sixteen stone." The fascination with his physical features led one fan to observe that his circle of chin whiskers could be seen only at close quarters. What such a description said about Ward's relationship with the observer one can only guess. Ward enjoyed the adulation yet never missed an opportunity to remind his audiences of his passionate commitment to the freedom of the slave and the elevation of his people. "I am devoted to black people," he told his listeners at a meeting of the Colonial Missionary Society; "I have none of the prejudices against their colour that some people have; I am married to a black woman."[2]

Although he was not closely allied with the Free-Produce Movement in the United States, Ward threw his weight behind the movement's revival while in Britain. The cultivation of sugar,

cotton, and other agricultural staples on which the British economy relied, its supporters maintained, could be more cheaply
produced by free labor in Britain's West Indian colonies, reducing
the country's reliance on slave-grown produce and thus helping
to undermine slavery where it still existed. The freedmen in places
such as the West Indies needed a guiding and helping hand if they
were to succeed. Ward's cousin Henry Highland Garnet had accepted an appointment in Sterling, Jamaica, as a missionary of
the United Presbyterian Church of Scotland just before Ward
arrived in London. Ward would soon follow. John Chandler, a
Quaker who owned land in Jamaica, offered Ward fifty acres on
the understanding he would raise crops for export. Success, Ward
and his benefactor hoped, would attract Black settlers from the
United States as well as encourage the cultivation of staples by
freedmen on the island. The fact that Ward had little experience
as an agriculturalist did not augur well for the venture.

Before sailing for Jamaica, Ward published his *Autobiography
of a Fugitive Negro: His Anti-Slavery Labours in the United States,
Canada, and England*. It took him mere weeks, cloistered in his
hotel room, to complete the lengthy manuscript. It was a remarkable feat of endurance and application. The book, as the title suggests, is divided into three parts: his American years, his brief stay
in Canada, and his tour of Britain. As such, it is an invaluable
source of information on his activities in the years up to 1855,
when he left London for Kingston. We know little about Ward's
years in Jamaica. On arrival, he settled in Kingston, where he became involved in the Baptist church. Not much was heard from
him until 1866 in the months following the Morant Bay Rebellion
of October 1865. Led by Paul Bogle, a Black small landowner, and
supported by George William Gordon, a Colored member of the
local Assembly, the rebellion was the most consequential political
event in the years since emancipation. It started as a protest by

peasants demanding more land, a demand the authorities resisted. Demonstrations outside a local courthouse turned violent when the mayor called out the militia. Shots were fired and the demonstrators retreated, only to return and set fire to the courthouse. That set in motion a rebellion resulting in the loss of scores of lives. Both Bogle and Gordon were captured and summarily executed. In a short pamphlet published in early 1866, and in testimony before a commission sent out to investigate the causes of the rebellion, Ward denounced the leaders of the rebellion and supported the actions of the governor. His position has continued to confound historians. Here was a proud Black man, who had made much of his attachment to and support of the rights of Blacks, a man who in the United States was a driving force in the movement to eliminate slavery and discrimination, taking the side of White colonists in their efforts to deny the aspirations of Black Jamaicans. We know little more of Ward's life in Jamaica.

If it is true that chronology is the biographer's best friend, then gaps in the timeline are his or her worst enemies. The many lacunae in Samuel Ringgold Ward's life may be the reason there has never been a full-blown biography of a person many contemporaries considered one of the giants of his era. Ronald K. Burke provided a few brief introductory chapters to his study of Ward's rhetoric published in 1995. Jeffrey Kerr-Ritchie has written a couple of informative essays that attempt to locate changes in Ward's ideology. Tim Watson has provided us with an informed analysis of what he calls Ward's "remarkable and strange career" in Jamaica. The present study, I can modestly claim, is the first attempt at a traditional biography. But the gaps are daunting. In his foreword to the 1970 edition of Ward's autobiography, the first since its original printing in 1855, Vincent Harding pointed to a couple of the major gaps in Ward's life story: there was little information on his early life and his marriage, and there was next to nothing on his involvement with the Liberty Party. These and other events, Harding writes, slip by in Ward's autobiography "with almost frustrating speed." At the time, Harding was amazed by how little we knew of Ward. What we did know, he writes, was "at once enigmatic and elusive." Since then, some of those gaps have been filled in, thanks largely to the work of C. Peter Ripley and his editorial staff, whose microfilm and published volumes, *The Black Abolitionist Papers,* collected and reprinted many of Ward's major speeches, editorials, and letters. Much, however, remains unknown. We know next to nothing about Ward's pastorate in Cortlandville, New York. We know a little more about his first church in Kingston, Jamaica, but nothing about his subsequent pastorates. His death remains a lasting mystery. Harding calls it a "kind of imploding alien death in which Black Americans have become so skilled."

Thirty years ago, I considered adding Ward to a series of biographical essays on nineteenth-century African Americans I was researching. Although I collected a considerable amount of information, what I did not know or could not find out about Ward prompted me to exclude him from the collection. The present time seems right for another attempt to write the life story of the elusive Mr. Ward. What we still do not know about him, we may never know.

Writing a biography in the midst of a pandemic, when visits to archives are impossible, had its own problems. Friends and colleagues helped by answering what they must have thought were interminable questions. Graham Hodges and Leslie Harris shepherded me through the thicket of New York City racial politics in the 1830s. Angie Murphy shared with me all she knows about the Jerry rescue, a pivotal event in Ward's life. Van Goose kindly sent me the page proofs of his voluminous history of antebellum Black political history. Karolyn Smardz Frost suggested leads on sources that helped me piece together Ward's years in Canada. Last but not least were my many friends in Jamaica, without whom I would not have been able to come to grips with Ward's years there. They include Swithin Wilmot, who responded to every one of my emails, some of them repetitive, even though he was suffering through dreadful performances by the West Indies cricket team. Suzanne Francis-Brown and Shani Roper pointed me to possible local sources. Jonathan Dalby, who is whiling away his retirement in France, kept such detailed records of his research in Jamaican court records that he could provide me with references to cases involving Ward. Gad Heuman helped to disentangle some of the mysteries surrounding the Morant Bay Rebellion.

My old friend from undergraduate days, Martin Crawford, read every chapter. They have benefited from his keen editorial eye and knowledge of nineteenth-century U.S. history. Angie Murphy added her touches to the first draft of the manuscript. (I would like to think she did so out of a keen interest in the topic—or was it that she felt the urge to return a favor for the many drafts of her dissertation and book manuscripts I have read?) So too did Jeffrey Kerr-Ritchie. He and I have been working in the same vineyards for years.

Archivists in lockdown still managed to respond to my inquiries even when they had little to offer. Teresa Gray of the Vanderbilt University Archives, where I had deposited all my research notes, managed to find the relevant boxes, digitize their content, and send them to me. Rachel Adams of the interlibrary loan office at Vanderbilt met every one of my challenges to find little-used nineteenth-century newspapers. This book could not have been completed without their assistance. Like me, the Maryland State Archives were stumped by Ward's life in slavery. Together, we came to the conclusion he was born in Kent County, but exactly where we do not know. Nor could we determine who his owner was. The folks at the Cortland County Historical Society knew only as much as I did about Ward's church, although they provided some useful leads on his children who were born and died in the county. Multiple federal archives in Boston and Suffolk County tried but could not find any records of Ward's insolvency case in 1851, although in his autobiography Ward mentioned he appeared in court as required by law. The moral of this story is that leads can take you down dead alleys. Persistence did not always help.

The pandemic posed one additional impediment: it denied me the opportunity to retrace the ground Ward traveled. It would have added to the story were I able to see the hamlets where the family lived in the Pine Barrens of Cumberland County, New Jersey, in the years after they fled enslavement. On a modern road atlas, I circled every town, village, and hamlet in New York where he lectured in an effort to paint a picture of his hectic itineraries. It was as close as I could get to seeing the locales for myself and experiencing the many miles he covered condemning slavery and demanding the rights of full citizenship.

In spite of the many helping and generous hands, there are still elements of Ward's life that continue to defy the best efforts of the biographer. All things considered, this is as full a story as is possible of a life that both inspires and frustrates. James McCune Smith gets the first word. Smith considered his schoolmate "the ablest thinker on his legs that Anglo-Africa has produced, whose powers of eloquence, brilliant repartee, and stubborn logic are as well known in England as in the United States."[3]

Samuel Ringgold Ward

CHAPTER 1

Taking Leave

IF SAMUEL RINGGOLD WARD suspected he had been born a
slave, he never confirmed it until the summer of 1841, when
his visiting mother revealed the fact. He was then twenty-four
years old. One can only imagine Ward's surprise when his mother,
Anne, informed Emily, Samuel's wife, that the family members
had been born slaves in Maryland. Ward told a few close friends,
but rarely spoke of it in public. The first details come from his
autobiography, published in London in October 1855: "I was born
on the 17th October 1817, in that part of Maryland, U.S., com-
monly called the Eastern Shore." Understandably, his parents
kept the exact location of their enslavement a secret for fear of
exposing themselves to recapture. Although the autobiography
filled in some of the details about his family's experiences in slavery, Ward left his public largely in the dark about his early life and
escape from slavery. Friends were free to put a heroic gloss on it.
When Ward got into a dispute with Lewis Tappan, the New York
abolitionist, over his planned visit to Britain, J. R. Johnson of
Syracuse dismissed Tappan's concerns as unwarranted and an insult to the memory of Ward's mother. "When your heroic mother

bore you in her arms, as she fled before the baby-hunters," Johnson declared, "she consecrated you by the baptism of her joyful tears; she just duly introduced you to the whole circle of suffering humanity." Ebner M. Pettit, who remembered meeting Ward in the early days of the Underground Railroad in upstate New York, penned an account of the family's escape that is nothing if not dramatic, but it contains numerous errors. Pettit writes that Ward's mother was born on a slave ship on its way to Baltimore and that she was enslaved on the Eastern Shore. Not long after she married, her husband was sold away after he refused to be whipped. Soon after, Margaret and her baby escaped with their mastiff, Watch, to New York City. It is a dramatic story of escape, but it bears little resemblance to what actually happened. Despite its embellishments, Johnson's account comes closer to the truth, if Ward is to be believed.[1]

The evidence points to Kent County, the northernmost county on the Eastern Shore, as the site of their enslavement. The area had undergone considerable economic and social change since the 1790s. Its plantation economy, based largely on the production of tobacco, had relied on a large slave workforce. Falling tobacco prices and soil erosion, however, transformed the area's economy over the following decades. Tobacco gave way to cereals that required a much smaller workforce. As a result, the enslaved population fell dramatically, from 5,433 in 1790 to 2,627 by 1850. Between 1830 and 1840, 14 percent of the enslaved population was sold at auction.[2]

Sometime toward the end of 1819, the family faced a threatened flogging because of a dispute between Ward's father, William, born around 1783, and his owner, whose name we do not know. Ward describes his father as a "pure-blooded Negro, perfectly black," who stood five foot ten. His mother, Anne, ten years her husband's senior, was part Indian, "a person of large frame," and as tall as William. She was a widow when she married William. Samuel was their second son; their first had died in infancy. Anne intervened to stop the flogging, angering the slave master, who threatened to sell both parents. But he delayed the sale, concerned that Samuel, who was a sickly child, would die without the care of his mother. Once Samuel's health was restored, and before a sale could be arranged, his parents took the decision to escape. According to Samuel's account, Anne was the driving force behind the resolution. The family fled during the summer of 1820, just before Samuel's third birthday. They headed to Greenwich, Cumberland County, New Jersey, on the banks of the Cohansey River, overlooking the Delaware Bay. The short journey was relatively uneventful. Ward later recalled they met a young man, a neighbor of their master, who tried to force them to return, but his parents left him the worse for wear.[3]

Slavery could not contain Ward's immediate or extended family. Samuel's family flight precipitated a series of escapes by the extended family over the next two years. There are few other instances of such organized flights from the Upper South. In late 1822 or early 1823, a husband and wife, members of the extended Ward family, escaped to York County, Pennsylvania, where, in September 1823, Thomas Myers Decatur Ward was born on a farm in Hanover. Thomas went on to become a prominent figure in the African Methodist Episcopal Church. After he was licensed to preach, the church sent Thomas to California as a missionary where, in 1868, he was elected bishop. Four years later, he became episcopal superintendent of the Pacific coast. Thomas would go on to hold many appointments in the South during Reconstruction.[4]

Months after Thomas's parents fled to Pennsylvania, a group of eleven members of the Trusty family, cousins to the Wards, fled Kent County, possibly following the route taken by the Wards to New Jersey via Wilmington, Delaware. The group included George,

Henrietta, their son Henry, and seven aunts and uncles. From New Jersey, Henry and his parents headed first to New Hope, Pennsylvania, where they remained for a few months before moving to New York City. The uncles and aunts opted to join Samuel and his parents in Cumberland County. Once in New York City, George, fearing possible recapture, changed their name to Garnet.[5]

Those fleeing slavery from Kent and Queen Anne's County, Maryland and middle Delaware, sometimes headed for southern New Jersey, as Ward later observed, because they knew it was free territory, a place where a "number of blacks [and Quakers] lived." Blacks had established communities such as Springtown and Gouldtown anchored by African Methodist Episcopal (AME) churches. The Wards settled in Springtown, a rural hamlet not far from Greenwich established around the time of the family's arrival. It and Othello, another Black settlement west of Springtown, became starting points on the Underground Railroad. The family later moved to Waldon's Landing, where Samuel attended school. The Wards' second son, Isiah Harper Ward, was born there in April 1822.[6]

William introduced Samuel to the finer points of gardening. Ward would grow almost rhapsodic in his recollections of the time spent in New Jersey, following his father around the family's garden with "fond childish delight." The plants, flowers, and shrubs he thought of as his father's creation. It was there that he learned valuable lessons: "to use the hoe, to spell in three syllables, and to read the first chapter of John's Gospel, and my figures." Ward would return to the memory of this rural idyll whenever times got hard, as they frequently did. On these occasions, he longed for a simpler time when he could retreat to his own piece of ground. Tilling the soil became a metaphor for escape from hardships and disappointments. As he wrote almost plaintively in 1855, had "I clung to the use of the hoe, instead of aspiring to a love of books, I might by this time have been somebody." Ward also implied that John's Gospel imposed on him a burden, one he bore willingly and unreservedly: to be a voice—sometimes a lone voice—crying in the wilderness against slavery and racial oppression.[7]

The quiet of Springtown was shattered in 1826 when slave catchers descended on the hamlet and took one of the extended family, whose name we do not know, back to Maryland. Soon after his return to slavery, he was on the move again, this time putting greater distance between himself and the Eastern Shore. His capture prompted Samuel's family to leave Springtown. They headed directly for New York City, arriving at the Garnets' apartment at 137 Leonard Street in early August 1826. The family soon moved into their own accommodation in the Five Points area in lower Manhattan. Exchanging the quiet, rural villages of New Jersey for the bustle of New York City must have come as something of a shock. The narrow streets of Five Points, in the jaundiced view of Charles Dickens, were permeated "everywhere with dirt and filth." Outbreaks of yellow fever in the 1820s were followed by a devastating cholera epidemic in 1832, and a major fire in 1835 leveled nineteen blocks of Lower Manhattan.

Yet Black New York City in the late 1820s was a vibrant place in spite of discrimination and a hostile white working-class population. By 1830, there were roughly fourteen thousand African Americans in a city of two hundred thousand. Law and custom denied them the right to ride city omnibuses and, like other former slaves, the Wards and Garnets lived in constant fear of kidnapping. *Freedom's Journal*, the first Black newspaper, appeared not long after the Wards' arrival. There were a number of Black churches: Episcopalian, Methodist, and Presbyterian. Blacks organized what would become the African Methodist Episcopalian

Church in 1821. Three years later, Samuel Cornish, co-editor of *Freedom's Journal,* became pastor of a new Presbyterian congregation. Social and mutual benefit societies, their membership both male and female, catered to the needs of the community. Four benevolent societies, all named for prominent British or American abolitionists, were chartered by the state in this period. Connected to the Black public school, the African Dorcas Society provided clothes and other support to the needy. Within a year of the Wards' arrival, Blacks in the city put on a massive two-day celebration to commemorate the final emancipation of slaves in the state. On the second day, three thousand to four thousand marched, to the accompaniment of music, to the AME church, where they listened to speeches. James McCune Smith described the celebrations as "full souled, full-voiced shouting for joy, and marching through the crowded streets, with feet jubilant with songs of freedom."[8]

Samuel enrolled in the African Free School No. 2 on Mulberry Street taught by Charles C. Andrews, an expatriate Englishman. The first school for Black children had opened its doors in 1787 under the auspices of the New York Manumission Society. Fire destroyed the school in 1814. Rebuilt the following year on land donated by the city, the new school was known as the African Free School No. 1. Five years later, African Free School No. 2 opened. The school provided a wide array of courses beyond the traditional fare. Its curriculum included courses in astronomy and natural history. Later, classes in navigational skills and mapping were added, offering training for those with an eye on a future at sea. The school produced an impressive roster of alumni who would go on to play leading roles in politics, education, culture, and civil affairs. They included Alexander Crummell, an Episcopalian minister who became the first bishop of Liberia. Denied admission to an American Episcopalian seminary, Crummell graduated from Cambridge University. William Howard Day went on to Oberlin College and a career in education, becoming the first Black to be elected superintendent of schools in Harrisburg, Pennsylvania, at the end of the century. No American medical school would admit James McCune Smith, so he enrolled in Glasgow University, where he received three degrees. Smith returned to New York City after graduation and established a successful medical practice. The Reason brothers, Patrick and Charles, were also contemporaries of Ward. Patrick became a prominent engraver; Charles was the first African American hired as a professor at an American college. He taught French at Central College in Mc-Grawville, New York. George T. Downing became a prominent restaurateur with dining establishments in New York City and Washington, DC. Earlier graduates of the school included Ira Aldridge, the Shakespearean actor who would leave his mark on the stages of Europe. Samuel would come to work closely (and sometimes cross swords) with many of his schoolmates.[9]

The slave owner who claimed the Garnets had not given up on retaking the family. Sometime in 1829, there was a knock on their apartment door. When George answered, a white man whom he did not recognize, but who he suspected was a slave catcher, asked if a George Testy lived there. He said he did and agreed to fetch him. Instead, George jumped through a second-floor window into the yard of the Crummells next door and made his escape. Henrietta hid with a neighborhood grocer. The slave catchers took Henry's sister but later released her. Henry happened to be at sea at the time. When he returned soon after and heard the news of the attempted kidnapping of his family, he bought a knife and roamed the streets looking for the slave catchers. Friends talked him out of it and took him out of the city to Long Island for his protection. A year earlier, slave catchers had captured and returned two of Ward's relatives to Maryland.[10]

Samuel's family may have escaped the clutches of slave catchers, but they, like other members of their extended family, were in constant peril. The teenager nonetheless had to make his way in the world. He was encouraged to pursue his studies by George Atkinson Ward, an Englishman, about whom Ward says little other than he encouraged the lad to persevere "in spite of Negro-hate." George Ward would become one of the White men who played a pivotal role in Samuel's life. Ward found a position with Thomas Jennings, a Black merchant and tailor and a leading light in the city's burgeoning civil rights struggle. Later, he and his brother, Isiah, were hired by David Ruggles, proprietor of a successful bookstore. Ruggles was the driving force in the city's first Vigilance Committee. Born in Norwich, Connecticut, he was "one of the most daring and active conductors of the Underground Railroad." It was to Ruggles's home that the young Frederick Douglass went on his escape through the city.[11]

Encouraged by his parents, Samuel looked to a future in the ministry. He was also encouraged to apply for a teaching position at a school for Black children in Newtown, Long Island. The school was established with a bequest of $2,500 from Peter Remsen, a successful New York merchant, whose father had been one of the largest slave owners on Long Island. Remsen's school was the first for the town's small Black population, whose children were refused admission to the public schools. The school's first teacher was James W. C. Pennington, who had escaped slavery in Maryland six years earlier and had settled in Brooklyn. Pennington's experiences help to explain what Ward was about to face in his first teaching job. On the first day of school, Pennington trudged seven miles through the snow from his home only to discover that the school had not been cleaned since the builders left. As he quickly found out, the existence of a schoolhouse did not guarantee that students would attend. He had to visit homes and encourage reluctant, skeptical Black parents to send their children to school. Even those who allowed their sons to attend, Pennington later recalled, were "ignorant of the benefits" and had little "knowledge of the merits of education." More difficult to address, however, was the parents' assumption that only Whites were competent to teach. Some of the parents were surprised when Pennington appeared, for they had taken it for granted that the new teacher would be White. As if these obstacles were not enough, Pennington started the job without books or slates, which he had to buy with his own money. It is not clear if Ward had to endure similar hardships as he left no record of his experiences in Newtown. This was teaching under trying circumstances.[12]

Months after Ward began teaching, proponents of the colonization of Blacks in Liberia led the resistance to the formation of the New York American Antislavery Society (NYAAS). This was the first in a series of "public altercations." Throughout the early months of 1834, city newspapers opposed to the abolitionist cause published a series of incendiary criticisms of the movement. Abolitionists, they claimed, supported intermarriage, or what some called amalgamation, which, as Leslie Harris argues in *In the Shadow of Slavery*, was "the most provocative rallying point for anti-abolitionists." The following year, on the eve of the society's annual meeting, an editor stoked racial animosity with a declaration that abolitionists had invited "the blacks to dine with them." More than that, they also sent "their children to school" with Blacks, invited and encouraged them "to seat themselves in the same pews with white ladies; to thrust themselves into their places in steamboats, and to obtrude their aromatic persons in places where the customs of society, and, let us add, the instincts of nature, have hitherto banished them." The worst fears of anti-abolitionists were confirmed when Lewis Tappan invited Samuel Cornish, the Black Presbyterian minister, to share his pew at the Greenwich Village Presbyterian Church.

Trouble began at a Fourth of July celebration, organized by Lewis and Arthur Tappan and several Black ministers, to celebrate New York emancipation at Chatham Chapel. David Paul Brown, the Philadelphia abolitionist, had just begun his address when about a hundred young White men stormed the hall, forcing Brown to abandon his speech. Three days later, Blacks gathered at the same venue for an emancipation celebration. A group of Whites disrupted the meeting, claiming they had reserved the chapel for their use. Blacks including Ward resisted, forcing the intruders to retreat. What followed was a full-blown riot, involving seven thousand to eight thousand Whites. It lasted over five days, during which Whites destroyed homes, churches, school-houses, and businesses, including the African Society for Mutual Relief. Eliza Day was at the meeting. As her son, William Howard Day, later recalled, Blacks barricaded their windows and "watched on our arms." Neighbors heated water "to give the mob a warm reception . . . and we had a man walking up and down with a sword on his side, to give the alarm when the mob came." The Black community was under sustained attack, but its members were not cowed. This may have been "one of the largest and most violent race riots in antebellum America." The bedlam did not end until the mayor called out the militia with orders to shoot.[13]

Ward was at the meeting on July 7 when the hall was invaded. People had gathered to hear Benjamin F. Hughes, one of the founders of the Phoenix Literary Society. The seventeen-year-old Ward was one of the group of Blacks that repulsed the initial attack. "The blacks were victors," Ward boasted. "Every white man was driven from the place." A larger group returned, however, and drove the defenders out. The "public watchman" arrested Ward and a few other "lads," not the attackers, and took them to the watchhouse for the night. Later, four other Black youths were brought to the cell in which Ward was held. While they were there, the mob continued its rampage, attacking Lewis Tappan's house and throwing his furniture and bedding onto a bonfire. The next morning, Ward and the others appeared before a magistrate, whom Ward dismissed, drawing on Shakespeare's *Much Ado about Nothing,* as "a sample specimen of the New York Dogberry." The magistrate abused them before remanding them to notorious Bridewell prison, where they were housed in a filthy cell filled with hardened criminals to await another hearing. It is possible that Ward was placed with a group of eleven men captured by the New York Kidnapping Club and awaiting rendition south. The following day, Samuel's father and G. A. Ward paid the turnkey to release him. His imprisonment, Ward writes, initiated him "into the anti-slavery fraternity."[14]

The mob attack and the destructive riots were defining moments in Ward's life. He may have been too young to appreciate the gravity of the slave catchers' attack on the family in Springtown, but the violence, his stand against the mob, and his imprisonment brought home to him the depth and pervasiveness of what he would later call "Negro-hate," that "peculiar American spirit" that was "ever at his elbow." Later, he tried to place the events of 1834 in some sort of historical context, partly, one suspects, to make sense of the irreconcilable tension at the heart of the country's existence, between its declared principles of equality and the existence of slavery and discrimination. That tension would continue to gnaw away at Ward's sense of belonging and commitment to the country but never at his sense of self-worth. They had gathered on July 4, as he put it, "just fifty-eight years from the very hour that the Declaration of 1776 was made." Rather than see it for the celebration that it was, the "aristocracy of New

York" took it as an affront to all the country stood for. This is why, Ward believed, the "gentlemen of property and standing" let loose the dogs of hate on those who had assembled peacefully to celebrate the country's founding and to promote the abolition of slavery. The lad of seventeen came to understand that his future in America was nothing if not fraught.

Sometime in 1835, Ward moved to Newark, New Jersey, where he taught school for the next two and one-half years. It is possible that his parents joined the move, anxious to put some distance between themselves and racial tensions in New York City. Ward has left us no information about the school. Newark, however, like the rest of the North, was undergoing a dramatic growth in abolitionist activities. Dozens of Black auxiliaries of the American Antislavery Society were formed between 1834 and 1837. One was Newark's Colored Anti-Slavery Society. Unlike comparable societies in other Northern cities, Newark's was a Black working-class association. Its president was the Reverend Henry Dayton, a former slave. Its officers included four laborers, John D. Closson, Abraham B. Ray, Benjamin B. Woodruff, and Peter Johnson; Pompy Pratt, a sexton in the First African Methodist Church; and Jacob King, a cooper. Ward would come to play a prominent role in the society during his time in Newark. While there, he became an agent of the *Weekly Advocate*, which first appeared in 1837, and its successor, the *Colored American*, both published in New York City. It was during this time that Ward made his first impressions as a public speaker. As Ward remembers, Lewis Tappan attended the first public speech he gave to a small New York City literary society in 1837. Ward was also the main speaker at a West Indian emancipation celebration in Newark in August 1838.

Eight months earlier, he had married Emily Reynolds of New York City. We know nothing of Emily's background except that she was one year older than Samuel. Although she would become her husband's rock of support, Samuel provides only a few glimpses into their life together. Their first child, Samuel Ringgold, was born ten months later.[15]

Samuel was on the move again, this time to Poughkeepsie, New York, where he taught at a Colored Lancastrian School. A "Colored American," writing from Poughkeepsie, gave an assessment of the conditions of Blacks in the town. There was one school, a literary society, several benevolent societies, and a Sabbath school. These, he reported, almost disappeared because of disputes between different sects, differences he labeled simply as "an ism." Conditions improved in early summer 1839 when, coinciding with Ward's arrival and intervention, the "ism" disappeared. Ward, "whose acquirement in education fully qualified him," took over the school, which at the time had about two dozen pupils enrolled. By the fall, their numbers had increased to sixty-seven. Ward organized a lending library and a debating society at the school. He also encouraged the formation of a couple of female benevolent societies.[16]

Something happened, however, while the Wards were in Poughkeepsie that would sour Ward on the town—and the country. Although Ward is guarded in his comments about the event, it had all the hallmarks of "Negro-hate." Evidently, he had been invited to attend a meeting to plan the formation of a literary society. The organizer, whose name we do not know, did not include Ward's name on the list of prospective members, worried that if he did, Whites would refuse to join. This was both patronizing and insensitive. Ward knew this person well; he was a friend as well as his tutor, with whom he had been furthering his studies. Furthermore, Ward had been actively soliciting members for the society. What, Ward asked, was "the use of my acting upright, seeking to win fame, and gaining it, if in this country a professed friend, a man who goes with me to the house of God, hearing me preach, visits my house, after all treads upon me to please his neighbours?" The snub hurt Ward deeply. Ward, "acting upright" and deeply committed to self-improvement, nonetheless had to deal with such racial slights. There seemed to be no future for him and his family in America.[17]

It did not help that the family also had problems making ends meet. We have no idea how much Ward was paid as a teacher. His first school at Newtown, Long Island, had paid Pennington $200 per year, from which he had to cover the cost of materials and even books. That may have been enough salary for a frugal bachelor, but it would not have covered the cost of maintaining a family. Ward thought he could rid himself of American racism as well as ensure the future of his family elsewhere.

Soon after the incident in Poughkeepsie, Ward wrote William Burnley about the prospects of moving to Trinidad. Burnley was the largest landholder and had been a major slaveholder on the island prior to emancipation in 1834. He was also the dominant political figure in the island's legislative council. Not surprisingly, Burnley had been concerned about the future of the island's economy following emancipation, when the enslaved left plantations in droves. The Emancipation Act had set in place what was known as the Apprenticeship Scheme, a period of adjustment that was to last until 1840, during which planters would be provided with a guaranteed supply of labor. Under pressure from British abolitionists and the freed people's reluctance to continue to labor on plantations, the British government abandoned apprenticeship in 1838. With the support of the legislative council, Burnley set out on a tour of the northeastern United States and the Maritime provinces of Canada in search of labor. He met with the American Anti-Slavery Society in New York City. The society had long taken a firm stand against all efforts, especially those of the American Colonization Society, to expatriate free blacks and freed slaves.

Burnley persuaded the society that his was no colonization scheme. As the society declared, while it regretted "to see intelligent and industrious colored citizens leaving their country and their brethren in bonds," yet it felt that "if any are determined to emigrate to a tropical region . . . the island of Trinidad offers greater inducements to emigrants than any other foreign country in our knowledge." Burnley provided the society with a lengthy report on conditions in Trinidad and the benefits of immigrating to a colony whose prospects were unrivaled. As Burnley promised, any emigrant who "wishes to raise himself in the scale of society" could do so in Trinidad because of the "political and social advantages which the colored inhabitants . . . enjoy over that of any other part of the world." The island's Council, he assured his readers, was composed of Blacks (or, more correctly, Coloreds) and Whites. The colony's laws protected the free practice of religious beliefs. There were seventy-six public schools attended by students free of charge. Much of the food consumed was imported. As a result, agriculturalists had an opportunity to expand food production and so prosper. Burnley ended his report with a rosy picture of conditions and opportunities on the island. Unlike those who went to Liberia, emigrants to Trinidad, he promised, would not find themselves "shut up in a distant part of the globe, in the midst of barbarians, but surrounded by a free, happy and prosperous population. They could correspond with their friends and relatives; could safely and easily remit to them money, by order of the colonial bank of Trinidad or their agents, Messrs. Maitland, Kennedy & Co., in this city; and whenever the fancy seized [them] could as easily pay a sudden visit to [their] associates and the land of [their] birth."[18]

Hurt by his experiences in Poughkeepsie, Ward seemed determined to cut his ties with America. He requested a letter of recommendation from Joshua Leavitt of the AASS. Despite the society's endorsement of Burnley's plan, Ward was the sort of person those opposed to colonization dreaded losing. On the other hand, Ward's departure would be a boon to those who insisted that Blacks had no future in the United States. Given what he had experienced in the New York City riots four years earlier, as well as the racial insensitivity of his Poughkeepsie associate, one doubts that Ward was concerned about what his departure meant for the struggle against colonization. He was looking for a place where he could live and prosper free of racial persecution. Rather than provide him with the letter of recommendation, Leavitt persuaded the society to offer Ward an appointment as a lecturing agent of the AASS, a position he accepted. Later that year, the AASS transferred his appointment to the New York Anti-Slavery Society. Suddenly, what was gloom became a period of renewed hope. Ward began his new position in November. It involved continual travel in all sorts of weather, he remembered. Although "denied the ordinary courtesies of civilized life," he was "combating some of the most deeply seated prejudices": it was a life of purpose that held out promise. He crisscrossed the state promoting the cause. It was the life of a wanderer that took him away from home for long periods, but he took comfort in the knowledge that he was now in the thick of the fight against slavery. In addition, he was licensed to preach by the New York Congregational Association in 1839. Things were looking up. Sometime in 1840, Ward moved his family to Peterboro, New York, to be closer to one of the hubs of abolitionist activity in the state.[19]

CHAPTER 2

Finding His Voice

CENTRAL AND WESTERN NEW YORK were Ward's principal fields of operation during the 1840s. William Wells Brown recalled that Ward "either preached or lectured in every church, hall, or school" in the area. Wells Brown did not exaggerate. The area was, as Ward later observed, "the very battleground of impartial Freedom." In this "favored portion of our native country and our adopted State," Black men and women, he argued, could attain "moral eminence." Theodore Dwight Weld had given anti-slavery agents their marching orders for organizing the state: "Let us take hold of the country—the yeomanry of the *country towns*," he advised, "leaving the cities to themselves for the present, and we will soon carry the question." This they did. By the end of the decade, every county in the state, bar one, had one or more organized anti-slavery society. No other town in the state had a greater reputation as a center of abolitionist activity than Peterboro. A hamlet in Madison County with a population of about three hundred, Peterboro, under the influence of Gerrit Smith, the largest landholder in the state, was "abolitionized" totally. A visiting minister was impressed by the inhabitants' depth and commitment to abolition: there was, he wrote in 1841, "abolition indoors and out—Abolition in the Churches and Abolition in the Stores—Abolition in the field and Abolition by the wayside." In the town, Gerrit Smith observed, Blacks and Whites mixed freely: "Colored persons sit where they please in our sanctuaries and I know not a family in our village that would reject a decent colored person from their table."[1]

Peterboro offered Ward a sanctuary from the racial tensions of cities such as New York, and an opportunity to stretch his wings as an anti-slavery lecturer. Here he met and befriended a number of the giants of the anti-slavery movement, none more prominent than Gerrit Smith. Ward first met Smith at the May 1838 annual meeting of the American Anti-Slavery Society held at the Broadway Tabernacle in New York City. On the occasion, he reunited with James McCune Smith, just back from his studies at Glasgow University. Gerrit Smith took the opportunity to explain why he had abandoned colonization and the reasons for his adoption of abolition. The speech left Ward in awe of Smith's intellect and his unwavering commitment to the cause. His support for colonization, Smith confessed, had been based on the erroneous assumption that Blacks were incapable of equality. This belief stemmed from "ignorance of the colored man's heart." Had "I communed with him, instead of those, who, though they were scheming about him, nevertheless stood entirely aloof from him, I should not have been the victim of color delusion for so long a time." That all changed when Smith entered into the "sympathies and sufferings" of Black men to put his soul in their "soul's stead; and in a word to make [himself] a colored man." At that point, he saw "how crushing and murderous to all the hopes and happiness of our colored brother is the policy of expelling the colored race from this country." Colonization, he concluded, was based on a "proud, aristocratic contempt of the poor." Such empathy startled Ward; Smith was the first White man he had met who saw the world through the eyes and with the heart of a Black man. Such empathy and commitment promised to undermine social and racial barriers.[2]

The speech left a deep impression on Ward. Almost twenty years later, when he was putting together his autobiography in London without the benefit of notes, Ward reproduced the speech almost verbatim. Their friendship blossomed over the years. After a trip together in 1850, Ward wrote of Smith: "His manners are the most easy and the most affable, without any strained efforts at condescension. But I always feel, what a poor, little, ignorant fellow is Sam Ward, besides Gerrit Smith. Still it is one of the supremest pleasures allotted to me on earth, to enjoy any moment, however small, of his association." Ward was not usually prone to flattery, but in Smith's case, he meant every word. This did not mean they saw eye to eye on all issues, but on the rare occasion when Ward disagreed with his mentor, his criticism was always restrained.[3]

Ward met other prominent abolitionists following his move to Peterboro. They included William Goodell, editor of the *Friend of Man*, Beriah Green, president of the Oneida Institute, and Elizur Wright Jr., who had given up his post at the Western Reserve College and moved east to join the anti-slavery cause. He was a founding member of the AASS. Ward first heard him lecture in 1834 in New York City just before the outbreak of the riot that had engulfed the city. A small balding man who described his looks as that of a "singed cat," Wright would later join the group that broke from the AASS to form the American and Foreign Anti-Slavery Society (AFASS). There were others, including Joshua Leavitt and Simeon S. Jocelyn, who came to influence Ward's thinking on the main issues of the day, among them abolition and temperance. Within months of Ward's move to Peterboro, the AASS split over the role of women and the efficacy of organized political activity. Ward sided with those who saw the future of the movement in what came to be called Bible politics, the belief that "the government of God and earthly states should be one and the same." Ward would soon emerge as one of the leading Black proponents of the movement. Yet, while he disagreed with those who continued to reject organized political activity as the best way to achieve emancipation, he never severed connections with them. He would later pay homage to Wendell Phillips, one of the leaders of the AASS, remembering him as the person who taught him his "hornbook on the subject of slavery when [he] was a poor boy."[4]

Sometime in 1840, the New York State Anti-Slavery Society transferred Ward's agency to the Western New York Anti-Slavery Society. His field of operation covered much of the state north of Peterboro. During a tour of northern parts of the state in February 1841, Ward made a stop in South Butler, Wayne County. His audiences were so impressed with his lecture and sermon that they began negotiations with Ward to take up the pastorate of the village's small Congregational church. The village lay three miles north of the railroad between Rochester and Syracuse. According to "RNS," who knew the village well, it contained a gristmill and a large furnace plow factory worked by steam, a tannery worked by skilled mechanics, two dry goods stores, a temperance hotel, four male and two female doctors, a large school, and three churches. The inhabitants, many of them settlers from New England, had a reputation, RNS wrote, for involvement in "Modern Reform." They were, Ward reported, "God-fearing descendants of New England" living in the interior apart from the "allurements and deceptions of fashion and so had the freedom to decide for themselves what was just in accordance with the Bible." Until recently, most supported the Whig Party and were political abolitionists of what RNS called the "most frantic and rabid kind." Following his lecture, George Candee and Dr. Clarendon Campbell invited Ward to tea. Several members of the church accompanied Ward to his next lecture stop in Walcott seven miles away. After another visit in April, Ward accepted the offer. He was ordained and installed as pastor in early September.[5]

The appointment of a Black man as pastor of a White congregation was, Ward said, paraphrasing Ecclesiastes 1:9, "a new thing under the sun." The congregation's decision surprised many. Ward knew the eyes of the country were on him. Failure of what many considered a risky experiment, Ward knew, could negatively affect the anti-slavery movement as well as relations between the races. Should he acquit himself creditably, he believed the "anti-slavery movement would thereby be encouraged." Should he fail, "the cause would be loaded with reproach." The appointment, he acknowledged, was freighted with unseen consequences for "the people of colour." To fail would be to confirm to "traducers and disparagers of the Negro" that nothing could be done to improve their lot. Failure would be a "complete and triumphant answer" to those who saw no future for the Negro. If he succeeded, young Blacks would be encouraged to "qualify" themselves for positions of usefulness among their "own people." At the same time, they "might also be so situated as to do good *to* others and *for* [their] own class." He was determined not to do "mischief to . . . the anti-slavery cause, nor to that of my beloved people."

To African Americans who questioned the wisdom of accepting the position, Ward replied that it was "a sign of hope and a token of encouragement." As Christ forgave, so should Blacks. They would be measured in the eyes of God, he insisted, by their willingness to forgive their enemies. As surely as the Whites were "our enemies . . . just so surely we must forgive them or lie down forever with them, amid the torments of the same perdition." He understood their hatred, given the treatment they had received from Whites. They must endure, however, if they were to be saved from an equally debilitating hatred. His congregation in South Butler had shown the way. If White America would follow their lead, it would mitigate the animosity felt by Blacks toward Whites by eliminating the cause of that hatred. All he asked was "even-handed justice" for the Negro. Yet he would not stoop to make a special plea for the Negro, for no other people, he declared, "in a state of partial subjection ever bore subjection so well, or improved so rapidly in spite of it." The achievements of his schoolmates at the African School No. 2 provided ample proof, even if America continued to deny these gifted men, "burning with an indignant sense of their wrongs, and the enslavement of their brethren" their constitutional rights as American citizens. Ward was proud of the fact that he and his small congregation had defied racial taboos. That accomplishment might be enough to bring the country to its senses. Even if the country resisted change, Blacks must still do the things they did best. Act well your part, he pleaded, quoting Alexander Pope, for "there all the honor lies." A noble sentiment, but it was a tall order.[6]

Ward also became a missionary attached to the American Home Missionary Society (AHMS). His quarterly reports to the society detailed his successes and frustrations. His weekly sermons were well received, he reported, as were his Bible classes. There was also a Sabbath school attached to the church. He was most proud of his successes in promoting temperance. As he reported, all the members of the church were "friends of temperance" and all but one had pledged "total abstinence." During winter revivals in 1843, four new members joined the church and several others were expected to join at their "next communion." In addition, "19 persons professed to have found peace." On average, thirty-five attended Sabbath school and eighteen Bible classes. He had added close to 150 books to the Sunday school library. These successes were marred, however, by the tendency of congregants to backslide and the rising popularity of a rival, the Campbellites, otherwise known as the Church of Christ, whose numbers were increasing dramatically.[7]

During his two and one-half years at South Butler, Ward kept up a grueling anti-slavery lecturing schedule, visiting many remote villages and towns. Some of these activities raised questions among the leadership of the AHMS, not because they were opposed to the anti-slavery movement, but because of Ward's willingness to use the pulpit to get his political message across. The Sabbath and the pulpit, some at the society believed, were neither the appropriate time nor place for such activity. Ward was unapologetic. He acknowledged that he frequently spoke on the topic of the nation's shame, calling on listeners to do all they could against this "sinful institution," one that a man is no more "at liberty (mostly) to vote for . . . than he is to pray for." No man, he continued, had a greater "right to commit a sin with his vote than with any other power or instrument." Ward made it clear he would not desist, for he was obligated to preach against all sins.

The society should not have been surprised by Ward's use of the pulpit to promote abolition. His very first letter to the press was a stinging rebuke of those who took the position that, if the state endorsed and protected slavery, then the church had to go along until such time as a political decision was made to abandon it. During an anti-slavery meeting at Cazenovia, New York, in February 1841, Dr. Fordyce Rice, a friend and supporter of the "third party movement," opposed plans to boycott ministers and churches that refused to take an active role in attacking slavery. It was no way, Rice argued, to convert "intelligent and rational men." Rational men had to be reasoned with using logical presentations of the cause of the "poor and oppressed." More could be achieved by "kindness and plainness" than by condemnation.

Ward responded that the church could not wait for the state to act. In fact, the "stronger the legal and custom-sanctioned bulwark thrown about a public sin, for its defense, the more unceasing should the religious bodies of the day proclaim against it." Churches that do not are "faithless to God," for when "planting the church," the author of the Bible said, "Ye are the light of the world." The purification of the church, Ward insisted, was vital to anti-slavery ends. His church in South Butler showed the way.[8]

Yet there were signs that all was not well. The numbers of those who converted and joined the church had fallen off by 1843. Ward also seemed to have attempted but failed to attract any of the over two hundred Blacks who lived in the county. It is not clear why his efforts at harvesting Black souls failed. Throughout his tenure, his family were the only Black members of the congregation.[9]

Ward's pastoral charge in South Butler ended on November 10, 1843. For months before, he had been complaining of poor health. A "disease of the throat" made it difficult to speak. It seems to have affected him most in the winter. Ward consulted doctors in Philadelphia and New York who recommended that he "give up speaking for a while," as continual irritation of the "vocal organ" would hinder a cure. He took their advice and cancelled most of his speaking engagements for the winter of 1843. Poor health would plague Ward for the rest of his life. If an illness had saved him from being separated from his parents in slavery, recurring health problems would now periodically limit his activities. Periods of convalescence invariably followed hectic lecture schedules.[10]

There were other problems. As Ward admitted, the family struggled with poverty during their time in South Butler. This too would become a recurring problem in his life. Rarely was he ever able to make ends meet. His $25 subvention from the AHMS helped, but it was never enough. Nor were the lecture fees he managed to collect. It did not help that Ward, as he admitted, was not a good steward of his finances. In spring 1842, he informed Gerrit Smith, to whom he owed $20, that a Mr. Cotton held "a kind of mortgage" on his house in South Butler. It seems Ward owed Cotton $40. To meet his debt, Ward proposed to give Cotton the house, which was worth $70. Cotton would pay off some of Ward's other debts, including that to Smith.[11]

In debt and unable to tour, Ward moved the family south to Geneva, New York, in December 1843, where he planned to study medicine, possibly hydropathy, with two prominent practitioners, Dr. Williams, formerly of Cleveland, Ohio, and Dr. Bell, who Ward later claimed was a "white Virginian." There were regular advertisements in local newspapers offering the services of spas and other water cures. Taking the waters was a popular treatment for many ailments. As Ward later recalled, it was the skill of his preceptors that eased his throat problems, making it possible for him to preach periodically at local Congregational churches. He later became a frequent patient at spas seeking relief from his ailments. Years later, he waxed almost poetic about the curative powers of Dr. Josiah Hoskiss Stedman's water cure in Tioga County.

Ward was engaged to preach for a year at a small Geneva Congregational Church. Founded in April 1843, the church had relied on visiting ministers to fill its pulpit. James M. Duffin solicited the AHMS for a $3 subvention to help meet its obligations to Ward. That was much less than Ward had received in South Butler. It is unclear if the society granted the request, or when Ward left Geneva. It is likely he moved the family back to Peterboro, a place he knew and one in which he felt secure.[12]

Within a few months of his return to Peterboro, he was back in the thick of the political struggle against slavery, much of it centered on his work with the Liberty Party. By 1843, Ward was an important figure in the party, of which he had been one of the founding members. As opponents were fond of saying, he was its "big gun." Other African Americans played prominent roles in the party, including Ward's cousin Henry Highland Garnet, who was living in Troy, New York, and Jermain Loguen of Syracuse. Ward, however, was its most visible Black proponent. The party was formed at a meeting in Albany, New York, on April 1, 1840, during a driving snowstorm. Opponents mocked it as the "April Fool's Party."

For those who believed the Constitution was, at its core, an anti-slavery document, participation in the political system was central to the destruction of slavery. Prior to 1840, anti-slavery proponents employed, as their counterparts had done in Britain earlier, the questioning system, interrogating candidates to determine where they stood on critical issues involving slavery. The questions posed to the Whig candidate for Congress by the Lorain (Ohio) County Anti-Slavery Society were typical. Where, the society wanted to know, did he stand on slavery in the District of Columbia, the internal slave trade, the possible annexation of Texas, and the recognition of Haiti? The candidate responded that he opposed slavery, "bodily and mental," wherever it appeared and especially its existence in DC. Slavery, he declared, was "utterly irreconcilable with our much vaunted declaration that with us all men are created equal." Then came the qualifiers. As a "practical question," he cautioned, he would do nothing to "hazard the existence of our government in a vain effort to break the chains of eight thousand slaves in the District." The Union had to be preserved at all costs. He also doubted that Congress had the power to abolish the internal slave trade. While he opposed the annexation of Texas, he confessed he knew nothing about Haiti. Abolitionists also interrogated candidates for state offices.

Were they in favor of trial by jury in fugitive slave cases? Would they vote to eliminate the $250 property requirement New York had imposed on its Black citizens before they could vote? Whatever their response, the questioning had little effect on candidates once they were elected. Some suggested an alternative approach: scattering their votes among the least "reprehensible aspirants."[13]

Neither approach had much effect. As Ward put it, opponents of slavery had one of two choices, given that both Whigs and Democrats bent their knees to Southern interests: they could refrain from voting or they could form their own political party. Many opposed the formation of a new party because it would be another divisive issue that undermined abolitionist solidarity. Supporters of the proposed party had gathered at a number of earlier meetings searching for agreement on its platform and candidates. Five hundred attended a meeting in Warsaw, New York, in November 1839 and nominated James Birney, a former Alabama slaveholder, for president, and Dr. Julius LeMoyne, a prominent western Pennsylvania physician, for vice president. Birney declined the nomination, worried that the time was not ripe for independent nominations. Proponents of the new party persisted. The Albany meeting in April 1840 was a smaller affair. Birney was again nominated for president, with Thomas Earle, a Pennsylvania Quaker, as his running mate. Supporters of the new party met in Syracuse in August 1840 at a Freemen's State convention to nominate candidates for state office. Ward, attending as a delegate from Peterboro, played an active role in the proceedings. The convention agreed to vote only for those who would work for emancipation by peaceful means, those who were committed to granting Blacks the franchise, declaring that no dedicated abolitionist should vote for either the Whig or Democratic ticket, for both had "bowed down before the slaveholding and piratical power of the South." To vote for either was to prop up the slave system.[14]

The new party labored under staggering odds in the 1840 presidential campaign. Its motto, "Vote as you pray and pray as you vote," proved an inadequate call to arms. The party garnered 6,225 votes, a mere tenth of the votes cast, 40 percent coming from New York State. There were, however, local areas, particularly in New York State, such as Gerrit Smith's stronghold in Madison County, where it had a "greater impact." The party did only marginally better in the 1844 presidential elections.[15]

While it never threatened the dominance of the two major parties, the Liberty Party's insistence that slavery was a national, not a state, matter kept the issue alive. Ward, Garnet, and other Black supporters in many ways became the public face of the party in New York State. Garnet was instrumental in winning support for the party at the 1843 Negro Convention meeting in Buffalo in the face of stiff opposition from Frederick Douglass and Charles Lenox Remond who, like other supporters of Garrison, viewed participation in the political process as an endorsement of the system that protected slavery.[16]

At the 1846 state constitutional convention, both the Whigs and Democrats dangled the prospect of equal rights for Blacks if the Liberal Party agreed to cooperate with either of them. In sections of the state where the party was strong, Whigs offered to cooperate in the election of delegates to the convention. Many in both parties promised to support the removal of the $250 property qualification. The promise of Whig support included, however, an appeal to the Liberty Party not to cooperate with Democrats. While both parties promised to support the removal of the qualification, they continued to believe that Blacks were not entitled to the vote. Neither party was committed to equal rights.

When, for instance, Governor Seward denounced the property qualification in his annual message, the legislature, dominated by Whigs, voted to retain it. The Whigs were swamped in the election to the 1846 convention. Few were surprised by the outcome of the subsequent referendum: 72 percent, including a majority of Whigs, voted against the elimination of the qualification. The Liberty Party had committed to the elimination of the qualification, and its rejection by the electorate proved disastrous for the party.[17]

Ward moved his family to Cortlandville in 1846 to take up an appointment as pastor of another all-White congregation. Unlike his time in South Butler, nothing is known of Ward's activities as minister of the Cortlandville church. The appointment, however, confirmed his willingness and ability to work with an all-White congregation.

By the time they left Cortlandville in 1850, the Wards had two boys and three girls. The second boy, William Reynolds, named after Ward's father and Emily's parents, was born and died in Cortlandville. We know nothing of the first daughter, Mary. The second, Emily Smith, was born in 1848 and died in Syracuse three years later. The last child, Alice, was born toward the end of their stay in the town. It is not clear if Ward sent his children to local schools; there is no evidence that he did so. Sometime later, he would publicly praise the local academy, yet felt it would not have enrolled his son. Friends thought it strange that a man who had pushed against racial barriers and who had managed, on a couple occasions, to break through, would acknowledge defeat without a fight. More significantly, there is no evidence that young Ringgold would have been rejected had he applied. Anticipating possible rejection, Ward may have decided not to put his son through the uncertainty and possible hurt of a rejection. Friends made it clear, however, that his fears were unfounded. Young Sam, they pointed out, was "a good boy." Moreover, the days of narrow-minded prejudice were over. "Friend Ward, think better of yourself, your boy and your community," they pleaded.[18]

Despite his formative years at the African School No. 2, in New York City, Ward believed his children should be taught at home. "I am very deadly opposed to sending children from under the parental roof for education. Education is emphatically home work," for the responsibility of the parent "cannot rightly be transferred to others." Who better to educate a daughter than the mother who bore her? Why should anyone else but the mother be "charged with the treasury, the mental and moral training of that daughter?" The same applied to the son, who should be educated "under the father's eye." Yet, he acknowledged, if a school was small, taught by an experienced teacher, and students were led to feel they belonged to a "well regulated Christian family," then he would have no objections to sending his children to be educated outside the home. There was evidence, however, of larger forces at work. The years spent at Cortlandville were not the most pleasant. Ward would recall that some of his "most laborious . . . services were rendered" there, a place where he "saw more of the foolishness, wickedness, and at the same time the invincibility of American Negro-Hate" than he ever saw elsewhere.[19]

This seems a rather harsh assessment of the people of Cortlandville and of his time there. It is there that he published his newspaper, the *Imperial Citizen*. There he found a measure of peace, if not always quiet, in his church. Yet he knew that, sooner rather than later, a racial incident would intrude. One occurred in 1847. Ward, long a proponent of temperance, had joined the Cortlandville Division (#55) of the Sons of Temperance. The membership, drawn entirely from his church, was presided over by John H. Thomas, a lawyer, member of the Executive Committee of the Liberty Party of Cortlandville, and editor of the *Liberty*

Party Paper. The clerk of the church was one of the division's vice presidents, as was the deacon. Soon after Ward became a member of the village's division, the Grand Division in New York City revoked its charter for violating the rules of the order. Thomas, the "Grand Worthy Patriarch" wrote, had acted improperly. Thomas was suspended and D. G. W. Cody appointed to visit and report on what had happened at Cortlandville. Cody reported he found "chaos and confusion." Thomas insisted he had the authority to admit "who he pleased, *black or white*, old or young" and declared proudly that he had "actually initiated a COLORED MAN." Cody confiscated the Cortlandville Division's records and wrote Ward explaining his decision. Ward responded publicly, admitting he had joined the division but rejecting the claim that he had been expelled. As soon as they learned of the Sons' policy on Black membership, the division, he insisted, had voted to disband and return its charter. The church had rallied behind him.[20]

The slight nevertheless gnawed at him. He would return to the incident frequently whenever he needed an illustration of the reach and pervasiveness of Negro-hate. In early 1850, Ward republished an editorial from Douglass's *North Star* excoriating the Sons of Temperance. The Sons, Douglass argued, seemed more interested in the "building up of caste and prejudice" than in promoting temperance. It was the only way to explain their refusal to admit African Americans. Their lodges were the "very spawns of slavery." The actions of the Sons were replicated in many other institutions that shut their doors to Blacks. Where Negroes were admitted, they were "stowed away like so much lumber, in some far-distant loft in the ceiling." No matter what the color of their skin, "whether black or white or brown . . . men who can rise superior to such degrading and demoralizing treatment, have in their composition a large proportion of the material of which heroes are made." There were few White men who could go through "this

ordeal and come out unscathed." Through their actions, North-
erners needed "to take the spirit of slavery" out of their hearts.

C. Robinson of Clarendon, Orleans County, west of Rochester,
responded, challenging Douglass and Ward on the best means to
address these issues. In what is a rather sympathetic letter, but
nonetheless emblematic of conventional views of race, Robinson
declared he was a proponent of abolition everywhere. The best
solution, he argued, was to free the slaves where they were, "under
a genial climate, most natural to them," among "whites of the
South," who were "less prejudiced against color, than we of the
North." Robinson's brand of anti-slavery informed his views on
the Sons' policies toward Blacks. Why, he wondered, should Negroes even wait on the Sons to act? Negroes were equally capable
of establishing and maintaining their own societies. If they wanted
to join the Sons, they could, as Blacks in New York City had, by
applying to the Scottish order for a charter. The claims of exclu-
sions, therefore, were not "well founded." Moreover, such criticisms were not "very generous." It was surely not the business of
the Sons to remove prejudice. To drive home his point, Robinson
pointed to the fact that abolitionists had been trying for years to
eliminate discrimination without much success. The objectives
of the Sons, moreover, were limited to the promotion of temperance, not the elimination of prejudice. That should be the aim of
churches. The Sons had acted in good faith. If, however, prejudice
seriously disturbed their harmony, he conceded, they must all
commit themselves to act accordingly, working for the elimination of slavery and discrimination.

Ward responded with a number of questions. Why, he wondered, conflate those who chose not to join with those the Sons
will not permit to join? What, he wanted to know, do the actions
of the Scottish Division have to do with those of the Sons in
America? By not attacking prejudice, were the Sons not endorsing

it? Finally, if the Sons will not admit Blacks, why do they deny them the right to form their own division? Ward then returned to his experiences with the Sons. Not only, he reminded his readers, were members of his local division chastised and expelled for initiating a Black man in Cortlandville, the Sons had done the same to Jermain Loguen in Syracuse. If, he asked, the promotion of temperance was the principal objective of the order, why did "they take so much pain to promote colophobia officially?" Robinson's claims to be anti-slavery only helped to confirm Ward's views of the failure of abolitionists and their tendency to defend, or turn a blind eye to, the effects of Negro-hate.[21]

His experiences with the Sons did not sour Ward on temperance. He remained active in the movement throughout the state. Two years later, he was elected to the Executive Committee of the New York State Temperance Society. Although he was deeply concerned about the effects of drink, particularly on the working class, Ward was not a teetotaler. Drinking in moderation was acceptable, he argued; the problem was when drinking led to intoxication. In that case, "immediate, lifelong, total abstinence was the only cure." Yet, as they used to say, Ward was a little "moist." When social conventions required it, he was not above holding a glass.[22]

The conflict with the Sons of Temperance came less than a year after the state referendum overwhelmingly voted to maintain the $250 property qualification. The defeat set the Black suffrage movement back years. Whigs had betrayed those African Americans who had voted for them. What purpose did it serve, Ward wondered, to continue to do so in the face of Whig intransigence? The only party openly committed to Black social and political equality was the Liberty Party. The referendum had demonstrated that the Empire State had refused "to do justice to the meekest, the most injured the most unoffending class of its citizens." A man's right to vote was sacred. "Because I am a *man*," he reasoned, and "a voluntary subject of government, my right to vote is *mine*, as much as any other man though I am black. The matter of complexion had nothing to do with it." That right was enshrined in the Declaration of Independence's principle that "the just powers of the government are derived from the consent of the governed." To deprive him of that right is to commit robbery. Those "professors of religion" who voted against the removal of the qualification were complicit in "wholesale robbery." Sham republicanism had voted to reject equal suffrage. There was no difference between hypocritical Whigs and "*cutaneous Democrats*"; they were "twins to all intents and purposes." Ward then turned to those African Americans who put store in the Whigs' commitment to equal rights. Can they not see, he asked, that there is but "one party in the State" that supports equal rights? The Liberty Party was the only party committed to equal rights, both by what they said and by what they did. He therefore called on Black voters to "bring forth fruits of repentance, by voting *with*, not *against*, the friends of the robbed and the down trodden." The state would only be redeemed when true republicans came together to ensure equal rights. Ward despaired that Blacks would ever see the connection between the two dominant parties, especially the Whigs, and continued oppression. If the vote were given to all, including the Negro, he had no doubt many would vote for the "very worst pro-slavery parties." That is the message Ward drove home in countless lectures and letters to editors. The Negro had to stand fast against the political forces of slavery and discrimination that dominated the Whig and Democratic Parties.[23]

Ward opposed any effort to water down the principles for which the Liberty Party stood. Following defeat in the 1844 presidential election, there were calls for the party to broaden its platform to include other reforms such as peace, abolition of the army

and navy, repeal of all tariffs, and land reform. Ward initially resisted, but by 1846, he and others came together to form the Liberty League, which incorporated a broader platform of reforms.
The nomination of John P. Hale, an independent Democrat of
New Hampshire, as the party's standard-bearer in the 1848 presidential elections, with a platform of not extending slavery, rather
than outright abolition, prompted many Liberty Party members,
including Hale, to throw their support behind the newly formed
Free Soil Party. Ward and other members of the Liberty League,
which in June 1848 became the National Liberty Party, refused
to condone the Free Soil Party's plan for limiting slavery to the
states and territories where it already existed. At a meeting in Buffalo, the new Liberty Party nominated a presidential slate headed
by Gerrit Smith. Ward received twelve votes for vice president.[24]

By early summer 1848, it was clear to Ward that a significant
number of African Americans and supporters of anti-slavery had
thrown in their lot with the Free Soil Party (FSP). There is some
doubt whether Ward was an official delegate to that year's Free
Soil Convention in Buffalo. He did attend part of the meeting,
held under a massive tent on a blisteringly hot August day and
attended by a crush of people estimated in excess of twenty thousand. Thousands who were not delegates arrived early and occupied many of the seats reserved for delegates, many of whom were
left standing. The convention started in chaos. Some of a "perti-
nacious disposition," a reporter with a sense of humor recorded,
made motions from the floor and seconded them, while the organizers were trying to bring some semblance of order to the proceedings. Near the end of the second speech, the stage collapsed,
as one reporter told his readers, "spoiling our gold pen, rasping
the epidermis from our shins, and committing sundry other out-
rages of a similar nature." He apologized for not doing Joshua
Gidding's speech justice because some "unmannerly fellows"

made it hard to hear. On the second day, he suggested, if speakers wished to have their comments reported, they should advance new ideas, as all the old ones had been used up long ago. Much of the important business of the convention was transacted behind the scenes. Led by Salmon Chase of Ohio, the party's plank called for the nonextension of slavery, and supported federal spending on internal improvement, cheap postage, and free land for settlers.

Frederick Douglass, Henry Bibb, Garnet, Charles Lenox Remond, Ward, Martin Delany, and other African Americans attended. On the second day, the crowd called for Douglass. Barnburner Democrats surrounded the chair, insisting that the "nigger" not be allowed to speak. Douglass did but only briefly as he had recently undergone surgery on his throat. The crowd was clearly disappointed. Bibb also spoke briefly about the difficulty of opening up the vote to Blacks in Michigan. Ward spoke, then dramatically stormed out of the convention as Martin Van Buren was about to be nominated.[25]

Ward would explain his position soon after he got home from the convention in his lengthy "Address to the Four Thousand Colored Voters of the State of New York," partly a plea to Blacks to demonstrate dignity and self-respect, and partly a warning to beware of those who would seduce them to vote against their better interests. Ward launched a scathing attack on the FSP and those Blacks who would support it. In the past, Blacks had voted against their self-interest by supporting the Whigs and in some cases the Democrats. To vote for the Whig ticket in the upcoming elections would be "treasonable deeds" against our common cause. The alternative, some would suggest, was a vote for Van Buren and the FSP. This Ward dismissed as the sentiments of "artful demagogues." They should be ignored, as the four thousand Black voters held in their hands the balance of power in the state. Ward conceded that the FSP had been slightly more progressive in its commitment to limit the spread of slavery, but that was still not enough to win the support of Black voters. He gave four reasons. The party platform did not include a commitment to equal rights, the cornerstone of the "doctrine of true Republicanism." No one should be surprised, as the party's torchbearer had not changed his stripes, nor had many of FSP's other leaders. Ward made special reference to John A. Dix, the New York senator and leader of the Barnburner wing of the new party. Dix had consistently opposed equal rights for Blacks, regarding them as an inferior race; he had rejected anti-slavery petitions to Congress; and he had opposed the abolition of slavery in Washington, DC. Ward, however, reserved his sharpest barbs for those who claimed to be Liberty men but who had consistently betrayed the party and were now trying to persuade Black men to vote for the FSP. Do not be seduced, he warned, by those who have "abandoned us, and have gone over to our enemies."

Second, the FSP had refused to take a position on the elimination of the 1841 preemption act, an odious pro-slavery law permitting White settlers the right to eject Blacks from government lands on which they had settled because Blacks, it was argued, were not free citizens. Ward wondered how anyone could vote for a party whose free soil principles were so "limited, so contradictory, so partial, so pro-slavery."

Third, Van Buren had consistently opposed the abolition of slavery in DC. Here was a man who had voted for the censoring of the press in 1833 and worked in 1840 for the return of the *Amistad* rebels to their Cuban owners. He gave no indication he was now prepared to reject these "deeds of dark depravity." He was as much the "friend of Federal Slavery, as . . . the friend of Free Soil." Blacks must use their vote to prevent the extension of slavery and promote "the extinction of slavery." A vote for Van Buren would be a vote for a "pro-slavery candidate with a pro-slavery party."[26]

Fourth, given all that the party's leaders had done, a vote for Van Buren and the FSP would demonstrate a lack of self-respect. How, he wondered, could Blacks approve of the "fosterers of the bitterest prejudices against" us, and our "most ruthless oppressors." To do so would be to send a clear message that Blacks did "not care about political equality." If by chance they were given the vote, he worried they would "barter it away for the smallest price to artful and designing demagogues." One way to show this was not the case was to "refuse to vote for pro-slavery men." Only then would "our enemies and pretended friends" acknowledge that the four thousand Black men of New York have "too much self-respect to be bribed, cajoled, cheated or flattered into pro-slavery voting." Ward's solution: vote only for those who abhorred slavery, advocating for its extinction, and who supported the rights of Blacks to vote. In other words, vote for the party that was "true to all the great instincts of the crushed, poor, black and white, bond and free"; vote to maintain "self-respect, so that your children shall not be ashamed to own you as father." There was only one candidate worthy of their vote: Gerrit Smith, that "outspoken, uncompromising, impartial, and truly-practical philanthropist." He was preferable to all the "huckstering, wire-pulling, aristocratic, pro-slavery politicians."[27]

It was a blistering indictment of the new party and its leaders. Ward knew, however, that Douglass would not be partial to his call because, like other Garrisonians, he "eschewed all political action." Douglass did not disappoint, but he did surprise Ward. Ward, he thought, was fighting a battle on old ground. Conditions had changed. Given present circumstances, he thought Ward's arguments were dated, even uncharitable. Douglass addressed each of Ward's points in turn. Blacks, he maintained, should pay less attention to what Van Buren, Dix, and others had done in the past, or even to what they said now. All that mattered was what they proposed to do. If Blacks thought their proposals were right and did not violate any of their cherished moral principles, "we should not hesitate to give our aid and vote to such a party." Forget Dix, Douglass seemed to say; he was not the party's candidate. He pleaded for understanding, for keeping in mind that men change their views and their positions. After all, Gerrit Smith was once a proponent of the colonization of Blacks in Africa. That should not stop Blacks from voting for him today. Dix, moreover, was not alone in his reprehensible views of Blacks. Even "professed abolitionists" held such views. One of the most effective ways of removing prejudice was "to act with such men, just so far as we can, without a compromise of fundamental truths."[28]

No one could doubt that Ward's presence at the convention and the several speeches he made were among "the most powerful blows ever dealt upon the thick skull of American prejudice against colored persons." Thousands had listened to Ward's "eloquent words with astonishment, mingled with admiration, and all probably went home with a higher and more truthful estimation of our race than they ever entertained before." Douglass quoted Ward at length, only to reject his insistence on the importance of preemption rights as "farfetched." He was confident that, once in power, the FSP would repeal the law as a violation of the principle of free soil. Douglass pointed out that Ward's condemnation of Van Buren's position on slavery in the District of Columbia was written before the candidate's letter expressing a commitment to emancipation in the federal territory had been published. (When Ward received news of Van Buren's new position, he sent a brief note to Douglass conceding that the new position was "very different," but insisting it was still far from satisfactory.)

In politics, allies sometimes made strange bedfellows, Douglass maintained. He used the analogy of a Black man traveling on a ship with Whites who abhorred his presence. A passenger fell overboard and needed to be saved. Would the Black man refuse to pitch in because those with whom he had to work disliked him? A reasonable man, Douglass maintained, would ignore the racist barbs and assist in the rescue. The moral of the story: "If the act be good, do it, and leave the motives of your fellows to be disposed of by the Searcher of all hearts." What bothered Douglass most was the likelihood that Ward's "Address" would benefit the established parties to the detriment of the very things Ward was anxious to ensure. The ways Blacks voted should never be determined by the "past transgressions of members of the Free Soil party, but by what they now are, and what they are now aiming to accomplish."

Given the drift of his argument, readers would have anticipated a full-throated endorsement of the new party by Douglass. After all, he agreed with Ward that the nation was drowning and needed to be saved. At the close, however, Douglass retreated to the safety of his Garrisonian position. "Our . . . course is clear," he declared; "we shall vote for neither of the candidates." Freedom for the slaves and equal rights for free Blacks could be achieved only if the Union was "broken up" and a "free republic" established in the North. The Free Soilers had "followed slavery up to the ramparts of the Constitution, and there they stop." Their approach would do some good, he anticipated, by "hemming slavery in, but the bloody ramparts of the Constitution must be scaled and battered down before the millions within its compass can gain their freedom." So long as Northern people assisted in the return of fugitive slaves, and were committed to putting down slave revolts, he could not vote "under the American Constitution."

Over time, the political distance between the two would narrow, but as it stood in the fall of 1848, neither had convinced the other of the merits of his argument. Ward, however, stood on

firmer and less ideologically questionable ground: he was opposed to any party that did not take an uncompromising stand
against slavery and Negro-hate, and that included the FSP. Douglass was unsure and tentative. At first, he thought the party had
taken a step in the right direction. Later, he would question even
that lukewarm support and call on Blacks to cast their ballots for
Gerrit Smith and the Liberty League. Weeks later, he would re-
verse course and come out in support of Van Buren.

Ward could not fathom the reasons for Douglass's vacillation.
As he told Gerrit Smith, he opposed all those who trimmed their
abolitionist sails to vote for the FSP. Blacks must vote, he insisted,
with "hope, courage and consistency." Ward knew he was in the
minority but that did not deter him. When Blacks met in convention in Cleveland in early September, there was a growing sense
of optimism that things were about to change for the better. The
new party, many believed, offered something significantly different from the established parties. Hanging over the three-day
meeting was whether to endorse the FSP. Ward and Douglass re-
prised their earlier dispute. Douglass, who presided over the convention, remained squarely in the Garrisonian camp. Ward called
for using the ballot box to elect Smith and the Liberty League.
There was also significant support for the FSP. Ward adamantly
opposed any such endorsement because of the party's refusal to
include an equal rights plank in its platform. After much maneu-
vering, the convention threw its support to the FSP even as members insisted on the need for more "liberal views."[29]

Ever since the FSP convention, Ward had been pushing Gerrit
Smith and the Liberty League to call a convention to select candidates to run in upcoming elections. In the face of desertion by
old friends and stalwarts to the FSP, the league, he insisted, must
name its standard-bearers and Smith must head the ticket, for, as
he told him almost despairingly, "*You* must be our Eternal Can-

didate." In mid-September, Ward chaired the league's county convention, held in Cortland. Given all that had transpired in the last few months, the convention members expressed a surprising level of optimism about the rise of opposition to pro-slavery parties. Even the FSP, they noted, had adopted portions of the Liberty Party's platform. As abolitionists and American citizens, the convention called on "patriots, philanthropists and Christians" to destroy the "slaveocracy of all parties" by upholding the "principles of the declaration of Independence at the ballot box."

The convention nominated Ward to contest a seat for the New York State legislature. Two days later, he issued an election manifesto laying out his positions should he be elected. It promised, among other things, to support abolition in Washington, DC, limit slave territory, abolish the 1793 Fugitive Slave Law, recognize Haiti, ban speculation of public lands, and defend indebted homesteaders from creditors. On the state level, he promised to work for a ban on alcohol and to repeal the 1821 law that imposed the $250 property qualification. It is not clear if Ward was ever committed to running for this or any other office, but no one could question his commitment to the Liberty League and to Smith.

In September 1851, days before he left the country for good, Ward called on the party to maintain its "platform of principles," to be both "radical and catholic." In its opposition to slavery and discrimination, it must be uncompromising, avoiding the mistakes of 1847, when it nominated John P. Hale, and of 1848, when some of its supporters were attracted to the siren call of the FSP. Such "deeds of folly" should never be repeated. Although reluctant to run again, "our beloved" Smith, the "representative and embodiment of our principles," had to be persuaded to lead the charge. The league had taken on the dimensions of a movement based almost on hope. The smaller it got, the more it saw a future for itself. Its numbers were reduced but not adherents' commitment and enthusiasm for the cause, which had lost nothing of its truth and importance. "You are seeking to bless the world," the 1850 convention declared, "with the realization of the Divine idea of Civil Government; and this object is no less great and glorious, than if millions were united with you in promoting it."[30]

Ward was nothing if not consistent and committed to the cause and the man who had come to mean so much to him. There was only one party, he liked to tell his readers, that "showed its contempt for negro-hate" by nominating in 1849 one Black man on its state ticket, three others for local offices, and yet another for the state Senate. Jermain Loguen of Syracuse, a fugitive slave from Tennessee, had been selected to run for the state Senate; Ward for secretary of state. Ward had received a dozen votes in the contest as the party's vice presidential candidate in 1848. In 1850, the party again nominated him as its vice presidential candidate, but by then it was an even paler shadow of itself. For years, Ward had, almost single-handedly, waged a campaign to persuade Black New Yorkers to abandon the Whig Party. He pleaded with them, sometimes berated, even insulted, them, yet they seemed unmoved. He cited the example of "a New York City black man" who took a "golden bribe" and used it to hire Black men to coax others to vote the Whig ticket. More troubling was the fact that "the most influential of the same class" had assisted him. He worried about the Whigs' success in finding people who were "*hirable and coaxable* enough to do the dirty deed of meanness." In Rhode Island, Blacks voted for the slave-holding Whig Party solely because that party claimed to have given them the vote. Ward dismissed them all as "pro-slavery negroes."[31]

George T. Downing, the restaurateur and a correspondent to Frederick Douglass's newspaper, took umbrage at Ward's characterization, even though he was not mentioned by name. Ward, however, had laid the blame for the Liberty Party's failure to attract a larger percentage of votes at the door of New York City's Black leadership. Downing dismissed the charge as a *"designed fabrication,"* a libel. He did not address Ward's charges directly but insisted that Black men must be free to make their own decisions based on their assessment of the conditions they faced. Black men in New York City had evaluated the situation and acted in their best interest. Downing then turned the tables on Ward. If there was a "dirty deed of meanness," it was not how Blacks in New York City voted, but Ward accepting an invitation to lecture to a segregated audience in Philadelphia. "A Committee of White Citizens" had invited Ward to speak on the topic of "Constitutional Slavery." The committee members had tried to secure a venue for the lecture but failed because of "prejudice against the Negro." They instead procured a room at the Black Second Presbyterian Church, then announced that the "lower salon will be appropriated exclusively to our White fellow citizens." Why, some wanted to know, was a committee of Whites selected to make such segregated arrangements? Were they afraid of being accused of promoting social equality?

Frederick Douglass got wind of the plans from Charles Lenox Remond, who was visiting Philadelphia at the time, and from George W. Goines, a city bookseller. Douglass promptly put out a special extra edition of his newspaper devoted to what he called the "most shameful concession to the spirit of slavery and prejudice." Given the aims of the meeting, "the well-known character" of Ward, and the fact the gathering was to be held in a Black church, Douglass thought it "the most cowardly, contemptible, and servile specimen of self-degradation which has ever come under my notice." It was an abandonment of the "doctrine and practice of human equality." How could Black men, he wanted to know, have agreed to such an arrangement? Seeking the elevation of the Black man in the "very pathway of self-degradation" would, he predicted, "end in disappointment, shame and confusion." Why had Ward agreed to such an arrangement? He could not blame it on the White organizers; troublingly, Ward had been aware of the arrangements ahead of time but had chosen to turn a blind eye. Why had he not denounced the plan and refused to speak under the terms laid down by the committee? Instead, he attended, spoke, and "treated his hearers to any quantity of fun." If this was fidelity, Douglass wanted to know, what was treachery? The time was long past, he concluded, for the people to demand that those "who stand forth as advocates" demonstrate "an inflexible adhesion to the principle of equal and impartial freedom."[32]

Remond was surprised to see the handbills announcing the meeting, astonished that a Black church had allowed an arrangement that sanctioned in "the most gratuitous, palpable and humiliating manner, the cruel and depressing customs and laws under which we have lived and suffered for a long series of years." He worried that this would establish an unwelcome precedent. George W. Goines also was surprised to see a "number of our oldest and most respectable seated in the gallery." He was even more alarmed that Ward said nothing about the segregated arrangements during his lecture.[33]

The criticism stung. Ward dismissed Goines's comments as "*shameless* but *characteristic* and *impudent.*" Goines knew, Ward responded, that he had turned from the advertised topic of the lecture to speak on the influence of slavery on the government and on "this very PREJUDICE, as the grand reason why black men are treated as they are, by the Government and the People." Three-quarters of his lecture, he insisted, covered the issue of "NEGRO HATE." Goines also knew that Ward's protest against the wording of the handbill announcing the meeting had resulted in the chairman removing the offending sections before they were circulated. According to Ward, Goines was also aware that the pew holders had resigned their seats voluntarily to accommodate Whites attending on the "same principle of comity that one gives up his rocking-chair, in his parlor, to his stranger guest." All this Goines knew, yet he and others, Ward concluded, thought it best to circulate false information. He expressed surprise that Douglass should print such misstatements but reminded his readers of "*like slips of his pen on more than one occasion.*"

Neither the characteristic editorial flurry nor the imagery of giving up the comfortable chair to the visitor did anything to mollify Ward's critics. Ward could not shake the image of voluntarily preaching to a segregated audience, an episode Downing characterized as "truckling, groveling and . . . disgraceful." As much as Ward argued that honest men could disagree about the merits of addressing a meeting under the conditions set at Philadelphia, he knew better. He had crossed a line, violating an almost sacred principle. Yet Ward persisted in his defense: he had spoken to similar audiences before. The examples he gave, however, may have been occasions when he addressed all-White meetings, not segregated gatherings. Martin R. Delany of Pittsburgh, Pennsylvania, a man equally proud of his Blackness as Ward was of his, tried to lower the heat of the exchanges. In a letter addressed to Ward, Delany was incredulous. He conceded he had not had a chance to speak to Ward about the incident, but wondered, as many did, how someone so widely praised for his commitment to the cause, someone of his unrivaled eloquence, could deign to accept such an invitation and say nothing about it. How could this "professedly high-toned anti-slavery man," he asked, allow himself to participate in such an event?[34]

Ward seemed chastened by the experience. It occurred at a time when he was at the center of the public debate over the Fugitive Slave Law. More immediately, the dispute was part of a low-level running competition with Douglass. They were both newspaper editors in proximity to one another, Ward in Cortland-ville, Douglass in Rochester, eighty-two miles apart as the crow flies. Both looked to Gerrit Smith for guidance and financial sup-port, although Douglass had yet to break totally with Garrisonian views of the best way to eliminate slavery; some members of the American Antislavery Society considered him a traitor to the cause. Douglass and his newspaper were the leading Black voices for Garrison's brand of abolition. Ward was the leading Black spokesman for the Liberty Party and political abolition. His news-paper was the official organ of the Liberty Party. Differences be-tween the two were always tempered by a respect for the other's talents and what each had contributed to the cause. Both were commanding orators whom people traveled long distances to hear.

In 1849, during the flurry of anniversary meetings (tradition-ally, May was the month when annual meetings of philanthropic societies were held), Ward challenged Douglass to a debate over the Constitution's relation to slavery. Douglass was both surprised and reluctant to debate but did not feel he could back down in the face of the challenge. The combatants met in late May in New York City, the topic "The Constitutionality of American Slavery." According to William C. Nell, the audience comprised "much of the intelligent, refined and reformatory, both white and colored." It was "Greek meeting Greek." The power of logic blended with genuine wit. The audience was riveted until "a late hour, and even then, the audience like Oliver Twist, asked for more of what was really a mental feast." By mutual consent, they did not submit the question to a vote. Nell declined to elaborate on the arguments each employed but insisted that the debate was a brilliant finale to the Anniversary Week in the city. The debate was a first for both men. Douglass thought it "proved a very pleasant and agree-able entertainment," one he would remember with "the best of feelings" toward his "respectable and very talented antagonist."

Despite the power of Ward's arguments, Douglass remained unconvinced about the merits of political abolition.[35]

Because of their mutual respect, Ward was taken aback by Douglass's criticism of his lecture in Philadelphia. They differed about the best means to achieve emancipation, but they had faced and vanquished the enemy together. Two weeks before the Philadelphia meeting, both were at the annual meeting of the AASS in New York City. Leaders of the society expected trouble. For days before, newspaper editors had whipped up resentment of the abolitionists. The *New York Herald* leveled its guns against the abolitionists, calling on its readers to make things hot for the fanatics who, they argued, had invaded their city spouting socialist, amalgamationist, and other absurd theories. William Lloyd Garrison expected a "stormy" meeting. He had only begun his remarks when a group of White rowdies, led by Isaiah Rynders, Tammany Hall boss of the Sixth Ward and nemesis of abolitionists, stormed the platform. Rynders, who controlled the streets of Lower Manhattan and was the terror of African Americans, insisted that a Dr. Grant be given the podium. It appears Grant, at one time, had been a pressman in the *Liberator*'s office. Grant's diatribe ridiculed Negroes, Indians, and "all sorts of bipeds" of different colors. They did not belong to the human race. Negroes, he argued, were descended from monkeys. As such, they had no human rights and so could be bought and sold like cattle. The absurdity of Grant's remarks reminded one reporter of Sir Joseph Banks, the eighteenth-century British botanist, who tried to prove fleas were a sort of lobster because when he boiled them, they turned red.

There were calls from the audience for Douglass, who began his remarks with Rynders standing "at his elbow" in an act of intimidation. He was there as a representative of his people, Douglass declared. He admitted he was born in slavery and had the marks of the lash to show for it. No one, and that included Grant, should be able to insult him without immunity. Look at me, he asked the audience, am I not a Negro, and a man? Rynders interrupted, insisting Douglass was only "half a nigger." What followed was classic Douglass. He admitted he was only half a Negro, the son of a slaveholder—which, he said, turning to his protagonist, made him "half a brother to Mr. Rynders." This produced roars of laughter from the audience.

A question lingered in the minds of a portion of the audience, one report suggested: if "the speaker had not been a white man's son and in that way half-human," could he "have exhibited these strangely human-like qualities?" These doubts could be expelled if they heard from a "full-blooded negro, with similar indication of having a genuine human nature." Douglass turned to Ward. As Ward came forward, Rynders was heard to say: "There's a regular black savage, and no mistake!" What followed was a masterful rebuke. "I care not for my lineage," Ward began, "and ask not whether I am descended from a man or a monkey." One thing he knew—he was a man, and the God who had made him intended he should "have the rights and perform the duties of a man." He did not care if his spinal column was not perpendicular to the base of his brain, as Grant said, but he was in no doubt that he had "the faculty of thought and the capacity of affection and emotion." He had a "human tongue to speak, and a human heart to feel." As far as the receding forehead mentioned by Grant, Ward wondered how many White men there were with "a low receding forehead, of which you might say of the schoolmaster in Dickens' Nicholas Nickleby. That if you knock there all day, you'll find nobody at home." The audience roared at what one reporter described as a "torrent of ridicule on the unfortunate Dr. Grant and his backers, shaking the house with roars of laughter." Ward's eloquence prompted another reporter to wonder: if color was a test of intellect, would Ward have been the last person in the place to come forward to speak? Ward immediately commanded the attention of the crowd, he reported. Everything he said, and the way he said it, "indicated education and culture." The pride he expressed in his color thrilled the audience. His wit "was set off by an intonation which gave the fullest effect to his thought." His triumph was complete. The thug Rynders, his ignorant White followers, and Grant were "put down, half covered by a couple of black noblemen."

The reporter then turned to a description of Ward that highlighted both his color and eloquence. Later observers would embellish this account, but sketches of Ward always contained similar elements: Ward's color, height, weight, and eloquence. As "unpromising as the appearance of Mr. Ward was, from his exceeding blackness," he began, "yet as he went on, his whole form transfigured. Intellect kept lightening behind the cloud. He seemed an animate statue of black marble, of the old Egyptian sort, out of which our white civilization was hewn. Every degrading association dropt away from his color, and it was as rich, in its blackness, as the velvet pall upon the bier of an Emperor." As the *New York Tribune* put it, Douglass made a "sad rent" in Grant's argument; Ward pulverized it. Rynders had the last word, however. The next morning, his followers packed the room and prevented the meeting from continuing. Garrison was forced to adjourn the meeting. It was the last annual meeting the AASS held in New York City.[36]

Days later, Ward was the main speaker at the annual meeting of the reorganized New York Vigilance Committee as the debate over the Fugitive Slave Law heated up in Congress. Protesters tried unsuccessfully to disrupt the proceedings. Ward criticized those good-hearted Americans who gave liberally to alleviate suffering in Ireland, Hungary, and elsewhere, but who closed their purses to the needs of American Blacks. Ward's declaration that he was an American met with laughter, hisses, and a shout: "a black one." Ward responded he was a citizen of New York, that he was indeed "gloriously black," but that he wore what Black he had only "on the *outside!*" At that point, rowdies in the gallery stirred. Ward called on his listeners to sit still. "If you want to see anything interesting," he told them, "look at me!" His reaction had the desired effect. Ward then went on—for possibly the first time publicly—to give a brief account of his family's flight from slavery. He was, therefore, a Southerner, yet he was "no more to be compared to a Northern doughface, than Daniel Webster [who was swarthy] to a Southerner, and the friends of Daniel Webster think it about as easy to find a Southerner like him as for a Nantucket eel to tow a shad boat through Long Island Sound." His audience roared approval. This was Ward at his oratorical best. Following a similarly commanding speech at the tenth anniversary meeting of the American and Foreign Anti-Slavery Society the previous summer, one newspaper had responded: Ward was a man "with a complexion considerably darker than that of Othello, in the Dusseldorf Gallery. His speech was a succession of brilliant coruscations, which could no more be put on paper, than the flashes of lightning, diversified with explosions of oratory, that rolled and broke on the astonished auditory, like an impending thunder cloud. His sallies of wit were genuine, and no mistake; with his gift of humor and sarcasm, we should rather listen to his oratory than be the subject of it."[37]

Ward's eloquence and erudition were, by now, legendary. People flocked to hear him. Yet his professional life, the things that he did for a living, as he would say, was in turmoil. The Liberty Party, to which he had devoted so much time and energy, had been ineffective for some time. Yet he never changed course. There was also the damning Negro-hate that hung like a pall over his life. For years, he had preached the need for the Negro to lift himself up by his own exertions. As he was fond of saying, a "depressed people cannot be elevated by other than themselves." The government might "sunder every chain and declare every slave free and clothe him with all that appertains to legal and constitutional equality." Friends of the Colored man might then invite him to "complete and perfect equality in the social circle, and in business relations." None of this would matter if Blacks did not "cultivate self-respect, dignity of demeanor, refinement of manners, intelligence, morality, and religion." They also needed to be "industrious, frugal, temperate, and chaste . . . not cringing, servile, and crawling, in [their] intercourse with whites." Then and only then would they command the "respect of the bitterest enemies the black man knows." Any Black man who faltered in this endeavor Ward dismissed as a "traitor alike to God, his friends, his family, his enslaved brother, and to himself."[38]

While these goals were admirable, even traditional, Ward's judgment was unnecessarily harsh. After all, he had been an editor, the proprietor of two newspapers, and had tried his hand at medicine, law, and teaching. Yet in the end, there were little material rewards to show for all his efforts at self-elevation. He could sway audiences with his eloquence, sprinkled as his orations always were with allusions to classical and modern literature as well as biblical exegesis. Yet the specter of debt and poverty haunted him at every turn. For a while, he managed to juggle his ministerial responsibilities with those of being the owner and editor of the *Impartial Citizen*. Months after the family moved to Cortlandville in 1846, Ward took over as publisher of the *True American*. He suspended publication a year later and merged the paper with Stephen Myers's *Northern Star and Freedman's Advocate* to form the *Impartial Citizen*. Myers acted as general agent until he left the paper in June 1849. Printed in Syracuse by Seymour King, the newspaper appeared twice a month for the first four months, be-ginning in February 1849. Ward hoped the traditional four-page broadsheet would not be a "mere local paper," but would reach readers throughout Central and Western New York. Prospects of reaching a wide readership looked promising for a paper that was both an organ of the Liberty Party and a voice for Blacks in Cen-tral New York. Ward, however, spent much of his time away from his desk soliciting subscribers and lecturing to raise money. With an annual subscription rate of $1, if paid in advance, Ward calcu-lated he would need at least fifteen hundred paid-up subscribers by the end of the year to stay afloat. That was easier said than done. Subscribers were tardy in meeting their obligations or never re-mitted their subscription. Ward begged and pleaded. Weeks had not elapsed before he found it necessary to apologize for the lack of an editorial. As he explained, it was due to his absence because of "constant duties in New York City" and his lack of funds, or, as he put it, "the extreme difficulty of getting money." The first issue of 1850 opened with a plaintive reminder: "Money which is due is needed now." He regularly published a list of subscrib-ers and other supporters both to acknowledge their contributions and, one suspects, to nudge delinquents to pay up. He also con-tinued to plead with delinquent subscribers. "We are put into very straitened circumstances, just now, for the want of what is due us. Could we realize what is honestly ours today, we need not owe any man tomorrow. Our debtors won't *let us obey the Scriptures*. We work hard and constantly, and had we received a respectable portion of what we have earned during the last eleven months, we might have been free from debt." He ended plaintively: "It's hard."[39]

Ward published a revealing and frank editorial at the close of the first volume. He had started the paper with a paltry $5 while carrying outstanding debts from the *True American*. Frederick

Douglass, by contrast, had started the *North Star* with a fund in excess of $4,000 donated by British friends, with promises of more to come. It cost $22, Ward estimated, to publish an issue. His partner, Stephen Myers, who left after three months, had reneged on promises of support. His problems were compounded, he told his readers, because he was a "hater of sectarianism." It did not help, he observed, that he started the paper in a "deeply pro-slavery, negro-hating community." Such harsh criticism would have surprised supporters in Cortlandville. The year 1849 was not the most propitious time to start a newspaper in Central New York. George W. Reynolds of Franklin, Delaware County, offers a possible explanation for the difficulties Ward faced: previously, residents in his area had subscribed to about one hundred abolitionist newspapers of "different shades." That number, he estimated, had dropped to about six. There were roughly two hundred Liberty Party voters in the county, but they had splintered into a bewildering number of what he called schools, to mention just a few, the Gerrit Smith, Tappan, William Chaplin, Ward, and the "everlasting hair-splitting prosy Goodell School." Reynolds nonetheless paid for a subscription and invited Ward to lecture in Franklin, pledging to cover his traveling expenses and offering what would have been music to Ward's ears: "a fair price for your labors."[40]

Ward also received regular donations of $25 from Gerrit Smith. When times were hard, as they frequently were, Smith would rise to the challenge by sending small donations. Smith's support of the *North Star* is illustrative. His contributions to Douglass were much larger, especially after Douglass broke with the Garrisonians. It is not clear why his support of Ward was less frequent and smaller. Ward also attracted support from a couple of women's groups. Julia Garnet, wife of Henry Highland, and eleven other Black women, including Charlotte Duffin and Caroline Loguen, announced plans for a fair in Syracuse in September 1849 during the city's Agricultural Week. The following year, the "Ladies Impartial Association" of Philadelphia organized a similar fair. The Syracuse ladies raised $34.12, welcome support for the struggling editor. Periodically, Ward also received gifts from closer to home.[41]

These tokens of support were never enough to run a weekly, nor did they pay Ward's bills. Unlike Douglass, Ward never had the backing of influential supporters at home and abroad. His English supporters, for instance, frequently rallied to Douglass's newspapers at moments of financial crisis. Without an endowment and with subscriptions sluggish, Ward had to go on the road in search of support. As he told his readers, he had to be away frequently and to "write as we run." In his absence, his printer sometimes had to get out issues. "When we have sufficient patronage either to afford to stay in our office, or to employ a clerk, we shall serve our readers better." Ward spent much of his time away from the office lecturing and raising subscriptions. These trips, many in the dead of winter, rattling over poor roads in unheated carriages or riding long distances on horseback between lectures, were physically and emotionally draining. On occasion, he was denied what he called the "ordinary courtesies of civilized life," such as the right to a cabin on a lake steamer. During a tour of northern New York, he was denied a saloon for the night on a steamer from Oswego even though the citizens of the town were "liberal towards the anti-slavery cause." Railway travel in certain areas was little better. On his way to Reading, Pennsylvania, he and his companions were forced to travel in the segregated cars of the Reading Railroad Company. The cars, he reported, were simply unfit for humans. There were no seat backs, no cushions, "no cleanliness, no decency, no anything, but just such an arrangement as is most perfectly suited to the demands of the pro-slavery negro-phobiaism of Pennsylvania." He reminded the conductor that those Whites who did make it to heaven would be grateful "to sit with anyone, white or black."[42]

These constant reminders of Negro-hate and his long and frequent absences from Emily and his children were his "cross to bear," the hardships he had to endure for the cause. Sometimes he attempted to ease the longing by taking Emily on a lecture tour. She was, he fondly recalled, his *vade mecum*, the guide that he needed close at hand. Having Emily with him was also a way of taking his home on the road. Home mattered to Ward although, as we shall see, he would spend long stretches of time away from his family while in Britain and Jamaica. "No place *can* be a substitute for home," he wrote almost nostalgically, "though the latter be a hovel, the former a palace. No observer can enter into one's feelings, live over again one's life, as does a loving wife. . . . In sickness, in sorrow, to be away from home adds mountain weights to what the wanderer's bosom must bear."[43]

Ward knew of what he spoke. He had become, by 1850, a wanderer who endured long spells away from home and the local causes to which he was connected. He missed, for instance, such major local events as the August 1850 Fugitive Slave Convention in nearby Cazenovia attended by more than two thousand and presided over by Frederick Douglass. His September 1849 lecture tour provides a glimpse into his hectic schedule. Ward gave ten lectures in thirteen days. He traveled east of Cortland through Chenango and Madison Counties, then east to Ovid, Seneca County, along Cayuga Lake to Lodi, south of Ovid, ending back at Homer, just north of Cortland. Autumn in New York was a pleasant time of year. The same could not be said of his tour of Jefferson County, north of Watertown, in early January 1850. In the fall of 1850, he gave sixteen lectures in three weeks with two brief stops at home. On some of the stops, Ward managed to gain several subscriptions. Twelve were added to the list of supporters in New Berlin and another half dozen or so in Hamilton. In mid-October 1849, he drove forty-six miles to lecture in Milan, Cayuga County, through one of the "severest storms." Yet, as he put it, sixty "waterproof Reformers" braved the elements to hear him. He enrolled sixteen subscribers in Troy and raised $6.10 in Albany.[44]

The political crisis created by the debate in Congress over the proposed Compromise of 1850, specifically the Fugitive Slave Law, increased the demand for Ward's services on the lecture circuit. Between March and May, he undertook a tour of ten weeks to Massachusetts, Connecticut, Rhode Island, and New York. He marveled that Emily did not start divorce proceedings. He spoke in Springfield at the first anti–Fugitive Slave Law meeting held in Massachusetts. He later met with William and Ellen Craft the same day Georgia slave catchers were "prowling about Boston" in search of them. He was one of the main speakers at the Faneuil Hall meeting on March 25 that condemned Daniel Webster for his infamous recent speech in support of the law. If the "moral influence" of that speech ever caught on with the young, Ward predicted, it would be so "deeply corrupting" that it would never be purged. Unfortunately, the law had attracted enough support from Northern doughfaces who were willing "to lick up the spittle of the slaveocrats, and swear it is delicious" when it suited their interests. They had gathered to "make a common oath upon a common altar that that bill shall never take effect." Senators and representatives might support it, but "we the people" would never be "human bipeds" howling upon "the track of the fugitive slave." The "law of Almighty God," he swore, would protect fugitive slaves who came to his part of New York State. Such crimes as the Fugitive Slave Law left Blacks no other option than to claim "the right of Revolution, and . . . that right we will, at whatever cost, most sacredly maintain." He would defend his right to remain free. He thought it ironic that the law did not mention color. That provided him an opening to riff on Webster's swarthy color, what he called his "honorable dark skin." Who knows? he observed ironically, "a local official might have to make a decision about Webster based on his color." Was it not odd, he observed, that some slave catchers were darker than Ellen Craft, whom Ward accompanied to the meeting? This led him to ask, quoting Alexander Pope: "If white and black, blend, soften and unite / A thousand ways, is there no black or white?"

The law had gone a step too far, he warned a meeting of Blacks at the Bleknap Street Church two days later. "We had always been true to our country, imitating the example of our fathers, whose unpaid services contributed to the nation's independence. Let us now be true to ourselves and the fugitive slave," he pleaded with the audience, and "if those with paler faces and blacker hearts oppress us, it becomes us to be united in the Phalanx of Freedom." He returned to the theme of Webster's betrayal. The former senator "did not commence falling in 1850." For years he had been "wandering from the path of freedom," demanding, for instance, compensation following the slave rebellion on the *Creole*, trying to return escaped slaves from Canada under the terms of the Webster-Ashburton Treaty with England, and doing nothing to challenge enforcement of the Negro Seamen's Act. These were bravura performances that, like all of Ward's major speeches, were littered with literary and historical allusions. Yet one gets the distinct impression that these were impromptu performances that drew from a deep reservoir of knowledge, driven by a passion for the struggle against slavery and Negro-hate.[45]

In September, Ward gave eleven lectures in twelve days in eastern and middle Pennsylvania. When he arrived in Harrisburg, the city was still abuzz following the failed rescue of three fugitive slaves from Virginia by the Black community. On his arrival in

Philadelphia, a "committee of 100" met him at the wharf and escorted him to the Philadelphia Institute, where he responded to a welcoming address by Dr. J. J. G. Bliss. That evening, he attended a concert of the talented Frank Johnson's band. The reception on this occasion was a far cry from the turmoil created by his earlier lecture to a segregated audience.[46]

These hectic lecture schedules took a toll on Ward's health. After speaking four times at Providence, Rhode Island, three times on Sunday, all while "writing, editing, selecting, conversing and debating," he was prostrate for over a week. He was confined "to the house, not daring to walk a quarter mile" following an address in Boston. Ward had a knack, however, for seeing the funny side of his troubles. He thought the pressure of engagements had caused his head to shrink in size. My body, he told his readers, "weighs on average 210 pounds avoirdupois. My head is the smallest I ever saw set upon so ponderous a carcass." Despite an intermittent fever that lasted several weeks, he continued to travel in Pennsylvania until the illness forced him to bed. Such were the demands of the "profession, the cause," his family, and his creditors that he was obliged, "against the remonstrances" of Emily, friends, and physicians, "to continue to travel, though the state of my nervous system was such that to write a half page produced intense pain in my head." By the time he returned to Philadelphia, he was diagnosed with influenza. All this was preventable, he pleaded with his readers, if only they would pay their subscription.[47]

Debt and the lack of money were Ward's Sisyphean burdens. From his time in South Butler, when he was forced to give up his home to meet an outstanding debt, Ward never seemed to be able to make ends meet. He was not profligate, but his ambition to be somebody of stature, recognized for the things he accomplished, cost him dearly. To have increased the cost of subscription would have been to cut off his nose to spite his face. He could have charged more for his lectures but, again, that would have had little effect. The need for money—or, more correctly, Ward's demand that he be compensated in a way commensurate with the services he provided—sometimes got him in embarrassing straits. One suspects that need may have prompted him to accept the invitation to lecture to the segregated audience in Philadelphia in defiance of his better judgment. It also got him in some tricky situations with friends and co-workers. In August 1849, Ward accused George Weir Jr. and other organizers of an August 1 celebration in Buffalo, New York, of reneging on a promise to pay him an undisclosed amount to be the main speaker of the day. When, he asked pointedly, will "black men learn to pay their own laborers as liberally as they pay white men"? Weir responded by publishing an exchange of letters showing that Ward had agreed to the terms of the invitation only to change his mind later on the grounds that the original agreement would have embarrassed him financially. Weir wondered if a man with a philanthropic soul, one with a deep interest in the welfare of bleeding humanity, would ever "make dollars and cents" the measure of his commitment to the cause as Ward had done.[48]

Yet few would have questioned Ward's commitment to the cause. Sometime in early 1850, he and his family moved to Syracuse in an effort, one suspects, to combine the newspaper's editorial and printing operations and, hopefully, to take advantage of a larger market. The move coincided with the stirring of public opposition to the Fugitive Slave Law. The public debate over the law had reanimated Ward's fight against inequality and this "most despotic law." Its passage was the "darkest page" in the country's history. Yet even in this dark moment, "when priests and Levite walked on the other side, neglecting the poor wounded man by the wayside," a host of "faithful men and women" stood in defiance against it. His 1850 tours of New England, New York, and Pennsylvania were largely devoted to an attack on the law and those who promoted it. After President Fillmore signed the measure into law, Ward published an editorial bristling with defiance. Senator James Mason's bill was nothing more than a Whig measure. Again, the party had shown its true colors, bending its knees to slaveholders. Those Whigs and Democrats who endorsed the law, he thundered, would "lick up quarts of slaveholders' saliva, and swear it is delicious, when said slaveholders so demand." Blacks such as those in Rhode Island who voted for Whigs in the last presidential election were "among the guiltiest" of those responsible for the law's passage. In denying the accused the right of habeas corpus, the law had violated a major legal principle and left Blacks few options but to rely on the "natural and inalienable right of self-defense—self-protection." Blacks, he promised, would protect themselves, even if in so doing they "put their lives in peril." Let the authorities know, he warned, that the "business of catching slaves or kidnapping freemen" meant open warfare upon the rights and liberties of the Black man. He saw signs of that resistance in the actions of the Harrisburg Black community led by Joseph Popel. "Let us make slave catching and all its parts," he thundered, "as perilous as it deserves to be."

He was cheered by what he saw on his way to attend a Liberty Party meeting in Oswego, New York, in early October. Traveling from Phoenix, where he had lectured the night before, he met "several fugitive slaves" on their way to the meeting. They left the conference buoyed, "encouraged, and determined to remain on the soil that their fathers fought for, and, if need be, die in the manly defense of their firesides." Like the small band of Greeks who, in 1821, attacked and defeated a larger force of Turkish occupiers, Ward believed, quoting a stanza from Fitz-Greene Halleck's tribute to the leader of the Greeks, that these fugitives would

> Strike! For their altars and their fires
> Strike! For the green graves of their sires,
> God, and their native land![49]

A couple days later, he was at the Syracuse meeting that condemned the law as unconstitutional and called on Congress to repeal it. The meeting pledged to defy the law by forming an eighteen-man interracial Vigilance Committee. Called on to speak, Ward issued a warning: should anyone come to "take him or his family into slavery, it would do well for him to first perform two acts for the benefit of himself and his family—*He should first make his will, and then make his peace with his Maker.*" Ward's friend Jermain Loguen also declared his determination to protect himself and family. Having spent twenty years in slavery, he was determined never to be retaken. "I don't respect this law," he declared. "I don't fear it. I won't obey it! It outlaws me, and I outlaw it."[50]

Ward declared the city a refuge for fugitive slaves. Should anyone invade that refuge, the people of Syracuse would make sure "his hide wouldn't be worth a Yankee ninepiece, to be tanned into shoe-string." The death of one of these "scoundrels . . . will scare a regiment of the same class. They will never produce a very long and brilliant list of martyrs." Following the meeting, Ward's friend Abner Bates informed him of rumors that slave catchers were planning to seize him. His friends, Ward reported, immediately sprang into action. They divided "into three classes—one class cried; another class prayed; and the third class cursed. I, meanwhile, did what seemed to me to [be my] duty in the emergency—a particular account whereof is not yet written." Such levity reflected Ward's sense of security and defiance when among friends.[51]

By then Ward had moved operations to Boston. He suspended publication of the *Impartial Citizen* in mid-June 1850, planning, as soon as he had the means, to resume publication in Boston. Money, however, remained in short supply. Gerrit Smith was willing to contribute $50 for two years if the newspaper remained an organ of the Liberty Party. In July 1851, Ward sent Smith the first number issued from Boston with a note pleading with his old friend to send him whatever he could spare. It is not clear if Smith responded. The paper folded soon after. In a requiem, Ward wrote a friend that the "*Impartial Citizen* breathed its last, after a lingering illness of the spine, and obstructions, impurities, and irregularities of the circulation. *Requiescat in pace!*"[52]

Ward's diagnosis captured the newspaper's structural weaknesses. It was never adequately capitalized, but then no other Black newspaper of the period, with the exception of Douglass's *North Star,* was. Samuel Cornish thought he needed at least fifteen hundred paid subscribers before he could begin the *Colored American,* and then he anticipated having to spend considerable time on the road raising additional funds. Ward generated similar numbers of subscribers, but began, as he said, with merely $5 and a partner who reneged on his promise to contribute financially to the effort. As he quickly found out, promised subscriptions many times never materialized. If only, he lamented, he could have collected 30 percent of those subscriptions, he could have made a go of it. His pleas largely fell on deaf ears. Funds raised from his many lectures went a long way to keeping the enterprise afloat. Gerrit Smith's donations were invaluable, but they were small compared to the support he sent to Douglass in Rochester. Support from two women's organizations, one in Syracuse, the other in Philadelphia, helped only marginally. His four years in the editor's chair ruined Ward financially and undermined his health. Having poured everything he had into the newspaper, he was left with a mere $2.50 to support his family of six. As he told Henry Bibb, he had allowed the newspaper to run "him hopelessly in debt," using all he received through subscriptions, what he had gleaned lecturing, what Gerrit Smith had contributed, and "what I had acquired otherwise." It is not clear what that last phrase means, but it suggests that Ward may have used questionable means in his effort to keep the newspaper afloat.

Bibb expressed surprise that Ward had suspended publication after spending the last three months soliciting subscriptions. Later, Jermain Loguen spoke of the newspaper's "sudden disappearance." Many supporters were surprised by the decision to cease publication. They had all paid in advance. Some had received one issue, others none. "I can tell you, friend Bibb," Loguen wrote, "it is a very hard matter for me that is not an editor to get along with such things. Editors," he surmised, may be able to "explain it much better" than he could. Loguen's comments were contained in a letter in which he tried to explain why he was having a difficult time procuring subscribers for Bibb's newspaper. It was clearly not meant to be published. That it was deepened Ward's sense of betrayal. They had been friends since Ward's move to South Butler. Ward had been a frequent guest at Loguen's. He had lectured and preached at Loguen's church many times. Loguen was the principal agent of the *Impartial Citizen*. Ward had been instrumental in getting the American Missionary Association to appoint Loguen one of its missionaries. All who had subscribed, Ward explained in response, had not paid. Had they done so he would have continued publishing. He conceded it was possible that Loguen's letter had been meant for Bibb's eyes only, yet he could not resist responding. This was not the first time, he told Bibb, that Loguen's "pen or tongue has been employed in secretly trying to injure a man, and therefore it is less manly and more base."

Rather than stopping there, Ward went on to accuse Loguen of overcharging Blacks who had received lands from Gerrit Smith "for getting deeds for them." In 1846, Smith, who owned 750,000 acres, had announced plans to give away 120,000 acres of wilderness lands to three thousand poor New York Blacks, land that would allow them to attain the right to vote. Both Loguen and Ward had acted as Smith's agents in helping grantees to secure legal ownership. Loguen responded that he was too busy fighting against slavery to quibble with those who "misrepresent and traduce" him. Yet quibble he did. He called on any of the grantees to come forward and give proof that he had charged them to procure deeds. He had in fact gotten deeds for twenty-five people living in Ithaca and not "charged them a cent for the service." Grantees in other counties, aware of the time he had spent volunteering his services, gave him "some 50 cents, some one dollar, some more as they chose, and others gave me not a cent." He dismissed Ward's accusation as "sheer falsehood." It was a bitter end to an old friendship.[53]

In retrospect, Ward had managed to produce a newspaper that compared favorably to its main rival, Douglass's *North Star*. His editorials were always pointed and frequently humorous. Almost every issue contained essays on the towns and villages he visited during his many tours. He had a keen eye for the physical beauty of the countryside, especially in autumn, when the foliage of upstate New York was vibrantly colorful. He was enthralled by the land's expansiveness. He spoke fondly of the many he met on his tours and paid homage to those who opened their homes to him. Like most of its contemporaries', the last page of the newspaper was given over to short essays and poems, some original, others reprinted. Yet in the end, it was not clear that the state could support another Black newspaper, especially one that covered much of the same material as Douglass's.

Sometime in late 1850, after the newspaper had folded, or early the following year, Ward was arrested for debt in Boston. At an insolvency hearing, he was ordered to "procure a bankrupt's discharge" which, as far as I can tell, required Ward to repay a portion of the debt. The exact size of the repayment is unknown. Ward turned for advice to old friends, especially George Atkinson Ward of New York City, who had bailed him out of prison following the 1834 riot, and Horatio Ballard, a prominent sawyer of Cortlandville, one of his old supporters.[54]

Ward then did what he did best: he went on the road, traveling long distances in the Midwest and Pennsylvania, lecturing to thousands. He was a rousing success. At least a thousand attended his lectures in Chicago. Crowds flocked to hear him in Detroit and Cleveland. He was the guest of George Vashon for an August 1 celebration in Pittsburgh. Jane Swisshelm, the newspaper editor and feminist, was impressed. Like other friendly White observers, she left us a picture of Ward that described his color, size, oratorical skills, humor, and intellect. She thought him as "fine [a] specimen of the black man as any friend of the race need wish to present as a refutation of all assertions of the inferiority of the African. He is so big and so black, so evidently at peace with himself, without a shadow of assumption of pomposity that at first glance one sets him down as a man of well-balanced intellect." He looked, she said, so "entirely good humored, yet calm and dignified, that we were not surprised to hear there was far more laughing than crying in his audience, and that the keenest edge is given to his satire by the perfect good humor in which it is uttered." That kind of reception and publicity must have lifted Ward's spirits, but it failed to generate the money he needed to meet his debts. Emily's presence on the tour must have helped to ease his disappointment.[55]

On the way home, Ward read an account of the shootout in Christiana, Pennsylvania, during which a slaveholder was killed attempting to reclaim a slave. The standoff occurred at a small Lancaster County farmhouse where William Parker and others had armed and barricaded themselves in anticipation of an assault by Edward Gorsuch and a band of Maryland slave catchers. Gorsuch was surprised by the speed with which the defenders had summoned support. He demanded that Parker hand over the fugitive slave. Parker refused and Gorsuch stormed the farmhouse. The result was a disaster. Gorsuch was killed and one of his sons seriously injured. Parker and two others fled to Canada. The events at Christiana were the last straw. After Emily had read the account of the shootout, Ward writes, they concluded that "resistance was fruitless" in a country "hopelessly given to the execution of this barbarous enactment." There was no hope of reforming such a country. It did not help that, as he put it, his "secular prospects . . . [were] exceedingly involved and embarrassed." He had come to the conclusion that lecturing against slavery did not put enough bread on the table. Neither did the anti-slavery cause provide "bread and education for one's children." They decided that the family's future lay elsewhere. They would move to Canada, buy "a little house and garden, and pass the remainder of [their] days in peace, in a free British colony."[56]

At times of disappointment and distress, Ward, as we have seen in his plans to move to Trinidad in 1838, thought of a future elsewhere. Canada had beckoned before—in the weeks after the Supreme Court ruling in the *Prigg* case in 1842 confirming the constitutionality of the 1793 Fugitive Slave Law. Now Ward's sense of disillusionment was compounded. How would a person born in slavery who had escaped with his parents as an infant prove he was free under the new law? It did not help that he was deeply in debt. There seemed to be no alternative but to leave the country. He planned to sell his home, he told Gerrit Smith, and move his family to Kingston, Ontario.[57]

There were other moments of despair when Ward seemed close to abandoning the fight against slavery and Negro-hate. In 1849, he wrote of the constant attempt to "array the white masses against the blacks, and to secure to the latter from the former, the most bitter and inhuman prejudices." Whites, particularly in the cities, treated Negroes as menials, denied them a "place in society," ridiculed and discouraged "all their best efforts at Self-Elevation," shut them out of schools, relegated them to "negro pews," denied them political rights, and from this drew "the sage conclusion that blacks and whites couldn't live on equal terms in the same community." If from among the crushed some dared to raise their heads "above the common level" and take themselves to "books, letters [and] learning," and through "patience, industry, energy and perseverance" acquire some means of influence, pro-slavery Whites demanded racial separation rather than "unstarch a little of their would-be dignity." How could those so utterly devoid of religion and democracy call themselves republicans and Christians? These Whites clearly knew no "*Bible—no God*—in respect to a black man's rights." If Christian "color-phobia on earth is a true representation of the same thing in Heaven, it were about as well to go somewhere else." Ward called on Blacks to be true to themselves and to each other. "Live above, not only the crimes and vices of the age, but above the mere fleshly and sordid [characteristics] of your nature. Be MEN in body and mind, and our elevation is certain." Despite everything, Ward insisted that the Black man's place was in America. Like an Old Testament prophet, Ward predicted, paraphrasing Psalms 12:5, that in "*a day to come,*" the Savior would "arise for the sighing of the poor and the crying

of the needy, and set him safely against him that puffeth at him."
The plea was uncannily autobiographical.[58]

The incident that greeted the Wards on their arrival in Syracuse on October 1, 1851, caused them to temporarily suspend their
plans to leave for Canada. Henry Williams, known also as Jerry,
an escaped slave from Missouri, was at work at his cooper's bench
when slave catchers seized him and took him before Commissioner Joseph Sabine, no fan of the Fugitive Slave Law. City church
bells tolled the alarm that a fugitive had been taken, bringing a
large group of Blacks and Whites, many of them attendees at the
Liberty Party convention, into the streets outside Sabine's office.
They were determined to resist any attempt to return a fugitive
from a city that they had declared a free zone. Earlier, on a visit
to the city, Daniel Webster had made it clear that the administra-
tion would do all within its power to ensure the law was enforced,
especially in an anti-slavery city such as Syracuse. "I am a lawyer
and I value my reputation as a lawyer more than anything else,"
he told his audience, "and I tell you, if men get together and declare a law of Congress shall not be executed in any case, and
assemble in numbers to prevent the execution of such a law, they
are traitors, and are guilty of treason, and bring upon themselves
the penalties of the law." Those gathered outside the commissioner's office were determined to make an equally forceful political statement. Before the hearing could begin, the shackled
Jerry threw himself across a table, "scattering papers and pistols,
Marshalls and constables," and headed for the door, surrounded
by supporters. He was retaken, however, half a mile from Sabine's
office before a carriage could arrive to take him out of the city.
Rather than return the bleeding prisoner to the commissioner's
office, officials placed Jerry in a room under armed guard. Ward
recalled that he and Samuel J. May, the Unitarian minister and

Garrisonian abolitionist, visited Jerry in his holding cell. It was the first time Ward had seen a "chained slave." A "short, thick-set, strongly built man, half white though born a slave," Jerry impressed Ward with his determination to be free. His pleas to visitors were fervid and eloquent. Ward devoted one page of his *Autobiography*, written four years later without the benefit of notes, to Jerry's soliloquy. The purported speech is so filled with standard anti-slavery and anti–Fugitive Slave Law arguments that one cannot help but think these are Ward's, rather than Jerry's, words.

By the evening, plans were in place for a rescue by a group Loguen labeled a "Congress of freedom" that included Ward, Loguen, Gerrit Smith, and others. They had anticipated that Sabine would release Jerry but thought that a forceful rescue would send a pointed political message to the authorities that the city had every intention of defending its status as a free zone. Ward addressed the large crowd gathered outside the police station. He called on "ye sturdy working men of Onondaga" to commit themselves to support those opposed to the law. He felt for Jerry as for a brother. "Yonder is my brother, in chains. Those chains press upon my limbs. I feel his sufferings, and participate in his anguish." Ward was careful to differentiate between the rowdies who had attacked their meetings in New York City in 1834 and the "glorious mob" gathered outside the prison in Syracuse. Loguen recalled that the crowd was led by the "young and active," followed by "the strong and middle aged . . . with elevated brow and firm tread—age-stiffened limbs brought up the rear—and the faces of all, relieved of every shadow that would obscure the brilliancy of their indignation." At a prearranged signal, the crowd stormed the building armed with clubs, stones, axes, and iron bars left, by arrangement, outside the hardware store of Charles Wheaton, a leading member of the Vigilance Committee. They "smashed the windows, chopped and pried out the casings and removed bricks from the building in order to gain entry." As if on cue, several men arrived with a ten-foot beam that they used as a battering ram. The door collapsed. An armed federal marshal guarding Jerry confronted the crowd, only for someone to strike his hand with an iron rod, breaking it. He escaped by jumping through a second-floor window. The crowd took the shackled prisoner out of the building to a waiting buggy and spirited Jerry out of the city. As one observer reported, it was "the sublimest scene my eyes ever beheld." Jerry was carried first to Mexico, New York, thirty miles away, then to Oswego, where he was placed on a steamer a few days later and taken across Lake Ontario to Canada.[59]

The resisters in Syracuse had made their political point. This "most daring and striving event," however, came at a cost to both Ward and Loguen, the two fugitive slaves who had played leading roles in the rescue. Knowing the government would be keen to make an example of those who defied the law, especially those who were still slaves under the law, Ward and Loguen left for Canada immediately. According to Ward, President Fillmore had ordered the arrest of all those involved in the rescue. Trial, Ward felt, would be as good as conviction, especially as the government had made it clear that opposition to the law was tantamount to treason. They had no alternative. As Ward said, if he did his "duty by my fellow men," he must "go to prison, perhaps; certainly, if the Government had their way, to the gallows." Loguen would later return once the crisis had blown over. Ward went into exile, never to return to his native country. The struggle in America against slavery and Negro-hate lost what Amos Beman, a friend and co-worker, called "our moral and intellectual Hercules." America's loss, many in Canada hoped, would be their gain.[60]

CHAPTER 3

———

Going into Exile

WHEN WARD LEFT SYRACUSE, he joined the exodus of fugitive slaves and their families to Canada following the passage of the 1850 Fugitive Slave Law. In December 1850, a Pittsburgh editor was genuinely surprised to discover that "so many of the colored people" who made the city their home "were runaway slaves." Two hundred had left in early September, even before the law went into effect. Six days later, 35 more left; three days later, 150 more. Three hundred passed through Cleveland, Ohio, in early October. Four hundred left Boston in the space of three days. There were reports of fugitives who abandoned their families in a desperate attempt to avoid recapture, hoping to be reunited later in Canada. The flood of departures continued, almost unabated, into 1851. Ward joined what Douglass called "a dark train going out of the land, as if fleeing from death." By 1852, there were an estimated five thousand to six thousand fugitives in Upper Canada, thirty thousand in Canada West. Rather than follow the route taken by Jerry through Oswego, or that of Parker and the others through Rochester in their flight from Christiana, the two logical options for anyone leaving Syracuse, Ward chose to travel first to Boston, then north to Montreal. Ward was aware that the authorities had issued arrest warrants for all those involved in Jerry's liberation, so his choice increased his prospects of reaching Canada safely. Demonstrating his knack for seeing the lighter side of serious issues, Ward told Henry Bibb he knew arrest for treason meant automatic conviction and that "conviction would be suspension," so he was "determined to let 'catching' precede any other step."[1]

In debt and with few prospects in sight, Ward contacted the American Missionary Association (AMA) as soon as he got to Montreal, offering his services as a missionary. Although he had remained active in the association, Ward hadn't held a missionary assignment since 1843, in Geneva, New York. Canada, he told George Whipple of the AMA, was to be his future home—here there was a crying need for missionary work among the growing number of refugees from American slavery. He promised to get to work as soon as he received a commission. He estimated he would need $400 a year to get the job done, $150 of which he could raise from Black settlers in Canada. That would help him to provide for his family of six. Should he be hired, Ward pledged to "make the field pay as much of the salary as possible." There is no evidence that Whipple responded.[2]

By the time of his follow-up letter to Whipple, Ward had moved to Toronto. Emily, the three children, and Emily's sister, Rebecca, joined him in mid-November. The family traveled across Lake Ontario from Rochester on the steamer *Admiral*, captained by Robert Kerr, a Scot, who refused them a cabin, insisting that his White passengers would be offended. His decision forced them to spend the night on deck unprotected from the elements. Please do not pronounce the captain's name "cur," Ward wrote sarcastically. Ward had a similar experience on a St. Lawrence River steamer traveling from Montreal to Toronto. He admitted that Negro-hate continued to hold sway on both sides of the border but somehow, he told Douglass, "negrophobia . . . and pro-slaveryism" were less prevalent in Canada. He would spend the rest of his stay in Canada trying to explain the nature of that difference.[3]

The family settled into their new home at 44 Duke Street and joined John Roaf's Congregational church. Born in England, Roaf came to Canada under the auspices of the Colonial Missionary Society. He was active in the city's short-lived anti-slavery society in 1837. When the society was revived following the Fugitive Slave Law, Roaf was one of its principal officers.[4]

Ward wasted little time severing his ties with his native country. Canada, he told anyone who would listen, was his "adopted country," its government was "my government." In speaking to Douglass and others of developments across the border, he distanced himself emotionally from "your country," "your Northern politicians," even from "your slaves." Later, he would dismiss the United States as that "bloated, besotted, rakish, unprincipled . . . republic." A country that did not love him was not a country he could love. In turn, he addressed Blacks in Canada as "my fellow-citizens of Africo-American origin." He grew almost rhapsodic about the St. Lawrence River's—and, by extension, Ontario's— "splendor of landscape," geographical features, and autumnal beauty. The colorful foliage on display on his way to Toronto gave the impression of an "immense vase filled with bouquets of unspeakable beauty and of most imposing grandeur." There were its beautiful fields of "early-sown wheat," elegant farmhouses, and "nice rustic gardens" dotting the banks of the Canadian side of the river, almost welcoming the visitor, stimulating a "sort of patriotic feeling." The whole vista gave him a sense of belonging, a "fellow feeling with its inhabitants." The country, in effect, had become to Ward, "in a sense in which no country ever was before, my own, and those people my fellow citizens." With the exception of the small villages and hamlets he had visited in upstate New York, and the fond memory of his boyhood in New Jersey's Pine Barrens, Ward never expressed a similar sense of belonging in the United States. It was his right, he insisted, to enjoy the political benefits guaranteed by its Constitution, but it never offered him social (far less economic) equality. He had done all that was expected of a man, yet he was unable to fulfill his ambitions, his hopes for his family and his people, because of Negro-hate. Years later, he told the Colonial Missionary Society in London, England, that he knew of no people, "not even my own people in the United States, [who] exhibit such marks of improvement" as those who came to Canada. There was an unspecified "something" in a man being free, shaking off the shackles and fetters, that gave him a "talismanic power." It was akin to a resurrection, when "the man becomes another altogether." There was "a development and a springing forth, like Minerva from the brain of Jove, armed and equipped for battle." The observation was nothing if not auto-biographical.[5]

To some extent, Ward had joined the struggle to improve conditions for the refugees long before he moved to Canada. He had visited Queenstown, Windsor, and Niagara Falls over the years while on lecture tours of the Midwest. Consequently, he felt he knew enough about Canada West to respond to a couple of editorials in the Colored American criticizing those who were planning to build separate organizations in Canada, arguing they were unnecessary in a country that imposed no legal restrictions on the Negro. The editorials were critical of the efforts of Hiram Wilson and others to establish a manual labor school that would cater to Blacks in Canada West. Wilson went to the area after graduating from Oberlin College in 1836. There he worked with Josiah Henson, a former Maryland slave, and others to establish the Canadian missions that ran schools for Black settlers. On the board of the missions were such prominent abolitionists as Gerrit Smith, William Goodell, and James C. Fuller. By 1839, Wilson had established ten schools taught by teachers drawn from Oberlin. Such organizations, editor Charles Ray argued, were only warranted out of "deepest necessity" where, as in the United States, "laws, common consent and usage" combined to "deprive us of some absolutely needful privilege, or to prevent our moral and religious improvement." Such was not the case in Canada. Schools there generally admitted Blacks, and churches had opened their doors to them. Finally, there was no need for a manual labor school as the University of Toronto "stands with open doors for the reception of students, without regard to color." For these reasons, Ray opposed Henson's mission to England to raise funds for the settlement and school.

Ward had visited James C. Fuller, the British-born Quaker philanthropist of Skaneateles, New York, and a supporter of the Canadian missions, at the end of one of his lecture tours. They discussed conditions in the area. From Fuller he learned that a Baptist church in Brantford had Negro pews and denied Black students entry to its schools. Two years earlier, Wilson had informed Ward that much of the prejudice against Blacks was the result of the influx of American settlers. Ward conceded that Ray might have been speaking of the attitudes of English immigrants, forgetting that, in many places, "the majority of 'the people' are Yankees." There is no doubt, he insisted, that "our people are excluded from schools and churches in all those places where 'separate schools' exist." As for newly arrived fugitives gaining admission to the University of Toronto, Ward dismissed Ray's "intelligent" informant and his "very unintelligent views of the matter" as patently absurd. Who would think that a newly arrived fugitive would have the necessary qualifications for admission to a college? Finally,

Ward wanted Ray's readers to know that schools established for Blacks were not racially exclusive; they were open to all, regardless of color. So too would be the proposed manual labor school. Ward would revisit many of these issues during his residence in Toronto.[6]

Canada, Ward believed, was to be the testing ground for Blacks fleeing American oppression. He had made similar claims for Central New York years earlier following Douglass's arrival in Rochester and Garnet's in Troy. But Canada was different. It was a "free country, where a man, if making any literary or other pretentions, is treated according to his actual worth, and admitted into circles for which he professes to be qualified, in a word, where a man stands rather upon his manhood than upon his complexion." There were numerous opportunities available to the exiles from the "slaveholding republic" in the cultivation of refinement, in manners, and in "manly self-respect." They would soon show themselves, he predicted, to be the "equal of European settlers." Their success, in turn, would provide abolitionists with ammunition "to refute the falsehoods of slaveholders and colonizationists." If, on the other hand, the refugees did not "come up to the mark," their enemies would rejoice and "point to us as a living demonstration of negro inferiority." Blacks were not "a pack of paupers," as many portrayed them to be. Fugitives, many of whom arrived destitute, did receive help, although he had to admit that through "intemperance and indolence," some "remain in want." Canada, he declared, is "free for us as for others." All fugitives needed was an opportunity "to help themselves." But they also had to demonstrate a commitment to self-improvement. That meant they should stop idling about towns, move to the country to "become tillers and owners of the soil," enroll in schools, and give up alcohol. Such commitments to self-elevation would help to overcome Negro-hate, some of which, Ward acknowledged, was due partly to "the bad manners and bad position and bad character of too many of us in the towns and villages."[7]

This new testing ground, he had to admit, also exhibited all the symptoms of the United States' malady: there was Negro-hate—Bibb called it "color-phobia"—poverty, and racial separation. This "contagious disease," which originated in the United States, was more destructive to the mind than to the body. It made Whites shout "nigger," it drove them to leave hotel dining rooms if a Black person sat at a table—but not if he cooked or served the food. It affected parents who, in turn, passed it on to their children. It got hold of the "dregs of society" who worried Blacks would become doctors and lawyers. It raised fears of amalgamation. All this, Bibb warned White Canada, was attributable to "the workings of a diseased imagination, of which you must be cured, or it will destroy your souls and bodies both." The remedy, Bibb suggested, was anti-slavery.[8]

Ward knew of what Bibb spoke. His and his family's arrival in the country had been marred by racial exclusion. His anti-slavery tours of the province only convinced him of the need for an expansive and vibrant anti-slavery movement, the only mechanism capable of attacking Negro-hate, what he called the "body-guard of slavery," and promoting the welfare of Blacks. Blacks also had to do their part. Ward was enthusiastic about the existence of an enterprising "colored elite" who in their "dress, manners, and all that sort of thing" were a "credit to any class of our community." Widespread "wine-bibbing" did worry him: even ministers' wives, he observed, drank "without blushing." But he was confident it was a shortcoming that could be overcome through the work of a vibrant temperance movement. Yet Negro-hate hung like a pall over all efforts to promote the cause in Canada.

Ward spent an inordinate amount of time addressing these issues and searching for solutions. In a series of three letters to the *Voice of the Fugitive*, he explored the nature and contours of Canadian Negro-hate. In the first and much of the second, he examined the history of opposition to the establishment of the Buxton Settlement, also known as the Elgin Settlement, by the Reverend William King, a Presbyterian minister, in 1849. King had inherited fifteen Louisiana slaves following his wife's death. They would become the nucleus of the settlement. Edwin Larwell, an Englishman and a tanner by trade, whom Ward dismissed as a "noisy, brawling Tory politician," led the opposition. Larwell condemned the settlement for promoting race mixing and introducing into the province a group of former slaves who, he predicted, would become a burden on society. King persisted and, with the active support of the governor, Lord Elgin, the former governor of Jamaica, the settlement thrived. It attracted some prominent Black Americans, such as Oberlin graduate William Howard Day, a schoolmate of Ward's at the African School in New York City, and William Parker and Shadrach Minkins, fugitive slaves who had escaped the clutches of the Fugitive Slave Law. By 1856, one thousand called Buxton home. The success of Buxton was proof that Blacks had as much right to "buy and settle lands" as did any British immigrant because, Ward argued, in Canada British law was applied evenhandedly and impartially.[9]

In his third and much longer letter, Ward reached for a wider analytical appreciation and understanding of the Canadian variety of Negro-hate. He and his family had felt the sting of that hatred. There was ample evidence of its existence, he argued, in the ways Blacks sometimes were discriminated against in hotels, public conveyances, and social interaction. Within a year of his arrival, he had accumulated enough examples of racial exclusion and denial of rights to assert that "Canadian Negrohate is incomparably meaner than the Yankee article," largely because it set one "poor ignorant people, against another." In Canada, where Blacks were equal before the law, such hatred was meaner than its American variant. This hatred did not have its origin, however, in Canada; it was an import, a "poor, pitiable, brainless, long-eared imitation of Yankeeism" introduced by some Canadians who had worked in the United States, and by American visitors who brought Negro-hate with them and infected the "smaller soil" of Canadians. The hatred, he insisted, was gratuitous because it was a pitiful imitation of Yankee views and practices. By pandering to their "aristocratic neighbors," Canadians benefited materially. Not one element of this despised history, he declared, originated in Canada. Those who peddled this hate were similar to Irishmen in the United States who trampled upon "blacks who helped to fight for the very liberties which these Irish paupers enjoy, and of which they seek to deprive the blacks." Unlike in the United States, however, such hatred was buttressed by neither "current religion, nor the civil law." In Canada, it lacked institutional foundations. Moreover, British law knew no man "by the color of his skin." Consequently, such hate could never be "eternal." He predicted it would recede in the face of pressure from anti-slavery activity and the "improvement, progress, and good demeanor of the black people." The pulpit and the press already condemned it wherever it raised its hoary head. Under such scrutiny and pressure, "negrophobia cannot long abide" for, unlike the United States, that made no pretense to social equality and democracy, Canada was "an aristocratic country." Here, a "black gentleman of good education, polite manners, and courtly address would be received as a gentleman, while a white man destitute of these would not be so received." As more talented and educated Black men entered the country, they would "give us

better character, and widen the circle of good society, among us."
Ward did worry that the actions of some, particularly the rantings
of unschooled ministers who were "really too ignorant to instruct
anybody," would increase rather than diminish the "prejudice
against us." Despite his many qualifications and reservations,
Ward was optimistic that if Blacks acted "rightly all will be well."
Not only must anti-slavery advocates commit to the education and
elevation of the refugees, they must fight against racial prejudice
wherever it existed.[10]

The task was not going to be easy. Wherever he went, Ward
found evidence that some refugees were acting in ways that justified the views of pro-slavery advocates. Some of the refugees,
he wrote, "talk about how they wish they were again with their
masters; others behave unbecomingly; our separate churches and
our evil demeanors fill the mouths of our enemies here and elsewhere." Separate churches had long been the bane of Ward's existence. As a Black man who had pastored two White congregations, Ward saw little need for the proliferation of Black churches
pastored by ministers who, to quote Douglass, made their congregations shout rather than think. Ward was also critical of Blacks
who chose to join churches that were soft on—if not directly
supportive of—slavery and racial exclusion. Of Episcopalians, he
wondered how any "high-minded black men [could] cling to this
miserably rotten pro-slavery establishment in spite of its abominable Heaven-abhorred practices." His schoolmate Alexander
Crummell had endured terrible mistreatment from bishops of the
Episcopalian Church, as had Isaiah DeGrasse, yet they chose to
remain members.[11]

American pro-slavery churches attracted a great deal of Ward's
attention. He devoted an entire chapter of his autobiography to
a devastating indictment of churches in America, excluding the
Quakers and Free Will Baptists, for their refusal to confront the

"corrupt, spurious, human system" of oppression, even as they never grew tired of proclaiming their Christianity and republicanism. They established organizations, including Sunday school unions and Bible, tract, and missionary societies, that all refused to address the question. The need to maintain harmony among the membership, many of whom were from slave-holding states, trumped tackling the "sin of oppression." How pure could a church be, Ward asked, that "smiles upon, fondles, caresses, protects, and rejoices to defend a system which cannot exist without turning out a million and three quarters of the women of the country to the unbridled lust of the men who hold despotic power over them"? Some of his readers may have winced at the imagery, but that was exactly Ward's point. He pointed to First Corinthians, 5 and 6: fornicators, adulterers, and other sinners could not enter heaven, nor could those associated with them.[12]

Many Black churches, too inward looking for Ward's taste, did little to alleviate the problem. He lamented their "execrable tendency" to sectarian division. They were too fond of "multiplying sects and churches." The proliferation of Black churches did little to help the cause or promote the welfare of their congregations. Before moving to Canada, he frequently commented on Black churches during his lecture tours. Why, he wondered, did the one hundred members of the Black population of Rome, New York, need a separate church? In such situations, what poor populations needed, whether they were Black or White, was a way to come together to break down "complexional distinctions in religion, for the purpose of abolishing such odious distinctions elsewhere." African or Colored churches did little to achieve these ends. He characterized the Black population of Springfield, Massachusetts, as "the most intelligent, most moral, and most industrious" he knew anywhere. Nowhere else did the "low, immoral and self-degraded class of blacks bear so small a ratio to the general mass."

Why, then, did they need to "sustain a separate and distinct" African Methodist Episcopal church? He rejected the need for any religious organization "whose very name is African instead of American," that, in too many instances, shut up Black people in ignorance. He conceded that some "pale-faced religionists . . . would rather go to Hell, than to do justice to a black man." Yet he had not the slightest doubt that both Blacks and Whites would be better in "head and heart" contending for their religious rights together. It was better, he wrote later, to teach "by intermingling than isolation. . . . It is by constant, every-day contact with the Negro, that his character—his faults as well as his virtues—can be learned." Blacks were neither independent, nor did they have the resources to build these churches. As a result, they went cap in hand to Whites for support. If they were lucky enough to raise the building funds, they then had to beg for support to sustain their ministers. (Ward seemed to forget that his church in South Butler, a White congregation, had to seek assistance from the American Home Missionary Association to meet his salary.) Ministers of these churches, he continued, became dependent and cringing, succumbing "to the pro-slavery public sentiment around them." There were exceptions, but these were usually in large cities with substantial Black populations. Even in such cities as New Bedford, Massachusetts, with a Black population of around twelve hundred, a place where Blacks, under law, enjoyed equal privileges, there were five Black churches. Blacks in Boston had built seven or eight churches. In Providence, Rhode Island, there were five. Why so many, Ward wondered, especially in places where "one man in one building could preach to them all, if sectarianism would permit?"[13]

In Canada, where a man who was working on improving himself could stand "upon his manhood," where, therefore, his complexion was not an issue, there was even less need for Black churches ministered to by uneducated preachers. Ward was particularly harsh on Jeremiah Taylor, an AME minister who, since his arrival in Canada in the mid-1840s, had built a congregation that, in ten years, became the third-largest AME congregation in the province. Ward saw no need for such churches in a country where Blacks were free, where "schools, churches, trades and professions [were] open to them." What was it that denied them opportunities for progress? Could it be their tendency to cluster into separate institutions? Ward vented his spleen on Taylor, a "miserable old man" who played the part of "a despicable pro-slavery pope." At his church, "the most indecent, disgusting, ranting and stuff is voided every Sunday that ever an audience listened to." Taylor's "disgusting, abusive, indecent language [and] his semi-theatrical gestures" that passed for a sermon disgusted Ward. His sermons were a "downright disgrace—a religious burlesque—a profanation of the Sabbath—a perfect public nuisance." Ward dismissed Taylor and other such preachers as "the greatest dunces we have." Ward must also have included the United States when he dismissed the "thousand and one black preachers" who preached from the "twofold desire to escape work, and to have and maintain a 'little brief authority.'" To think that the majority of Blacks approved and admired such antics depressed Ward. These preachers and their behavior, he concluded, "bedarken our prospects."

Ward was not a lone voice. Mary Ann Shadd, born free in Delaware, migrated with her father and brother to Canada West in 1851. She settled in Windsor, where she taught school. Shadd was as scathing in her denunciation of the "corrupt clergy . . . sapping our every means, and, as a compensation, inculcating ignorance as a duty, superstition as true religion." She dismissed their "gross ignorance and insolent bearing" and suspected they were motivated solely by money and "not the good of the people."[14]

While harsh, Ward's criticism of the Black church and ministers such as Taylor should not be uncoupled from his view of the struggle against slavery and Negro-hate, a struggle that should be seen in the broadest and most comprehensive terms, reaching beyond the freeing of slaves to the elimination of racial exclusion and to the elevation of the Negro. The keystone of American religion, he argued, was its hatred of the Negro. Those who bellowed loudest about Christianity and republicanism, setting themselves up as "universal reformers," held slaves and persecuted free Blacks. Those who supported charities at home and missionary activities abroad were the greatest culprits. Many of the most learned divines, whom he dismissed as "pulpit parasites," defended slavery using the Bible. Others refused to condemn slavery as a sin. To do so would be to condemn slaveholders who were members of these churches. When a "system of religion" became so corrupt as to uphold and defend an abominable system of inequities such as slavery, it was not to be trusted about anything else. Ward dismissed all calls for reforming the church as unworkable and impractical.

Why then, one wonders, was Ward so harsh on a church that had severed ties with established denominations to create a space of freedom where Black men could lead congregations of Black people? Ever since his move to Peterboro in 1840, Ward had joined the chorus of those calling on men of conscience to establish nonsectarian churches. He was a pivotal player in a group advocating the creation of a Christian Anti-Slavery convention in Auburn, New York, in 1841. Among other objectives, the convention planned to explore how best to purify churches and ministries from the great sin of slavery. The result was the establishment of a number of independent churches throughout the state, churches that held firm against slavery. All of which suggests Ward should have been partial to Toronto's AME church. Yet, as he never failed to insist, not only must slavery and Negro-hate be attacked from all angles, it must also aim to cultivate "all the upward tendencies of the coloured man." All who, by dint of hard work, had elevated themselves and had "acquired a skill" were, he declared, "anti-slavery labourers." By doing so, they lived down "the base calumnies of heartless adversaries." He regarded "all the upright demeanor, gentlemanly bearing, Christian character, social progress, and material prosperity of every coloured man, especially if he be native of the United States, as, in its kind, anti-slavery labour." His was an expansive vision of the anti-slavery struggle that relied on "the doctrine of the Bible, and not creeds of sects—a religion which loves its neighbors, is without partiality that *does* as well as *says*, that makes war upon all manner of sin, and preaches repentance of all classes of sinners." The struggle presupposed its leaders would be drawn from men like Ward who elevated themselves by dint of hard work, not such as Taylor.[15]

Within forty-eight hours of his arrival in Toronto, Ward was at work lecturing in support of the Anti-Slavery Society of Canada (ASSC) and promoting the cause of Black American refugees. He spoke at Roaf's church in late October on the condition of Blacks in the United States, on slavery and Negro-hate, and gave what the *Toronto Globe* described as an "amusing narrative of the rescue of Jerry" and his participation in it. Jermain Loguen followed Ward with an account of his years in slavery in Tennessee and his escape.[16]

The society was organized at a public meeting in Toronto's city hall in February 1851, with Michael Willis, principal of Knox Theological College, as its president, Thomas Henning as secretary, and Andrew Hamilton as treasurer. Three Blacks were named to its Executive Committee, including Henry Bibb, who had escaped slavery in Kentucky in 1837, settling first in Michigan before moving to Sandwich, where he and his second wife, Mary, pub-

lished the *Voice of the Fugitive*. Although not an officeholder, George
Brown, editor of the *Globe* and one of the country's leading abolitionists, was a vital part of the society, together with his extended family. The *Globe* provided the society with a valuable
organ for reaching the public. Following extensive correspon-
dence with British and American abolitionists, the society invited Douglass, Samuel J. May of Syracuse, and British abolitionist George Thompson to deliver a series of lectures in Toronto.
Thompson had recently arrived in Boston at the start of his second tour of the United States. Douglass spoke on the way slavery
separated families, its reliance on the lash to maintain itself, and
the many ways churches and ministers sustained it. "The Altar
and the Auction Block are near each other," Douglass declared.
In tones reminiscent of Ward, he condemned ministers who "tor-
ture the Bible" to justify the system's existence. The cause had
nowhere else to go but to appeal to people at home and abroad
to "awaken an interest in their hearts in the sad condition of the
slaves." Give us your aid, he pleaded, "for we can never strike down
Slavery till we add to our power the moral power of the world
around us."[17]

The society hired Ward as an agent soon after his arrival in
Toronto. Speaking of the need for anti-slavery agitation in Canada, Ward observed that the province was, much like the Northern states, dominated by "pro-slavery feeling . . . and Negro-hate."
Toronto, like Syracuse, was similarly committed to the cause.
Generally, Canadians needed to be educated on the political nature of slavery and the ways Northern politicians sustained it by
being subservient to the South, which "rules and controls the
country." Ward began his agency in December 1851 with a series
of lectures in and around Toronto at Stouffville, Whitechurch, and
Markham and at a meeting of Blacks at Toronto's First Baptist
Church. The society reported optimistically that Ward's eloquence

had been instrumental in spreading and increasing support for the cause and weakening prejudice against the refugees. At Whitechurch, Ward picked up the thread of an old slight when he invited the local division of the Sons of Temperance to attend his meeting. He called on them to sever ties with the American organization and establish a local division free of prejudice. At the end of Ward's speech, a Dr. Creel justified the Sons' Negro-hate on the old worn-out grounds that to act otherwise would encourage race mixing. Ward must have taken some satisfaction when the audience barracked Creel for his comments. By the end of the year, the society reported on the formation of a number of auxiliaries.[18]

Ward toured continually during 1852 and the first few months of 1853. Beginning in early January 1852, he traveled, by his own estimates, 565 miles, visiting, among other places, Windsor, Brantford, Hamilton, St. Catharines, Niagara, London, and Buxton in the west, holding anti-slavery meetings and fighting against "the rising tide of Canadian racism," speaking in "that masterful style of convincing argument" that, as Bibb reported, was "his peculiar *forte*." He called on refugees, whenever possible, to avoid settling in towns and doing manual labor. Settle in the country, he advised, and become "tillers of the soil—[your] own soil, if possible"; cultivate your minds and you "shall soon cease to hear of the stupidity and rascality of blacks." Wherever he went, he saw progress. There were thriving Black businesses led by enterprising men, churches, civil societies, and, especially in Buxton, expanding landownership. He predicted the settlement would soon "contain 1000 inhabitants." He was surprised by how little prejudice he saw even in St. Catharines, reputed to be the hotbed of Canadian Negro-hate. There, he reported, "the prejudice against our people was not so strong, so prevalent nor so unprovoked" as he had heard. The sources of the problem were some "natives of the

United States" working to find a "Canadian soft sapling" to infest. That work was also aided by some "foolish actions of our people," the nature of which he did not explain.

Later, Ward would spend much of the first chapter of the Canadian section of his autobiography explaining the source of local Negro-hate. The country's soil was "polluted by the unholy tread of pro-slavery men." Some were former plantation owners in the West Indies dispossessed by the Emancipation Act of 1834. Others were former slaveholders in the United States who found it difficult, he wrote, quoting Numbers 11:5, to forget the "'leeks and the onions' of that Egypt in which they once luxuriated as small-sized, very small, Pharaohs." Some of these "pharaohs," he pointed out, were Colored men. Yet others had gone south, seeking their fortune on plantations, where they found work as overseers and slave drivers. They had returned to Canada "self-seeking, pelf-seeking devotees of the institution." Finally, there were those Englishmen who visited the South and became enamored of its social traditions. With eyes wide open, they saw nothing "but just what they wish[ed] to see." Canadians were not immune. Although not confined to the "lower order," Negro-hate was most prevalent among the "lowest and least educated," those who did not have the "training of gentlemen" and were not "accustomed to genteel society." Class—or, more correctly, gentility—mattered to Ward. He asserted, without reservation, that he had never seen "the slightest appearance" of Negro-hate among those in Canada who were recognized as gentlemen, men of education and manners who were respectful of others. Among them, he declared, "the black takes just the place for which he is qualified."[19]

The tours led to the formation of chapters of the ASSC but failed to add much to its coffers. Yet the society was convinced Ward had helped to lay the foundations for an expanding anti-slavery presence in the country. Although his health had suffered because of the demanding travel, Ward was equally optimistic about the result of his work. It also convinced him that Canadian Blacks were as well off as their White neighbors. They were not in need of emissaries going on begging missions to the United States. What the "recently arrived refugees" most needed was not "land-buying societies, not old clothes, not any substitute for labor, but stimulation to *self-development.*" Ward's ire was directed at the Refugee Home Society (RHS), a Detroit-based organization formed in 1851 under the leadership of Michigan abolitionists. The following year, it joined forces with the Fugitive Union Society, a Black organization based in Windsor. The Union Society was formed following a convention of Blacks in Windsor that called for the acquisition of land to address the needs of approximately four thousand destitute refugees in the Amherstburg area. The combined society aimed to address the needs of incoming refugees by settling them on land close to Windsor. The society would purchase large tracts of land and resell plots to refugees. Settlers received five acres with the option of buying an additional twenty. One-third of the money received from the sales would go to support schools, the balance would be deposited in banks, and the interest accrued used to purchase additional land. Controlled by a group of Whites in Michigan, the society was led locally by Henry and Mary Bibb and David Hoskiss, the American Missionary Association's agent in Amherstburg.[20]

The Bibbs considered it a "glorious foundation" on which the settlers could build. The project soon ran into opposition, however, from the settlers as well as from a group of Blacks, including Ward and Mary Ann Shadd, opposed to segregated Black settlements as contrary to the refugees' best interests. Ward insisted such settlements were undesirable. He questioned why the RHS was "encouraging, and creating separate settlements, churches and schools" among the settlers. Experiments such as Buxton, he admitted, had proven their worth, but he saw no need for any more of them. As he had said many times before, it was better to intermingle than to isolate. Shadd insisted that the insularity of such communities denied Blacks the benefits that came with exposure to the culture, education, and "moral refinements of western society." She leveled even more pointed criticisms at the leaders of the organization. She accused them of fraud, of skimming more than 60 percent of the funds raised for personal use, and of distrust between White and Black members of the Executive Committee. After a year of collecting funds, only eight families, she pointed out, were living on the land. The fugitives distrusted the society. Henry Bibb was dishonest, collecting money that never reached the refugees. Instead, he used the money to build a lavish house and to purchase a vessel. He also bought his wife a farm. The society, she predicted, would fail. "God's approbation may not be looked for of a scheme whose advocates as a last resort, are driven to make a wreck of private character to sustain it."[21]

Ward and Shadd were pulling against a strong current. Most of the leadership of the ASSC supported the RHS, as did such prominent American abolitionists as Lewis Tappan. Frederick Douglass kept a studied neutrality. After first reading its constitution, Ward wrote Bibb that he liked what he saw, but at a meeting of the RHS in August 1852, he denounced the society as "unrighteous and despotic" and "insulting to our manhood." He leveled much of his criticism of the enterprise at the Reverend Charles C. Foote, whom the RHS had hired to solicit support in the United States. A Presbyterian minister who had moved to Michigan in the late 1840s, Foote, like Ward, was an active member of the Liberty Party in New York. The party had nominated him as Gerrit Smith's running mate in 1847. When he came out in support of the Free Soil Party, however, Ward, a competitor for the vice presidential slot, successfully pushed for Foote's removal from the ticket. While Foote was in Pennsylvania soliciting funds, someone (it is not clear who) asked Ward for his views on the RHS. Ward obliged with a lengthy letter documenting his criticisms of the society. There was no need for a land-buying or land-selling organization in Canada, he contended, as government land could be had more cheaply, could be obtained with "equal (if not greater) facility," and could be held under a "much better *tenure*." Only one-tenth of the cost was needed at the time of purchase, the remainder to be paid in nine annual installments, with interest limited to the unpaid portion. By any measure, government land was cheaper and better than anything the RHS could acquire. In comparison, under the terms laid out by the society, fugitives were limited to twenty-five acres, which Ward dismissed as much too limited. Five of those acres were given to the settler; the remaining twenty would cost $50. Even when the land was fully paid for, the settler could not transfer it for fifteen years. Should the settler attempt to do so, the land would automatically revert to the society. More damagingly, Ward contended, agents of the RHS misrepresented the "condition of the blacks in Canada." They gave the impression that the former slaves could not "acquire such money for themselves." Ward admitted that fugitives did need assistance to get by soon after their arrival, but he insisted they could find work within three days. "I repeat that immediately upon their arrival, they are destitute, and most grateful are we for any aid we may have from the United States or elsewhere." But the refugees did not need Foote to "beg money to buy lands for them." Neither did they need "boxes and barrels of *old clothes*, which cost twice as much for transportation as they are *worth*," nor did they need "a set of land jobbers to beg money to buy lands for them." Such "LAND JOBBING, *under the sacred name of benevolence towards negroes*," was nothing more than "injustice and tyranny." This sort of land manipulation, at the expense of Negroes, had been a cardinal feature of the Liberty Party's condemnation of the federal government land policy in the West. Furthermore, the society's agents received 20 percent of what they raised. It gave settlers one-fifth of the land bought with the proceeds of this begging and sold them four-fifths. There was no greater example, Ward repeated, of the injustice and tyranny of land-jobbing.[22]

Ward then provided an account of a meeting he attended in Detroit in August 1852 to discuss the RHS's constitution at which he raised a number of questions—none of which, he insisted, were answered adequately. The acreage allocated, he pointed out, was much too small and destined to keep the settlers "poor, dependent and a sort of peasantry." Because the bulk of the money raised came from poor people, he was told, they would be irate if the settlers were given land larger than twenty-five acres. The reversion plan for land sold before fifteen years had elapsed, Ward insisted, reduced the fugitive to "a sort of serf." If the fugitive was allowed to sell the land on the open market at the time he thought best, rather than have to hold on to it for fifteen years, he would be able to act independently and possibly reap a profit. Ward was mistaken, supporters of the plan responded; it was meant solely to protect settlers from speculators. When he complained that "this was the equivalent to saying that men who had bought 20 acres of land, were unable to take care of themselves—the old pro-slavery story of the negroes"—the society "virtually admitted it." When he insisted that these abolitionists were being patronizing, Foote replied that, were they ruling for White men, they would have imposed even more stringent requirements. Ward's move to drop the "abominable" reversion clause met with only limited support. Failing to win any concessions, Ward rejected efforts to add his name to the list of the society's officers. When someone suggested Joshua Giddings as an alternative to Ward, the militant abolitionist congressman, Foote objected, arguing that opponents of Giddings—and abolitionism more generally—would be reluctant to contribute to the cause if Giddings was listed as an officer. This only convinced Ward that the RHS was "pro-slavery in its doctrines concerning the capacity of the ne-groes," false in its assertions of the "condition of Fugitives," and willing to "pander to the pro-slavery appetite" of those who opposed Giddings "on account of his anti-slavery course in Congress." To withhold his "solemn and earnest protest" against the society, Ward concluded, would be "false to [his] abolitionism, to [his] love of truth, and to [his] manhood." Earlier, Ward had denounced what he called the "systematic charity seekers" who begged in the United States, even in the South, "partly for fugitives, but chiefly for their own pockets." As if to demonstrate the society's deviousness, Ward added a postscript, pointing out that the reversion clause had been omitted from the version of the constitution published in the *Voice of the Fugitive*.[23]

Ward's was a devastating indictment of the society and its agent, one that Foote could not ignore if he hoped to have any success in his begging missions. He lamented the fact that "friends of the colored people" had yet to learn to disagree without being disagreeable, without employing, as he put it, "unlovely epithets." Foote then strung together a list of what he considered Ward's unsavory words, most of them taken out of context. If he was not a "graduate of Billingsgate," Foote asked, why did Ward "resort to such a dialect?" He doubted "friends of the fugitives" would be influenced by such "denunciations and hard names." Clearly, Ward's public rebuke hurt Foote. In the past, he reminded Ward, they had "acted politically, publicly, socially and privately even to night-slumbers." Was Ward charging him with "bribery and ve-nality" when he claimed Foote received 20 percent of what he raised? Ward, he believed, had relied for such misinformation on an "old rogue," a "professional slanderer," someone who also had nasty things to say about Ward for receiving handsome payments for his lectures. It is not clear why Foote adopted this line of defense. If he was not paid 20 percent, why did he not just say so? Foote pointed out, correctly, that Ward had originally supported the aims of the RHS. He found it ironic, moreover, that Ward would object to the twenty-five acres as too small when Ward's farm in "this State" covers "*hundreds* of broad acres." It is not clear who was the source of this information. It is possible that Foote was alluding to the land Ward received when Gerrit Smith distributed lands to New York Blacks, providing them with property to meet the constitutional requirement needed to vote. Were he referring to this, Foote must have known that Ward's allotment was never that large. Reversion, Foote insisted, was meant to protect "unlettered Fugitives," who were at best "adult children," from grasping predators, the kind, he concluded, almost gratuitously, who would have sent Ward back to New York to be hanged for his participation in the Jerry rescue.[24]

Ward had raised all these objections at the 1852 meeting, Foote recalled, where they were "routed, horse, foot and dragoons." The meeting was attended by the tried and true friends of the "colored people," men who had "devoted their substance and unpaid time to their elevation." Foote listed the members of the society's Executive Committee, many of them leading reformers in Michigan, as well as those from outside the area who had endorsed the work of the RHS, including Michael Willis, Thomas Henning, William King, and George Whipple, "all great rogues," Foote concluded sarcastically, for commending a monstrous species of "land-jobbing, injustice and tyranny." Ward simply was not the best judge of what fugitives needed once they got to Canada. Refugees, for instance, were unable to get homes from the government on short notice. As a result, many went homeless. The RHS had stepped in to fill that void. Every day penniless and destitute fugitives arrived "feeble in Knowledge, and often with a moral constitution fearfully dwarfed and perverted by a system which confounds and confuses every principle of Christian ethics." Exploiting one of the major flaws in Ward's argument, Foote insisted that Ward must have known that the newly arrived needed more than three days of support.[25]

Within four months of Ward's arrival in Toronto, Michael Willis had written the British and Foreign Anti-Slavery Society (BFASS) seeking its aid to hire Ward. Aiding fugitive slaves, Willis pointed out, was a vital part of the society's work and he thought the most effective way of promoting its efforts was to hire the services of a "talented Negro" such as Ward, whose skills as a "speaker and pleader" he compared to those of Douglass. Willis also suggested that both societies could benefit if the BFASS invited Ward to tour and lecture in Britain. There is no evidence the BFASS responded. Two years later, the ASSC announced its decision to send Ward to Britain, hoping to "take advantage of the anti-slavery feeling of Great Britain, quickened and intensified as that feeling had recently become by the unprecedented influence of Mrs. Stowe's *Uncle Tom's Cabin.*"

The announcement came not long after Ward's public denunciation of the RHS. Lewis Tappan declared his opposition to the plan. Like many in the abolitionist community, he was troubled by Ward's public chastisement of the RHS, an organization he considered an important cog in the fight against slavery and in the efforts to improve the lives of fugitive slaves who had escaped to Canada. Ward, he insisted, had maligned the commendable efforts of the RHS and the men who led it, which, he feared, could scuttle the society's efforts. He wrote Thomas Henning that he had known Horace Hallock, one of the society's leaders, for many years. He was a merchant and well-regarded philanthropist. He did not know H. D. Kitchell, another of the leaders, but he was told he was an "intelligent and excellent man." Because the society included men like this as well as Foote, who had a "good reputation," possessed a solid constitution, and received glowing testimonials, he had agreed to have his name added to the list of officers, although he had not attended any of the society's meetings. If Ward did not cease his public condemnation of the society, Tappan pledged that neither he nor the American and Foreign Anti-Slavery Society would provide Ward with letters of recommendation to British abolitionists.

Many saw Tappan's letter, published by Douglass, as a threat. J. R. Johnson, an old American Missionary Association co-worker and Liberty Party stalwart, came to Ward's defense. When Ward escaped slavery in his mother's arms, Johnson declared, she consecrated her child "by the baptism of her joyful tears" and introduced him to "the whole circle of suffering humanity." For many years, Ward had "battled for the cause of Liberty." Now, because of his opposition to Foote and the RHS, he was being told, "in what has the appearance of intimidation," that he must cease his opposition or he could not expect "certain papers of recommendation." Such public condemnation, as we shall see, may have persuaded Tappan to relent.[26]

Just before he left for Britain, a new newspaper, the *Provincial Freeman*, announced that Ward had agreed to become its editor. It was the brainchild of Mary Ann Shadd, who persuaded Ward to lend his name, prestige, and reputation to the enterprise. Not surprisingly, given his experiences, Ward did so very reluctantly. As he told Douglass, being a "burned child," he dreaded the editorial fire. Because of a "very severe and painful experience," he told readers, he had promised himself never again to associate himself with a newspaper. But he had been persuaded to take on the task for one year on the clear understanding that he was "unable to invest a single penny" in the newspaper. In his one and only editorial, he announced that the newspaper would devote itself to the elevation of Black people by promoting temperance "in the strictest and most radical acceptation of that term," would be an outspoken proponent of anti-slavery, would direct its energies to promoting the cause of refugees, and would be free of sectarianism. It was to be, in many ways, a Canadian version of the *Impartial Citizen*. The first issue was published from Windsor, but Ward announced that once it had attracted enough "*cash subscribers*," its headquarters would move possibly to Toronto. The paper next appeared a year later from Toronto while Ward was in England.[27]

Three weeks after the first issue was published, William Howard Day announced that Ward had agreed to serve as corresponding editor of his new newspaper, the *Aliened American*. It was a reunification of sorts with an old schoolmate. The first issue appeared in April 1853 and was generally well received, although some, such as the *New York Tribune*, questioned the wisdom of publishing another Black weekly. Day, the editor of the *Tribune* warned, was fishing "with a naked hook—or rather with the frying pan—and so is quite unlikely to catch any but the slowest chubs." The warning was unnecessary. Day had already announced that the paper would continue only if it attracted a substantial number of subscriptions. A second number was issued the following August.[28]

Unfortunately, only one issue is extant. It contains a curious piece from Ward about the reasons he went to Canada. He was searching, he wrote, for a life a "little more stable than the soap-bubbles and cob houses" of his boyhood. He hoped to enjoy greater liberty than the "Black man ever had, or ever will have, in my native country." He longed to enjoy "the bosom of his family," to get away from the toil of thirteen years, during which his "dependent family had been sacrificed." Moving to Canada allowed him to avoid the relentless rounds of traveling, lecturing, and editing. Yet he had to admit he gave his first lecture within forty-eight hours of arriving and since then had maintained a grueling travel and lecture schedule throughout the province. Despite his best efforts, he lamented, he had failed to escape grinding poverty, and, at the relatively young age of thirty-six, could see the telltale signs of "progressive premature old age." It was a sad admission of personal failure and despair compounded by a recognition that maybe, just maybe, the "great fundamental principles" of the American republic would never be "practically applied alike to whites and to blacks." Was it even possible, he wondered rather forlornly, to "excite in our Anglo-Saxon Spoilers" a sense of justice? The emotional and psychological separation from America that he had so clearly articulated on the trip down the St. Lawrence River on his way to a new life in Toronto in 1851 was harder to attain than he had thought.[29]

Ward left for England a week after his piece appeared in the *Aliened American*.

CHAPTER 4

———

Going on a Mission

WILLIAM J. WILSON wondered if Ward was the best man for the job, yet he was willing to give him the benefit of the doubt. On the eve of Ward's departure, Wilson told his readers, drawing on Mark 4:5, that Ward planned to use his "strong arm" to "hoe the good seed sown there by *Uncle Tom*; and otherwise culture the stock and blade till the ear comes." He could think of no better person than Ward to fulfill such a mission but only if Ward kept "proper command over his inner self." Wilson chose not to elaborate. But Wilson, who wrote under the byline "Ethiop" for *Frederick Douglass' Paper*, knew Ward well. They had worked together on the formation of the League of Colored Laborers in the summer of 1850 during the political crisis caused by the Fugitive Slave Law. The league elected Ward president, Frederick Douglass one of two vice presidents, and Wilson to the Executive Committee. The league aimed to improve the lot of Black workers, to "promote union and concert among the people of color in means of their own improvement; especially in their social and physical condition." It seemed less interested in trade union activity and more in industrial education, Philip Foner has written. Nothing, however, came of the effort. In his doubt about Ward, Wilson may have been pointing to Ward's tendency to flay those with whom he disagreed, to use what Charles Foote called "unlovely epithets" when expressing differences. He was particularly harsh on African Americans who chose to stick with the Whig Party in spite of all its shortcomings. Wilson knew that those sorts of public disputes in Britain would have worked against the interests of the transatlantic movement, which African Americans saw as critical to the maintenance of a united front in the war against slavery.[1]

Although Ward's departure left a gap in the ranks of the Anti-Slavery Society of Canada—one, Alexander Murray argues, it was never able to fill—the society considered his mission critical to its work among the increasing number of exiles from the United States. He was going to raise funds to aid fugitive slaves, to speak on the "subject of slavery generally; to give facts in relation to the demands and progress of the Anti-Slavery cause in Canada, and the actual condition of the coloured refugees in Canada." Ward added to his remit. He was also going, he later recalled, to continue the effort to win British support for emancipation and the fight against Negro-hate. British anti-slavery societies must do everything they could to warn British emigrants to the United States "against the guilt and danger to which they will be exposed ... when settled in the United States," and to rebuke them if they fell into "the trap of adopting American pro-slavery ideas and anti-black attitudes."[2]

Ward, who had so strenuously opposed begging missions to the United States, saw nothing incongruous in a mission to England to raise funds to aid the cause of fugitives. He was following a well-worn path. As early as 1838, British abolitionists had contributed to the establishment of schools for fugitives in Canada. A visit by Hiram Wilson and James Fuller in 1843 netted £1,000 for building schools and employing teachers. Josiah Henson's visit in 1851 raised more than £7,000 for the Dawn Settlement, in spite of controversies that dogged Henson throughout his tour. Alexander Crummell, in England to attend Cambridge University, also raised money to build the Church of the Messiah, the second Black Episcopalian church in New York City. British supporters established two committees to oversee Crummell's fundraising: one for the church, the other to support Crummell's family while he attended university. The church appeal raised nearly £2,000 between 1848 and 1851.[3]

Ward carried with him a satchel full of letters of recommendation to many of the leading figures in English philanthropy. John Scoble, former secretary of the British and Foreign Anti-Slavery Society, in Canada on a mission to evaluate conditions at the Dawn Settlement run by Josiah Henson, recommended to the ASSC that it provide Ward with letters of introduction to Bible, tract, and missionary societies as well as the Congregational Union. Ward's pastor, John Roaf, added letters of introduction to the Colonial Missionary Society as well as to prominent British Congregational ministers. Scoble also provided him with a "memorandum of useful hints." In a letter to the BFASS, Scoble praised Ward for his "cultivated mind" and his eloquence. Characterizing Ward as a "pure Negro, of noble personal appearance," Scoble believed he would "lose nothing by comparison with Frederick Douglass." He also felt it necessary to point out to his former colleagues that Ward was not a Garrisonian abolitionist. If there was one thing that worried Scoble, however, it was Ward's "tendency towards a belligerent spirit." The angry Black man had long discomforted white co-workers in the movement. This was, in part, behind Charles Foote's reactions to Ward's opposition to his begging missions in the United States. Frederick Douglass's insistence that he be treated as an equal generated similar reactions from Richard Webb during his visit to Dublin in 1845. Douglass, Webb thought, was too quick to take umbrage.[4]

Ward had to travel to New York City to catch the Liverpool boat. The fact that he spent less than forty-eight hours there suggests that he was still concerned he could be arrested for his involvement in the Jerry rescue. He took the opportunity to visit his mother, who had moved back to the city from Newark following the death of William, apparently from a stroke, in May 1851. Ward had visited William a couple of times while he recuperated from his first stroke; he heard of his father's death as he was about to deliver a sermon at Amos Beman's church in New Haven, Connecticut. The visit in New York before he sailed was the last time Samuel would see Anne. Word of her death would reach Ward while he was at breakfast in Liverpool with the Reverend Thomas Raffles, a prominent Congregational minister, in September.[5]

A reconciliation between Ward and Lewis Tappan in the weeks after Ward's public condemnation of the Refugee Home Society increased the mission's prospects for success. At the height of the controversy, Tappan had vowed to oppose Ward's mission. Without Tappan's endorsement and letters of recommendation to the leadership of the BFASS, the mission likely would have been doomed. Tappan not only paid for the ticket to Liverpool, he also provided Ward with a letter of introduction in which he declared that Ward "had the confidence of the great body of abolitionists" in the United States.[6]

The journey, however, did not start as Ward had hoped. Soon after he boarded the *Europa*, a Cunard steamer built in the Glasgow shipyards in 1847, Edward Cunard, the company's agent, introduced himself and explained that he had made it clear to Tappan when he purchased the ticket that Ward would have to take his meals in his rooms. Tappan had protested but Cunard would not budge. It was, Cunard admitted, company policy meant to appease White American racial sensibilities. The company simply could not allow its ships to be an "arena of constant quarrels" over slavery and social equality. When confronted by similar exclusionary policies on a St. Lawrence steamer in October 1851, Ward had looked for another boat to get him to Toronto. Now he had no choice if he wanted to be in London for the start of the anniversary meetings. Here, Ward lamented, was "an Englishman perverted . . . like the Yankee, making a dollar come before right, law, or anything." Cunard pleaded he did not share "Yankee feelings" on race. Even if that were true, Ward condemned the liner's policies for pandering to arrogant White Americans. They preached freedom, yet constantly imposed their own views on other nations. They claimed to believe in equality, but only their variety of it. Worse than this arrogance was the ease with which a "Yankeefied Englishman" accommodated himself to it. As compensation, Ward was given a superior stateroom. Later, when the second steward invited Ward to the second-class table for dinner, one passenger, a squirt of a Welshman, "four feet nothing and a half," who had lived in Texas and became a slaveholder, protested. That was too much for Ward, who ignored the protest and took his seat at the table. Not long after, he and his *little friend* were reconciled.[7]

Ward devoted six pages of his autobiography to the episode, eager to explain, if not understand, what lay behind the steamship's policy. As a businessman, Ward acknowledged, Cunard had to be sensitive to the views of his customers. White Americans were frequent passengers; Negroes were not. The company maintained its business by constantly bowing to "Yankee sensibilities" and conciliating the Black passengers who occasionally sailed on its ships. Negroes, he concluded, seemed made to be "kicked about" for White men's convenience. Whenever confronted by situations like this, Ward would search for their deeper meaning, hoping to find a solution. There were, he observed, Black men of stature, of learning—ministers, educators, and orators—but few of wealth. "Black men must seek wealth," he declared. Then and only then would businesses like Cunard's, faced with the prospects of losing customers, adopt a different course. When Negroes, like Quakers and Jews, he concluded, were widely known for their "pecuniary prosperity and independence," when they had elevated themselves, through their own exertions, then and only then could they expect to be treated equally.[8]

Ward knew of Frederick Douglass's treatment in 1845 on the *Cambria*, another Cunard ship, when the captain had to threaten to clap in irons passengers who were disrupting a speech the captain had asked Douglass to deliver. After that experience, the company had pledged to treat all its passengers equally. When, however, Henry Highland Garnet and William Wells Brown's two daughters later traveled to England, the company failed to fulfill its pledge.[9]

The crossing was pleasant and comfortable. The bishop of Montreal visited, as did William Makepeace Thackeray, the English novelist, on his way home from a successful six-month tour of the United States, during which he had visited and lectured in a number of Southern cities. Unlike Charles Dickens, who had found little to praise in the country, North or South, Thackeray maintained a studied silence about slavery. As he told friends, "Blacky" was not his "man and brother." He predicted he would be "sadly unpopular at home by confessing that what I saw of negro-life seemed anything but unhappy." Thackeray, Ward recalled, spent an hour every day with him in his cabin. They struck up a friendship that Ward implied endured once they landed in England. The ship's doctor also visited daily. Yet of the several American travelers on board, not one paid Ward a visit. His loneliness was reflected in how precise Ward was about the length of the voyage; it took, he remembered, "ten days, fifteen hours, and fifteen minutes."

Then, at last, he was in England, "the England of my former reading, and my ardent admiration. . . . I was in the land of freedom, of true equality." He had landed in a city, he acknowledged, "whose merchants, but sixty years before, had mobbed Clarkson for prying into and exposing the secret inhumanities of their slave trade." Unlike other Black visitors, Ward made it clear that his arrival in England did not instantly make him feel like a "man." Regardless of the conditions under which he lived, he had always thought himself to be the equal of any of "those who trampled upon me." Throughout his visit, Ward would try, not always successfully, to maintain a balance between his reverence for the country and the people who had abolished slavery in its colonies, and an acknowledgment that Britain bore a heavy burden and responsibility for the treatment of its former slaves.[10]

For Ward, as for so many other Black American visitors, first impressions mattered. He was surprised by the "comfort and cleanliness" of the working classes. He had read and heard that their conditions were "far worse than the American slave," that they were destitute and forced to work for 6 pence a day. Those were the claims of American protectionists in whose camp, he admitted, he once belonged. In Liverpool, he saw "abundant refutation" of that claim. In subsequent travels through Lancashire, he came to realize that the "factory women" dressed as well as those in Lowell, Massachusetts, and other New England factory towns. Wages were comparable, as were the hours of labor. He visited a factory in Manchester where he found the work "as easy, and the health and cheerfulness of the operatives as good" as he had seen "in the same class on the other side of the Atlantic." The same was true for men. Formerly, he conceded, operatives had suffered "much from the want of care exercised by themselves,

and more from the want of humanity on the part of their employers." These conditions were changing, led, in large part, by government regulations and the work of philanthropists. This was
Ward's way of dispelling a myth promoted by pro-slavery advocates that the Southern slave was much better off than the British
worker. On a more personal note, men and women of all ranks
received him warmly wherever he went. "Genteel society" knew
how to make strangers feel perfectly at home with their "capti-
vating kindness."[11]

Ward set immediately to work once he got to London. Within
a month, he had attended and spoken at all the anniversary meetings, including the Bible, tract, Sunday school, missionary, and
peace societies—an honor, he pointed out, he had never received
in the United States. He spoke at the Colonial Missionary Society's annual meeting eight days after his arrival. The society supported Congregational churches in Canada and Australia. At the
meeting, held in the elegant Poultry Chapel in Cheapside, rebuilt
after the Great Fire of London, Ward prefaced his remarks with
expansive acknowledgments of the prominent men who sat on the
stage behind him. Such introductions, he observed, came to him
"like a cooling, soothing balm." When necessary, Ward knew how
to flatter. He praised the society for the dedicated men it sent
to Canada, such as his pastor, John Roaf, men who labored under
trying circumstances on "very small pittances." Despite these
hardships, the church had flourished in Canada. The future looked
bright, but it could be secured only with increased support. The
speech was a superb first effort littered with humorous asides. He
announced his determination to return to Canada, to go to his
farm, and to work for the sustenance of his "small wife and large
family." Ward was at his oratorical best.[12]

Exeter Hall, the venue for the annual meeting of the BFASS,
was packed beyond its capacity of five thousand. Tickets for the

event had been sold out weeks earlier. Pickpockets had free rein, relieving patrons of their possessions, until the police intervened. There were many Americans in the audience, including William Wells Brown, a fugitive slave who had been in England a number of years; Sarah Pugh and J. Miller McKim, prominent Philadelphia abolitionists; and William G. Allen and his wife, who had recently escaped a mob in Central New York when they announced they planned to be married. Allen, a professor at Central College, was Black and his wife-to-be, Mary King, was a White student. William and Ellen Craft, former slaves in Georgia who had escaped attempts to recapture them in Boston, were also in the audience.

Lord Shaftesbury, the chair, was half an hour into his welcoming speech when Harriet Beecher Stowe, her husband, and her brother entered the hall. Pandemonium broke out, Wells Brown reported; there were "waving of hats and handkerchiefs, the clapping of hands, the stamping of feet and the screaming and fainting of ladies." The crowd had come to see the famous author whose novel had transformed the debate over American slavery. It had sold over 1 million copies within eight months of its publication in Britain. Lord Palmerston, who claimed he had not read a novel in thirty years, admitted to reading it three times. Everyone seemed to be reading it, from boys in London streets to people in country villages. Ward recalled that he met with an emaciated and bedridden child in Aberystwyth, Wales, who had read *Uncle Tom's Cabin* and as a result had developed an "interest in the slaves, and daily prayed for them." The lad had set aside part of his allowance to give to the cause of the fugitive slaves in Canada. Wells Brown observed that the novel "had come down upon the dark abodes of slavery like a morning's sunlight, unfolding to view its enormities in a manner which has fastened all eyes upon the 'peculiar institution,' awakened sympathy in hearts that never before felt for the slave."[13]

According to Wells Brown, Professor Calvin Stowe gave a sub-par speech. He evidently wished there was "no agitation on the subject and said it would do no good as long as England purchased American cotton." As far as Wells Brown was concerned, Stowe was a mere "child in the antislavery movement." Ward, on the other hand, gave the "best speech of the evening." He exposed the hypocrisy of American pro-slavery churches, leaving Professor Stowe visibly uncomfortable. Wells Brown admitted he placed little hope in the America clergy, White or Black, but he had to concede that Ward was one of the most honest, uncompromising, and "faithful advocates of his countrymen." Ward's speech combined a scathing attack on the American church with his personal experiences. He seemed to speak directly to Professor Stowe as a representative of the American clergy who, as the false prophets in the Old Testament did, pandered "to the vices of the nation, while the true prophets reproved them." He spoke of his "pious mother" whose faith, he acknowledged, was the one thing that had saved him from infidelity. He also told the story of a Black girl who once rejected a religious tract from a White woman because Whites, while they were anxious to save Black souls, would not condescend to sit next to them in church. The White woman persisted, finally persuading the Black girl she was different. The girl relented. She took the tract, read it, and was converted. That girl, Ward announced, was his wife. Ward then recounted his experiences on the trip across the Atlantic. It did not seem to matter that he "was a British subject, and Mr. Cunard was an Englishman." Such prejudice against the Negro had to be "rooted out, and the coloured man, if worthy of it, ought to be allowed to occupy a position in society on equal terms with his white brethren."[14]

Two days after the Exeter Hall meeting, Ward participated in the anniversary meetings of the Societies of British Missions, made up of the Home Missionary Society, the Irish Evangelical

Society, and the Colonial Missionary Society. Days later, he, Calvin Stowe, and Charles Beecher attended the annual meeting of the Congregational Union of England and Wales. Ward would attend and speak at both their annual and autumnal meetings while he was in Britain.[15]

He and Calvin Stowe also attended the National Temperance Society's annual meeting. The editor of the *Temperance Chronicle* was deeply impressed by this "unflinching advocate of the cause," and recommended that local societies try to "obtain his services" whenever possible. Ward, the editor observed, did not restrict his sympathies to his own race, nor to one object such as abolition, but "gives them a scope wide as the sphere of philanthropy." In a letter to the editor, Ward had declared, "I cannot turn my back upon one good cause because I am an advocate of another. As I travel, my principles must be known; they were made on purpose to be known. Indeed were I a man of wealth, feeling as I now do on this great subject, and desiring as I do the best weal of my fellow subjects, and seeing how much total abstinence has to do with this, I should devote no small portion of my time to the advocacy of this holy cause."[16]

Ward and Harriet Beecher Stowe attended a musical recital by Elizabeth Greenfield, known as the Black Swan, at Stafford House, the palatial home of the Duke and Duchess of Sutherland. The duchess was the patron of both Stowe and Greenfield. After the performance, guests toured the house and grounds to the strain of bagpipes. Stowe was struck by the attention Ward attracted at the event and the ease with which he circulated among the guests. She described him as a "full-blooded African tall enough for a palm tree." She observed him "in conversation with lords, dukes and ambassadors sustaining himself modestly, but with self-possession. All who converse with him are satisfied that there is no difference between the African and other men." When Ward read her description of the evening in her published account of her tour of Britain, he was unimpressed. It was another example of Whites pandering to American Negro-hate. For all her praise, Stowe could not bring herself to tell her readers that she entered the hall on Ward's arm. To have done so, Ward reasoned, would have cut into the sales of the book in the United States. His reaction was reminiscent of the hurt he felt when his mentor in Poughkeepsie refused to name Ward a sponsor of a society they were about to form. Such slights by those who claimed to be working for the cause pained and angered Ward.[17]

Ward called a preliminary meeting of potential supporters of his mission at Radley Hotel in London on June 6, 1853, attended by Lord Shaftesbury, Louis Chamerovzow, secretary of the BFASS, and the Reverend James Sherman, the Congregational minister of Surrey Chapel, among others. Sherman, who had written the introduction to the official English edition of *Uncle Tom's Cabin*, opened his home to Ward and the Stowes. It must have been a new experience for Ward to have a White person open his home to him for over three weeks, especially since they had only recently met. Although Ward had lived in Peterboro for many months, there is no evidence that he spent a great deal of time at Gerrit Smith's mansion. What Sherman did was different, and it struck Ward as a meaningful gesture of friendship and disinterested philanthropy. The two developed a lasting friendship—Sherman became one of Ward's most important confidants. Sherman's friendship, Ward wrote, was that of "a man of feeling, as well as a man of honor; it is that which places at one's disposal whatever he has, whatever he can do, and rejoices in any sacrifice to accommodate whoever may have the good fortune to be admitted to his intimate acquaintance." Not since the death of his father had he met a man who "in adversity and prosperity, in sunshine and in storm" he could "so safely trust," one in whom "he could so implicitly rely in any and all the varying and trying circumstances of life and fortune" as Sherman. Smith would have been surprised to read that.[18]

The provisional committee called a public meeting for Freemason's Hall two weeks later at which Ward laid out the purpose and objectives of his mission. All the fugitives in Canada needed was to be "taken by the hand," to be put into a "position in which they could obtain work and provide for themselves." There was prejudice in Canada, he admitted, but unlike in the United States, the law was on the side of the fugitives, and religious groups there did not "sanction prejudice." These were rather rosy claims that Ward knew would not stand up under scrutiny. Blacks could appeal to the law, yet discrimination, as Ward had amply documented, was widespread. What they were able to achieve in Canada, he argued, would set an example in the United States and "work out most important results." A committee composed of lords, ministers, philanthropists, and bankers, headed by Shaftesbury, would guide Ward's activities for the ten months of his mission. The committee issued a public appeal for support. The success of the fugitives, they insisted, would demonstrate "the fitness of the slaves for freedom . . . the perfect capability of the negro to live and to advance under the same government and upon terms of political and social equality with the anglo-saxon race or any of the great human family."[19]

Ward left on an extensive tour of the provinces and Scotland in late summer. He estimated he visited "almost every county in England." If he did not, it must have felt as if he did. He attracted large audiences on many of his stops. Despite inclement weather, over twelve hundred attended his meeting in Birmingham; fifteen hundred heard him lecture in Leeds. September saw him in Kent, Sussex, and Northampton. He preached twice in Cheltenham, made famous for its spas. In late November, he spent most of his time in and around London. Much of December was spent in Scotland, where he visited Sterling, Dunfermline, Edinburgh, Dalkeith, Hamilton, Stewartown, Cumnock, Kirkaldy, Falkirk, Rutherglen, Greenock, Campbeltown, and other places north of the border. He estimated he held two dozen meetings in Scotland. While there, he was employed by the Glasgow New Antislavery Association for twenty days. Formed in 1850, the association was meant to be a counterweight to the Glasgow Emancipation Society, which supported the Garrisonian wing of the American movement. Henry Highland Garnet and J. W. C. Pennington had earlier worked with the association, for which they had won the ire of Garrison's supporters. In Edinburgh, however, Ward worked with Jane Wigham, one of Scotland's most effective supporters of Garrison.

As had been the case in the United States, the heavy schedule of lectures took its toll on Ward's health. The Scottish winter did not help. He suffered from congestion of the lungs and took solace from James Thomson's poem "Hymn of the Season": "In Winter, awful Thou!" He also had problems of the spine that at times "completely prostrated him." Ward retreated to Ramsgate on the Kent coast to recuperate after one of these bouts of illness. Once he was on his feet again, Ward lectured in the Huntingdonshire village of Kimbolton, where he met Florence Edger, the three-year-old daughter of the pastor of the church where he preached, who gave 1s. 3d. to the cause. After his lecture in Upper Clapton, a servant girl rushed home and returned with a gift of 5 shillings. In Poplar, many of those who donated, he recalled, were "poor persons, widows and others who generally do much more, in proportion to their means, than the rich do." A Black seaman, living temporarily at the local Sailors Home, contributed 5 shillings. As far as Ward was concerned, these were the highlights of his mission and a statement of working-class solidarity with the cause.[20]

Ward also found time to deliver major lectures and sermons. He returned to Cheltenham in late November where he gave a lecture titled "Origin, History and Hopes of the Negro Race" to the city's Literary Society. Blacks were universally mistreated, their "peculiar features . . . made the badge of inferiority and enslavement," he declared. He traced the race's history back from Noah to Adam and from Adam to God. The Negro, he declared, as he had so many times before, belonged to the human family. Europeans derived their history from the Greeks and Romans who, he argued, had it from "Jews—the Jews from Egyptians and Ethiopians—in other words, from Africa." Having established the genesis of man in Africa, Ward turned next to biblical exegesis to explain early history, especially Chronicles 4:40, which declares that the children of Israel "found fat pastures and good, and the land was wide and quiet and peaceable; for they of Ham had dwelt there of old." Ancient history had acknowledged the importance of such Africans as Hannibal and Euclid. On the other hand, the modern history of the race had been dominated by slavery, during which they were "trodden under the heels of those who made no records of those on whom they trod." They had peacefully endured a "slavery unparalleled for 240 years." In that regard, the Negro was equal to any race that has had to endure slavery. Not only was he "patient and gentle, but he has such religion as we see but few specimens of in this country." This "Christian patience" had sustained the Negro in the face of a remorseless tyranny that denied him the Bible, letters, and marriage. Despite all this, he had maintained a moral character "equal to any depressed people." Yet Negroes had made invaluable contributions to the societies that oppressed them. For instance, they fought bravely in the Revolutionary War to guarantee America's independence, only for some of them to be returned to slavery. "If the ancient negro was a soldier, the modern negro has shown himself one whenever opportunity" has been afforded him. Even where opportunities had been limited or denied, as in the case of the United States, Ward provided a list of those who had managed to break through racial barriers. It was an impressive list. It included his cousin, Henry Highland Garnet; Alexander Crummell, who had recently graduated from Cambridge University; Daniel Payne, bishop of the African Methodist Episcopalian Church; William Douglas, the artist who had studied in London; J. W. C. Pennington, awarded an honorary doctorate from the University of Heidelberg; Charles Reason and William G. Allen, former professors at New York Central College; William Howard Day, editor and graduate of Oberlin College; Ira Aldridge, the Shakespearean actor; Frederick Douglass; and Ward's co-editor of the *Provincial Freeman,* Mary Ann Shadd. Yet all had been denied their constitutional rights. Only in five Northern states were they allowed to vote. In this sense, the United States was the exception, for "in every other country . . . the blacks who are free meet with respect." Freedom in the United States, he predicted, would come either peacefully or by "some powerful eruption among themselves." Ward's prescience must have startled some of his listeners. But he did not flinch from the significance of his prediction. He repeated the lecture in Liverpool, Dundee, Glasgow, and Ulverstone, Lancashire. At the latter stop, he took time to visit the home and chapel of George Fox, the founder of the Society of Friends, "an honored branch of the Christian Church to which my people are very much indebted."[21]

On some stops on his tour, Ward also preached at prominent chapels and churches. In Ralph Wardlaw's chapel in Glasgow, he took as his text John 15:7: "If ye abide in me, and my words abide

in you, ye shall ask what you will, and it shall be done to you."
Wardlaw, who was gravely ill, could not attend. Over two thousand were there to hear Ward preach. He connected his text to
the tenth verse: "That whatsoever ye ask of the father in my name,
he may give it to you." His was a message of hope and the power
of faith, both needed at a time when "sin so much needs to be
checked—when the heathen needs to be converted and when so
many of our crowded towns and villages need a word of caution
in their ears—take heed, beware of covetousness." Christ was
"the door" to salvation and the Bible the only standard of faith.
One had to live by Christ's commands, the ways he "expresses his
will." We live in guilt, Ward declared, when "we live not in the full
faith that what Christ literally promises is not literally expected."
Britain had a promise to fulfill, for "God has made it the home of
the poor—an asylum for the outcast—God caused it to be planted
as a city of refuge to receive those who fled to it as the manslayer
pursues." By contrast, America, with its slaves, did not receive the
word of God. We wish Britain, Ward concluded, to be "God fearing, sin hating . . . that from it the light of truth may spread to the
ends of the earth."[22]

In a lengthy editorial, John Campbell, editor of the *British
Banner,* discussed what the sermon meant for the future of the
Negro. A Congregational minister, Campbell was one of the first
to suggest raising money to buy Frederick Douglass's freedom in
1846. Douglass impressed him. Reacting to a three-hour speech
by Douglass at Finsbury Chapel in May 1846, Campbell described
it as the sort of speech British abolitionists "would have taken a
voyage around the globe some forty years back . . . to have heard
. . . from the lips of a slave." It was, he said, a speech of "much
logic . . . much wit . . . [and] much eloquence."[23]

The editorial, however, had less to do with the future of the
Negro and more to do with the man who delivered the sermon.

The Negro, it opened, had been "subjected to such oppression and neglect" that his "real character is but ill determined." Some believed that this oppression had so "crushed and downtrodden" Blacks that they had lost "the higher developments of a mature manhood," making them fit only to serve, never to rule. Ward gave the lie to all such conclusions. In him, Campbell saw not "the crouching sycophant, not the timid, furtive glance, not the quivering, hesitating voice, not the fawning obsequious manner of one wishing to secure the good grace of superiors," but a man in full possession of all "the feelings and faculties of a fully developed humanity." If, given all the suffering the Negro had had to endure, the race could produce such a specimen of "dignity and authority, what may not be expected when it shall have been restored to all the heaven-born privileges and improved with all the advantages of high civilization, and a still more elevating Christianity." Ward, by his appearance and eloquence, had "dissipated another popular error." His was no "cold philosophy" but one "expressed by logic on fire." Campbell did take issue with what he saw as Ward's indecisiveness about who constituted the poor. He wondered if Ward was referring to the "virtuous poor and not those who make themselves poor and keep themselves poor through their own misconduct." Yet he remained totally convinced by Ward's argument that Negro inferiority was a fallacy. Given Ward's background, Campbell was impressed with his clear intellect, "an imagination as fertile, reasoning faculties as acute, and judgment as sound as the great majority of those who occupy the pulpits of our country." Campbell concluded his analysis with a biography of Ward from his birth in Maryland to his escape to Canada. Following an earlier speech of Ward's at a Sabbath school celebration, Campbell marveled at his "intellectual power and rhetorical ability," which he considered to be of a "very high order." In no case had Ward failed to "acquit himself with honor." His resources,

Campbell asserted, were "inexhaustible, and his vitality is such that he is always at home, while his tact would make him a formidable antagonist for the astutest man among us." It could not be explained logically that such a man, "and the race to which he belongs, should be seized and robbed of their inalienable rights, on the simple ground of their color, when given proof of fitness for fellowship, not of horses and oxen, but of the most cultivated portions of white men!" Campbell was not alone in praising Ward, who left his mark wherever he went.[24]

Throughout his agency, Ward gave regular accounts to the *British Banner* and other publications of the moneys raised for the fugitive slaves in Canada. At a public meeting at Crosby Hall with Samuel Gurney in the chair, the secretary of the committee, S. Horman Horman-Fisher, a lawyer and banker, reported that the mission had netted over £1,900: £400 of this was remitted to the ASSC; a little more than £320 was used to cover traveling expenses, the cost of arranging meetings, and Ward's salary. The committee retained £424 that later would be transmitted to Toronto.

Assessing his efforts, Ward insisted that the slave system was getting worse and more entrenched. Under the terms of the Kansas-Nebraska Act, it was now expanding into free territory. He spoke mostly of the hardships facing fugitive slaves, particularly the fear of recapture. "Men who could do all or any of these things and encounter unspeakable hardship for the purpose of being free, deserved their freedom." These hardships notwithstanding, once the escapees got to Canada they became "good servants, diligent scholars and, in the majority of instances, made their way up in society and obtained some little property for themselves." They bought plots of land and built homes, setting an example to White Canadians. Recently, attempts had been made to exclude them from schools, but Ward continued to insist, erroneously, that the courts had stepped in to stymie those efforts. With the aid they received, they had shown themselves capable of helping themselves.

Ward wrapped up his ten-month mission in March 1854. The tour, by all measures, was a rousing success. Back in Canada, Mary Ann Shadd declared the tour the "most important ever made by a colored man to England." Ward helped to refute the notion that all fugitives in Canada were destitute. He also made a point of differentiating between those in need and those who were self-reliant, which only helped to strengthen them against slavery and discrimination. He was not only the indefatigable agent of the Toronto Society, he was also "the representative *par excellence* of colored Americans, in capability, energy and address." Campbell thought it a bit of good fortune for the cause, a happy conjunction, as he put it, of two events: the publication of *Uncle Tom's Cabin* and Ward's arrival in England. Playing on the title of Stowe's second volume, Campbell declared that the key was "even more effective than the lock; but the arrival of a man, six feet high, and we presume sixteen stone weight, gifted with a vigorous understanding, endowed with a rich original eloquence, to turn the key—that was the finishing stroke."[25]

Many expected Ward to return home at the end of his mission, but there was continued demand for his services by British philanthropic societies. More important, he needed the money. It is surprising, and a testimony to Ward's frugality, that he managed to make ends meet on such a small allowance. He must have had to cut corners and rely on the hospitality of friends to have survived on the portion of the £320 set aside for traveling and lecturing expenses. A few weeks after the end of the mission, Ward wrote Shadd that his "private and professional engagements, were never more numerous." Then he added a telling phrase: "My own personal business [was] never more embarrassing and perplexing." The old problem continued to haunt Ward.[26]

Ward took up where he had left off, following a hectic schedule of lectures and sermons. He attended meetings of the Irish Evangelical Society, the Home Missionary Society, the British and Foreign School Society, the Congregational Union of England and Wales, the British and Foreign Sailors Society, the BFASS, and the Colonial Missionary Society, which hired him for one month. Unlike Garnet, Crummell, Pennington, and other Black clergy, who had established a record of promoting missionary causes, Ward seemed to become more outspoken in his commitment to missionary activity once he got to England. He commented on the role of missionary societies in the colonies at the annual meeting of the Colonial Missionary Society. He reminded his listeners that God had given England her "great provinces" for the "purpose of sending the Gospel to the distant parts of the earth and to tell all nations that this was her glorious privilege." The inhabitants of Africa had conferred upon the British a very large portion of her literature and her art. The names of Euclid, Augustine, and others were associated with "that land." He dismissed Thomas Carlyle's "long-eared book" on the West Indies, *Occasional Discourse on the Nigger Question,* as beneath contempt. "How pitiable it was for the descendants of the Anglo-Saxon race to put the Negro people into the scale, and so much weight of sugar or cotton into another, and then sell or exchange them, as though he was no more value than a mere bale of goods." There were those who believed that God gave Canada to the English for "effecting great objects, not merely in the matter of corn and gold, and tallow, but also to teach us that our dominion was universal in its mental, moral and religious aspects." Crummell went out to Liberia following his graduation from Cambridge University. Garnet had gone to Jamaica under the auspices of the Presbyterian Church of Scotland. Shortly after his arrival, he reported that "surely the wall is broken down, and the field is all grown over with thorns, and nettles cover the face thereof. This remark is true of our church, both in the temporal and spiritual point of view. Yet I think—ay, I know—that these walls can be raised again by God's help." This was classic missionary zeal and optimism.[27]

A few days later, Ward found himself embroiled in a dispute over the responsibility of missionary societies to promote abolition. In America, abolitionists—and that included Ward—kept up a constant criticism of the American Board of Commissioners for Foreign Missions for its refusal to expel slaveholders from its churches among the Choctaw and Cherokee Nations or to reject contributions from slaveholders. The board's missionaries responded that there was no alternative to slave labor available in the regions where they operated and that attempts to reform or destroy slavery, an integral institution of the Indian nations, would meet with vigorous opposition from local leaders and eventually lead to a cessation of missionary activities there. Confronted with a choice between espousing anti-slavery and furthering the spread of Christianity, the board, like most nineteenth-century missionary societies, opted for the latter. Ward knew better. He was an active member of the American Missionary Association, formed in 1846 with a clear anti-slavery mandate. In February 1854, the Reverend James Vincent appeared before the Congregational Union to ask its support for the American Reform and Tract and Book Society, another organization that had refused to take an anti-slavery position. While praising the work of the society, the union declined to endorse it to avoid creating a precedent that might lead to difficulties in the future. Vincent accepted the decision. Then in May, the Reverend Cuthbert Young appealed to the union to support the work of the Turkish Mission Aid Society

(TMAS), a British arm of the Board of Commissioners for Foreign Missions. Young argued that the union's support might prompt the board to oppose slavery. Ward rejected the argument. He had no confidence, he told the meeting, "respecting the probability of imparting to the Mission Board of New York Anti-Slavery feelings by any assistance which the Christians in this country might give the Turkish Mission." Yet even though he dismissed Young's hope as an "idle dream," he asked the union to aid the "good work" of the missionaries by supporting the TMAS.[28]

The decision, not surprisingly, brought immediate condemnation from Vincent's supporters, including the BFASS. Its newspaper devoted three pages to an exposé of the board's views on slavery and its work among the Indian nations. It was, the editor concluded, "inexpedient and dangerous" for British abolitionists to give aid to the TMAS, an offspring of the pro-slavery board. Ward found himself in an awkward position. The decision also violated a bedrock principle of the Anglo-American abolitionist movement: the isolation of American pro-slavery churches and organizations. It is very likely Ward was influenced by his respect for Lord Shaftesbury, his British patron and head of the committee that supervised his mission. Shaftesbury was president of the union. He was also involved in a wide array of benevolent organizations, including those promoting factory and mine improvements, reform and reorganization of asylums, the ten-hour workweek, and better housing for the poor. He had shepherded Ward through the thicket of English philanthropic societies in his early days in London. Shaftesbury not only lent a guiding hand, he introduced Ward to London's high society. No other Black American visitor had moved in such circles so regularly. Ward had been a guest at Mansion House, the official residence of the lord mayor of London. He was impressed, but also did not miss the irony of what he saw at Elizabeth Greenfield's concert at Stafford House:

"What a sight for my poor eyes! Stafford House, British nobility, and a Negress!" James Sherman had welcomed him to his home, as had the Tod family in Scotland. Ward considered Shaftesbury a "prince of noblemen" and the "great prince of British beneficence," his "dearest personal friend." Shaftesbury's work and commitment to benevolent causes, Ward wrote, made his name "fragrant among all lovers of freedom." It was an odd choice of words, but Ward was susceptible to the blandishment of the nobility that showed him favors and supported the causes he represented.[29]

Despite his differences with the BFASS over the Turkish missions, Ward joined George Thompson, Parker Pillsbury, the Garrisonian abolitionists, and William G. Allen at the society's annual meeting. Ward addressed two themes that would come to dominate his speeches for the rest of his stay in Britain: Britain's responsibility to protect its Black citizens imprisoned in Southern port cities and the free-produce movement. The former became a regular theme of his lectures. The British government, he told the meeting, had a moral duty to protect its subjects imprisoned in the United States simply because they were Black. For over thirty years, either through connivance or actual consent, the government had done nothing to stop free Black British sailors being imprisoned in Southern ports—or sometimes sold into slavery. A number of Southern states, beginning with South Carolina in 1822, following the suspected slave uprising led by Denmark Vasey, had passed Negro Seamen Acts. All Black sailors entering one of their ports were held in custody until their ships were about to sail, at which point the captain had to pay the expenses of the sailors' detention. If the captain defaulted, the sailors would be considered slaves and sold. Ward estimated there were between thirty and forty Black British citizens detained in Georgia and South Carolina prisons. When British consuls attempted to protect Black seamen, South Carolina responded that habeas corpus did not apply to Blacks. British representations to the federal government were equally unavailing: petitions from the BFASS in 1846 and 1850 fell on deaf ears.

Ward turned to the case of John Glasgow brought to the attention of the British public by John Brown, a fugitive slave from Georgia, who had recently arrived in England. Brown relayed the case of Glasgow under oath. Glasgow was born free in British Guiana. He went to sea as a boy on ships trading first around the Caribbean and later to England. Glasgow had settled in Liverpool, married, and started a family. On a voyage to Savannah, Georgia, he was imprisoned under that state's law. Unfortunately, the ship was detained longer than expected. The captain could not afford the prison charges and Glasgow was sold into slavery, where he met John Brown. Ward dismissed the federal government's argument that this was a matter only states could settle. This was contrary to their demands for compensation for slaves who had escaped to British territories from U.S. vessels. This problem could have been settled long ago if the British government "had not been most culpably negligent in their duty." The Negroes were "simply turned over to the tender mercies of the slaveholding States." The government could go to the aid of the Turks against the Russians, but when "the wrongs of the British negro demanded redress, that same lion became a very harmless creature" divested of all power, "without either teeth or claw." This was a disgrace to a nation that claimed "Britons never will be slaves." The truth of that boast seemed to depend on where they were caught and the color of their skin. How, he asked, could the government and its people allow this to continue? They worried, he surmised, that any action would affect trade and interrupt the flow of cotton. "What was the negro made for but to be oppressed and trodden underfoot, that trade may go on, and white men make fortunes?" He was not asking the people of Britain to "pity these poor negroes;

he was too proud to ask pity either for himself or his persecuted brethren from any man. What he did ask was justice—common justice, simple justice, even-handed justice . . . and to demand of the Government . . . that not another subject of the British Crown be made a slave for no other crime than the color of their skin."[30]

Ward returned to this issue frequently in later lectures. It was one of the subjects of a lecture at Boston, Lincolnshire. At the conclusion of his speech, a petition was sent to the House of Commons calling on the government to renew its efforts to fight for the abolition of the laws that one local newspaper called "barefaced Yankee interference" with free trade and the rights of British subjects. At a large anti-slavery meeting in Manchester in August 1854, he insisted that the British government had done nothing to free its Black subjects and citizens from Southern prisons. In that regard, they were like the old man's two sons: "John did nothing, and Tom helped him." It was one of Ward's priceless aphorisms.[31]

Before giving most of his attention to the free-produce movement, Ward had to complete his obligations to the Colonial Missionary Society. He did so in a stirring speech in Bradford at the end of May. August saw him in Manchester, where he attended the North of England Anti-Slavery and Indian Reform League meeting. The league was the successor of the short-lived Manchester Union Anti-Slavery Society formed by George Thompson in 1853 in an effort to cooperate with the BFASS. The rapprochement did not last. The Manchester meeting aimed to compete with the BFASS's conference set for later that month. Ward joined a number of prominent British and American abolitionists, including Thompson, William Wells Brown, and Parker Pillsbury. William P. Powell, who had moved his family from New York City to Liverpool in the wake of the Fugitive Slave Law, also attended. Wells Brown was waiting anxiously to hear if his former owner had accepted the offer of British friends to buy his freedom. The negotiation had been going on since early in the year, but Wells Brown had yet to receive the signed document. In a long, rambling speech covering many issues of interest to abolitionists, Pillsbury mentioned that Wells Brown had to be ransomed before he could "set foot on the soil of his native country." He was safe in England and Pillsbury wished he would stay, for he had no "faith in his free papers." When it was Ward's turn to address the meeting, Joseph Barker leaped to his feet and asked to be given the floor as he had a train to catch in five minutes. The mercurial Barker, who spent a great deal of his time crossing the Atlantic and less time changing his abolitionist affiliations, had only recently returned to England. The chair ruled against Barker, explaining that Ward also had a train to catch but he had shown the courtesy of asking the chair's indulgence to speak earlier. The decision set off a short-lived row that ended with Barker leaving the meeting. Ward opened his remarks with a sarcastic glance at Barker: "If order does reign in Warsaw, which it has not done for the past half-hour," he proposed to make a few remarks. One wonders how many in the audience were familiar with the reference to the crushing of the Polish uprising by Russian forces in 1831.[32]

Ward left for a tour of Wales as the guest of Richard Griffiths, who acted as his interpreter and translator. Ward gave two lectures on slavery at the Tabernacle chapel in Bangor. He also lectured at Beaumaris, which he described as a "fashionable watering-place," Holyhead, and Caernarvon on slavery and temperance. He spent four days at Aberystwyth, where he lectured, and at Welshpool, where he spoke on temperance. While at Caernarvon, Ward and his host, a Mr. Hughes, climbed Mount Snowden. At 3,650 feet, it is the highest peak in Wales, notorious for its dramatic changes in weather. It normally takes six to eight hours to complete the ascent and descent. There was nothing in Ward's background to suggest he enjoyed the outdoors or strenuous exercise. Lugging 222 pounds up the mountain must have taken some effort. At the end of the hike, he drove eight miles to lecture at Caernarvon that night. Next day, he traveled ninety-seven miles by coach to keep three engagements.

Ward thoroughly enjoyed his time in Wales. He had high praise for the Welsh peasantry and laboring classes. Unlike in other parts of Britain, he saw no begging. The one major drawback to their development, he thought, was the tenaciousness with which they clung to their language. They needed to abandon their isolation and "mingle with the other elements of [the] British population." He was no prude, but "bundling," a form of courtship, disgusted him. Bundling occurred when a couple shared a bed for a night to get to know each other, a bolster placed between them "to keep a decorous distance." Evidently, the practice grew during the mixed "night prayer-meetings" of the Nonconformists. Ward thought it the one blot on "the most moral and religious country" he knew.[33]

In many of his recent lectures, Ward revisited a theme that had dominated his talks beginning in early 1854: the free-produce movement and its potential to undermine the slave system. Ward had a long association with the movement. It was one of the planks of the Liberty Party and he had made a point of promoting it in his newspaper. As he argued in an editorial, "Abstinence from the fruits of slavery is, in my view, the duty of all Abolitionists, and an important agent in the work of emancipation; since to me it is clear that he who buys stolen goods encourages the theft and that when the demand ceases, the supply will stop also." But abstinence without a regular supply of free-labor produce stunted the movement's ability to affect policy. As Ward told the BFASS meeting, Britain had already done something for the development of its former slave colonies in the West Indies, but it needed to do much more. Continued success there, he argued, would work against American slavery by demonstrating that goods produced in these colonies could compete with American goods in European and world markets and in doing so undermine the slave economy. In a note to Mary Ann Shadd, Ward envisaged a system of trade centered on British colonies. Canadian wheat, flax, and pork could "command a good price in England and the British West Indies." Canada, he suggested, could refine Jamaican sugar. "Thus, the free in Canada can trade with the free of the West Indies," both profiting from and contributing to "the elevation of our British American colonies." His approach addressed the need to develop the resources of the West Indies while at the same time "sustaining the fugitive slaves in Canada." As he told the meeting, it was all well and good to boycott slave-grown products, but it would have even greater effect if the articles were "successfully cultivated on a large scale in other regions by free labor." Such activity would also challenge what he called the "pecuniary connection" of Southern slavery and Northern merchants, undermining, in turn, "the political and ecclesiastical control which the abominable institution has obtained."[34]

Garnet had led the revival of the free-produce movement in Britain. The failure of British abolitionists to stop the rising importation of slave-grown produce, especially after the equalization of import duties in 1846, had led to a sputtering revival of the movement. That changed when Henry and Anna Richardson, Newcastle Quakers, assumed leadership of the movement in 1848. The Richardsons invited Garnet to join their effort in 1850. He was an immediate success. Thousands attended his meetings. Garnet reported the formation of twenty-six local societies by the end of January 1851. Other Black American visitors, including Pennington, Crummell, and William Wells Brown, lent their support to the movement. Supporters of Garrison were not enamored with

Brown's support of what one dismissed as "quack medicine." Although it never became a mainstay of the larger movement, free produce continued to attract public support. Ward did his part. In July, he attended a meeting with Louis Chamerovzow of the BFASS in Woodford, Essex, to promote the formation of a local auxiliary of the Ladies' Free-Labour Association. Stephen Bourne, a former stipendiary magistrate in Jamaica and British Guiana, chaired the meeting. Magistrates such as Bourne were sent to the West Indies following emancipation to adjudicate disputes between the freed people and proprietors. Ward called on his audience to abstain, as far as possible, from consuming slave-grown produce. Developing the resources of Britain's colonies would augment the supply of free-labor staples and undermine those economies that depended on slave labor.[35]

Ward was developing a keen interest in Jamaica as a result of his growing commitment to the free-produce movement. He read John Davy's recently published *The West Indies: Before and since Emancipation* and James Phillippo's *Jamaica: Its Past and Present State*, published in 1843. It is possible he saw Garnet's published reports of his experiences at his mission station in Sterling, Jamaica. In February 1854, Ward wrote Hugh Fortescue (Viscount Ebrington), a Whig politician, about the possibility of going to Jamaica. Ebrington invited him to dinner, where Ward reported he met "several persons of distinction." But it was his conversations with Stephen Bourne that may have been most influential. Bourne had returned to England sometime around 1850 and became very active trying to influence anyone he could about the need to increase the development of West Indian resources. He spent his time speaking and writing on economic conditions in the area. His efforts led to the formation of "the British West Indian Association to encourage the growth of cotton and sugar" as well as the opening of "industrial schools in British colonies."

Little came of the effort; it was an association a little ahead of its time. By 1855, the Cotton Supply Association was promoting the need to find alternative sources of cotton as a way to ease Britain's reliance on the Southern United States.

As concern rose over the supply of cotton in the summer of 1862, as war raged in America, Bourne called on the authorities to "pour a half-million of emancipated negroes from the Southern States of America" into Jamaica, insisting it was one way to "realize the sanguine expectations of the friends in the production of the valuable staple." Earlier, with conditions worsening in Jamaica, a person who signed himself "B" (who, I suspect, was Bourne) issued a circular calling on free Blacks and fugitive slaves to immigrate to Jamaica, where land was available at £1 per acre. Five thousand fugitives, "under the guidance and instruction of such a man as Mr. Ward," the circular claimed, could produce a number of crops there, and "4 or 5 acres of good land" could earn £130 to £140 annually. Following in Garnet's footsteps, Ward wanted to lead "industrious and skilled families" to Jamaica and hoped for the "final settlement there of many thousands of fugitives from the land in which they are now, not only enslaved, but treated as an inferior and incapable people."

Shadd would have none of what she considered a harebrained scheme. Why, she wondered, would "hardy and industrious men and women" move from a free country where land was cheap to benefit "some absentee proprietors?" She followed with more questions: why leave a temperate climate to face tropical diseases; why give up the prospect of becoming "independent yeomen" to join a "peasant class?" The plan involved "an absurdity so glaring, that we very much doubt any gentleman would attempt to make such proposals to any but the supposed stupid fugitives of Canada, and the coolies of the East." Shadd doubted that Ward would be interested in such a scheme, given his long-held view of the importance of Canada as a "home for black men."

Shadd was also aware that Black Canadians had rejected a similar scheme three years earlier. In the wake of the crisis created by the 1850 Fugitive Slave Law, the Jamaican government had commissioned William Wemyss Anderson to tour the Northeast and Canada to determine African Americans' interest in settling on the island, which was in desperate need of labor. Anderson's message was a familiar one: America, he told his listeners, was steeped in discrimination and prejudice against the Black man; Jamaica offered a refuge for people of color, including fugitive slaves—a place where they could enjoy social and political equality in an overwhelmingly Black society. He found few takers in New York City, where he and John Scoble spoke at meetings in Pennington's church. He was equally disappointed in Buffalo, New York. A visit to Toronto boosted his hopes, if only temporarily. Two weeks before his visit, a convention of Blacks had called for the formation of an "American Continental and West Indian League" to aid those who had fled slavery to settle on farms in either Canada or the West Indies. Unfortunately, nothing came of the organization or of Anderson's plans.[36]

Shadd could not have known that Ward had already settled on moving to Jamaica. In December, Ward told a Boston, Lincolnshire, audience that he aimed to raise funds to "establish sugar and cotton plantations" on the island to compete with American slave-grown goods. He repeated his plans during an anti-slavery lecture in Chelmsford, Essex. In the audience was John Candler, a local abolitionist who owned 150 acres in Portland, Jamaica. Candler offered Ward fifty acres on which to conduct his experiment. Candler knew Jamaica. He had spent twenty months in the West Indies over two separate visits. In 1839, the Society of

Friends had commissioned him to report on the condition of the recently freed people in Jamaica. He undertook a second trip in 1849, this time with G. W. Alexander, treasurer of the BFASS. His 1839 meetings in Jamaica attracted large crowds. He laid the foundation stone for the chapel and school at Sligoville, one of the first free villages built on land purchased by Phillippo. Candler was delighted with the scenery and bracing air of the Blue Mountains. He reported that coffee plantations were thriving in the area, but the men and women who worked them were unhappy with the high rents they were charged for poorly constructed huts. They also complained that they were forced to work five days a week, leaving them no time to tend to their own gardens and provision grounds. In his report, Candler expressed concern about the "low state" of plantation workers. Candler visited Bourne and his family at Strawberry Hill in the mountains northeast of Kingston, where Bourne worked ten acres planted in "vegetable and root crops." Seven boys helped in the cultivation, "to whom in return he gave lodging, food, clothing and instruction." Bourne, his two sons, and his daughter were teachers in what was a "small industrial school." On his return home from his second visit, Candler stopped off in the United States and visited Washington, DC, while Congress was debating the Fugitive Slave Law. He met with President Taylor at the White House, and Senator William Seward and Gamaliel Bailey, editor of the city's anti-slavery newspaper, entertained him.[37]

Ward seemed set to leave for Jamaica in December 1854 but, for some unknown reason, did not. He later wrote that he planned to spend a portion of each year in Jamaica until his son was old enough to take care of the property. Instead, he reentered the fray, in January 1855, with a series of three letters entitled "The Modern Negro," which he sent to Douglass. The letters were prompted by Douglass's commencement address to the students at Western

Reserve College in July 1854 entitled "The Claims of the Negro Ethnologically Considered." The "vital question of the age," Douglass argued, was "the unity of man." Recently published ethnological analyses, such as those of Samuel George Morton, had argued against the unity of man. Blacks and Whites stemmed from different sources. Douglass dismissed these claims, based on "*prejudice* rather than from *facts*," as nothing more than "scientific moonshine." Morton's historically inaccurate analysis, which attempted to show that Egyptians were not Africans, was no more than a transparent attempt to write Black people off as unequal, the better to justify slavery. Not one of these studies addressed the "mental endowments of the negro." Douglass listed a number of what he called "undiluted black men," including Ward, whom these studies ignored. "To be intelligent," he concluded, is "to have one's negro blood ignored."[38]

The lecture provided Ward an opportunity to explore an old peeve, the fraught relations between Blacks and White abolitionists, as well as to investigate the origins and nature of Negro-hate. He had written earlier that although White American abolitionists wished Blacks to be free, they did not treat them as equals. They wished "to keep us [wearing] the short frocks of childhood." They only loved "the colored man at a distance." He compared American Quakers and Garrisonian abolitionists. The former had "purged their sect of slaveholders" and no longer condoned or supported slavery, nor did they abuse the Negro. While they supported the education of Black children, they did not welcome them in their schools alongside their own children. What they did for the Negro, they did at arm's length: "noli me tangere." No other sect produced "specimens of deeper . . . more religious negro-haters." Garrisonians likewise did not believe in "negro equality." They refused to hire Black clerks in their offices. They paid Black lecturers less than their White counterparts.

Ward then turned to Parker Pillsbury, with whom he had had a frosty relationship since Pillsbury's arrival in England. Pillsbury had attacked the "three Maryland lads"—Pennington, Garnet, and Ward—for claiming that Garrisonians were infidels. As far as Ward was concerned, Pillsbury was jealous of the fact that the three had been welcomed in places where Pillsbury was not. In a scathing letter to a Glasgow newspaper, Pillsbury had dismissed the "lads" as insolent and not worthy of British support. That support, he almost demanded, should go to the AASS, the only genuine American abolitionist organization. In letters home, Pillsbury dismissed all Black visitors except William Wells Brown as "an outrage on all decency, and a scandal to the name of anti-slavery." Ward thought Pillsbury's animus was that of a slighted overseer.

He recalled his and Douglass's encounter with protesters at the 1850 AASS meeting in New York City. Together, Douglass the mulatto and Ward the Negro had defended the "manhood and equality of our African ancestry and our Africo-American brethren." Ward was fond of differentiating himself from Douglass this way, but it always seemed to be done in jest. The issues of Black manhood and equality were, Ward believed, the questions of the hour. They dominated discussions about the experiment of freedom in the West Indies. They bore directly on the future of slavery, especially the justification that the Negro was inferior. Blacks had to take the lead in this fight. They needed a new breed of historians. He listed three existing histories that broached the issue: Abigail Mott's *Biographical Sketches and Interesting Anecdotes of Persons of Colour* (1826), Wilson Amistead's *Tribute to the Negro* (1848), and William C. Nell's *Services of Colored Americans in the Wars of 1776 and 1812* (1851). Interestingly, he omitted mention of Pennington's *A Text Book of the Origin and History of the Colored People* (1841), considered by many contemporaries as the first history of the Negro in the United States.[39]

Ward revisited and amplified some of these themes in his autobiography. All the world knew that the history of the Negro was wrapped up in slavery and the slave trade: "the chain, the coffle gang, the slave ship, the middle passage, [and] the plantation hell." Scraps, "patches, anecdotes, those are all that bear record of us." But he saw signs of hope, for there were a few living souls who could illustrate and vindicate their manhood. He pointed out that he had given a number of lectures on this topic throughout England and Scotland, drawing on what he called sacred testimony and profane history to argue that, although "the road to distinction" was more hazardous for Negroes than it was for others, they had nonetheless contributed to world civilization. Other races also faced hardships, but for them the road to improvement was not blocked totally. European peoples had "enough to cheer, encourage and stimulate them." Not so the Negro. For him the "sky is sunless, starless; deep, dark clouds, admitting no ray of light, envelop his horizon." Ward supported his argument with brief biographical sketches of capable Black men, including James McCune Smith, Alexander Crummell, and Martin Delany, who were all denied admittance to colleges and universities because they were Black. They struggled on, however, despite these impediments, only to be then denied the full rights of citizenship. "The educated Negro in America is a greater sufferer than the uneducated: the more his feelings are refined, the more keenly he feels the sting of the serpent prejudice." He was "out of place." Whatever progress Blacks had made in America had been accomplished "under the frown" of many obstacles. Although Ward continued to insist he was not one of the educated, he was well aware that he had done all that could be asked of him, and yet he continued to find himself on the outside, unaccepted and unrewarded.

Yet all was not gloom. The ways of progress, he thought, lay through admixture. Through the domestic slave trade, the more intelligent slaves of the border states were mixed with the "less intelligent in the far South." Like James McCune Smith and others, he predicted increased admixture because of the rising number of interracial marriages. He saw hope, too, in the fact that major European countries had freed their slaves, that Brazil had abandoned the slave trade, and that commerce with Africa was on the increase. Friendly feeling "towards the Negro is in the ascendant everywhere, except in America, and it is increasing even there." God had a plan for Negroes; he was preserving and educating them "for some great purpose," yet unknown—first through their enslavement, then by their emancipation. The two races seemed destined to be "associated in some important future service to the family of man."[40]

In his final letter, Ward insisted that in defending their "claim to equality" Blacks, of necessity, had to compare themselves to the "Anglo-Saxon race." There were two branches of the latter: the British and the American. Both thought themselves superior to all others, but Americans went "the farthest in claiming that superiority distinctly." But how was that superiority to be measured? Ward suggested that the ways the countries fought wars and the levels of education they provided their citizens were useful measurements. He sent Douglass a report of a recent discussion in Parliament on the poor state of education in the country to prove his point that all was not well in Britain. As for the art of war, the country's dismal performance in the Crimea put to rest talk of England's military superiority. The American branch of Anglo-Saxons had no way to explain the existence of 3 million miserable and ignorant Whites in the South. Neither had it shown itself capable of fighting a war without the aid of others. The country had to rely on foreign intervention and Black support in both the Revolutionary War and the War of 1812. Its only victories

had come against minor powers such as Mexico and against Indian nations.

He then returned to an issue that had engaged his thinking for
years: the source and nature of Negro-hate. Ward dismissed the
idea that it was the result of a "natural antipathy betwixt whites
and blacks"; it was not true that the more Whites associated with
Blacks, the more they came to believe Blacks were inferior. On
the contrary, those who "know most of the Negro," Ward argued,
were "his best friends." Nor did the antipathy stem from slavery,
for in places such as Brazil, Cuba, Puerto Rico, and the British and
French Caribbean possessions, where slavery had once or still
existed, free Blacks were not treated as they were in the United
States. He argued that class and education were the major deter-
minants of Negro-hate. The lowest classes in Britain, he pointed
out from experience, would "stare impudently at a black person,
and frequently make some stupid, vulgar remarks concerning
him." The "well-bred," on the other hand, were "incapable of anything of that sort." In Britain's possessions, prejudice was confined "to the lowest, dirtiest, most contemptible." These different
attitudes, he posited, had been transferred to the United States
at its settlement. In New England, where the "refined and educated" had settled, there was less prejudice against the Negro
than among those who went to New York, New Jersey, and eastern Pennsylvania. He offered no explanation for why that was
so among Pennsylvania's "stolid Dutch." It was the "low pauper
scum, offscourings of [England] and Ireland" who became the
"bitterest persecutors of the Negro." Putting it all together, Ward
concluded, "Our disparagement had its origins where it now has
its chief seat, in the low degraded minds of the early semi-savage
settlers of America." Blacks, he concluded, had a duty to expose
the sources and consequences of this hate, "to seek its destruc-

tion, to claim and to vindicate our natural God-given equality, to recover our enfranchisement and to take back our liberty."[41]

Still smarting under criticism from his former allies among the Garrisonians, Douglass fully endorsed Ward's views in his first two letters. He had always admired Ward's "characteristic boldness and plainness of utterance." The elevation of the race, he concurred, depended almost exclusively on its own exertions. They must dash "their fetters to the ground." Outside assistance was always helpful, but the "oppressed nation" had to take the lead in the struggle for its freedom. Ward understood that, in expressing his views candidly, "he sets himself up as a target." Ward had even dared, "in his insolence, to peep into the headquarters of American Garrisonianism, to look at the colored mailwrappers, and waiters in general, who, we fear, will be kept in their 'waiting' position, till they satisfy their superiors, that they are able to 'keep pace' with them, and that they 'understand' the illiberal policy of *their* 'operation.'" The struggle against slavery and Negro-hate, whatever its source, required men such as Ward to return to America and engage the enemy. "Come home, then, brethren, and help us perform the '*disagreeable duty*,' of telling the truth, and the whole truth, though the promulgation make enemies of 'our best friends.'"[42]

There was, however, little sign that Ward would soon return to Toronto. The few remittances he sent Emily were never enough to cover the needs of the family. He also continued to struggle to make ends meet for himself. He had written Shadd in May 1854, at the end of his agency with the Colonial Missionary Society, that at this stage of his life, he needed a more lucrative job. But no other agency was forthcoming and there were no other jobs in the offing. He continued to survive on lecture fees. It also appears that, at least during the ten months of his mission for the ASSC, the society had agreed to cover the cost of the family's rent. Why, then, did he not return home? At the end of his mission in April, Douglass had called on him to return to the struggle in America. Shadd expected him at the completion of his agency with the Colonial Missionary Society in June. Others anticipated he would be back in September. But to what would he return? Picking up where he had left off with the ASSC had little appeal. He needed a job that would provide him with the means to support his family. What that job would be no one, including Ward, knew. As a result, he continued to linger in Britain, giving lectures wherever he could.[43]

He returned to Scotland for a brief lecture tour in late May. At its conclusion, he sailed from Glasgow to Belfast for his second visit to Ireland. The first, in September 1854, was largely for rest and recuperation after a heavy summer schedule. His first stop on this visit was Sligo. He was still in much demand. The Colgher Anti-Slavery Society had hoped he would join William G. Allen at its annual meeting, but his Sligo commitment prevented him from doing so. Ward preached there on the 3rd and lectured on the 4th. The reception was enthusiastic. The sermon, the local newspaper reported, was "remarkable for a combination of vigorous thinking, sound good sense, and experimental feeling." His lecture covered a familiar topic: "American Slavery and the Claims of the Colored Population in Canada." The house was packed, and many had to be turned away. According to one observer, the town had seldom seen such a meeting. A local reporter could barely contain his enthusiasm. Irrespective of his color, Ward was not

a common man, his person and bearing are very striking—his manners are those of a polished gentleman—his vocabulary is copious and well chosen—his mind is more matter of fact, quite so than imaginative—more of an English than what we usually conceive as the African type. He has plainly the hot blood of the line; but it is greatly regulated by

> sound sense and sincere piety. On the existing subject of the wrongs
> of his race, and especially on the laws, etc., of the United States, he is
> almost fierce, quite too much so probably for good, easy, excellent
> people, who have all their lives long lived undisturbed beneath to[o]
> cool shade of the broad British oak. We are scarcely competent critics
> here. "Oppression maketh a nice man mad." We should be most
> grateful that we are not similarly tried, we are right glad of Mr. Ward's
> visit, and we cordially wish his mission great success.

Ward could not have asked for better press. Here was an observer who recognized his talents, manners, and fierce commitment to the struggle of his people for social justice. It was all he asked, although, as he knew from bitter experience, it rarely put enough bread on the table.[44]

The following day, he was headed to Limerick over what can only be described as a most circuitous route. He traveled a bone-jarring sixty miles to Mulligar in a coach "of no very ample dimensions" on his way to Dublin. The next day, he caught the train for Limerick, the next stop on his tour. Another full house greeted him. The leader in a local newspaper predicted that the time for the Black race to rule would soon come, and if Whites did not wish to be enslaved, they should rise up and crush slavery now. World opinion should say to America: Free your slaves. This must have been music to Ward's ears. The report of his lecture was even more glowing. If "manhood in mind and body" was an argument in favor of the redemption of his race from shackles, then Ward possessed it. "If burning oratorical power together with fascinating, playful, laughter-causing wit be arguments in favour of his cause," he possessed them. "If excellent education, self-gained, and cool, intrepid judgement be arguments for his brethren," he embodied them. "If a voice of thunder—which would at the head of an advancing column in the battle field rival the peal of artillery, but scientifically suppressed to suit his audience—be the argument for suffering manhood," he brought it to bear in his delivery. He had been honored with the friendship of lords and earls, "or at least he honours them with his friendship." He "brings with him no sectarian prejudices—he carefully, to his immortal credit, avoids any offence in a religious point of view; he disdains to pander to prejudice, or traffic on it, but the soi disant religionists of America he denounces as the vilest slaveholders." A race that produced the likes of Toussaint L'Overture and Ward ought not to be enslaved, the report concluded. As in so many other accounts of his lectures, the reporter could not pass up the opportunity to comment on Ward's color, his height, and what he called his "Herculean frame," even though on this occasion he was on crutches as the result of an unknown injury. Incidentally, in this speech Ward made reference (for only the second time during his sojourn in Britain) to his family in slavery, mentioning that his mother's great-grandmother was owned by an Irishman named Martin. There is no way to confirm the claim.[45]

Ward gave his final lecture at Cork before returning to London. Like many other Black American visitors to Ireland, Ward was struck by the level of poverty he saw. Despite all its promises, the island was economically distressed, due in part, Ward believed, to the Roman Catholic Church's stranglehold on the people—or, as he put it, the "Papal power." Improvement would come, he predicted, when education was increased, and when there was material improvement and "an increase in wealth." He thought he could discern some signs of improvement between his two visits. But the working classes continued to be held under the thumb of the papacy. These same folks showed marked improvement once they got to the United States, where opportunities were opened to them. At no time did he mention the effects of the Great Famine that had ravaged the island, taking close to 750,000 lives between 1845 and 1849, although his past comments showed that he was familiar with its economic and social devastation. Ward was stunned nonetheless by the depths of poverty. The residents of the countryside were "as dirty, as unthrifty, as scantily fed and clad, as those who swarm in the most densely populated towns." He had seen poverty in the worst sections of Northern American cities, but nothing to compare to the conditions in Ireland. The "degradation, idleness, filth, such as abounds in Irish dwellings—and beggary, the abominable profession of a very great number of hale, strong, Irish men, women and children" were largely self-inflicted. He was also a member of a degraded race, but he could not fathom the dirt and filth of their cabins; they were nothing but pigsties. They chose to beg rather than work. Everywhere he went, he was dogged by beggars, "sound in health and strong of limb, with rags and reeking with filth." One would be hard pressed to find anything like this among his "unfortunate people, in any part of America." Ironically, the man who "in his native bog is unwashed and unshaved, a fellow lodger with his pig in a cabin too filthy for most people's stables, when he arrives in the United States, the Negro's birthplace, the free country for which the Negro fought and bled," was one of the first "to ridicule and abuse the free Negro." He is, without parallel, the "bitterest, most heartless, most malignant enemy of the Negro." Yet Ward, the Jeremiah prophet, could see a better future and improved relations between the Negro and Irish immigrants. Were the Irish true to the "sentiments" Ward witnessed throughout his travels, they could "with a little exertion turn the tide of persecution from the Negro." The two would then "grow up as brethren." The "wit, warmth and enthusiasm—the capacity to imitate, to improve, and to endure—the cheerfulness, bravery and love of religion—said to be peculiar to the Celt, are well-known natural characteristics of the Negro." Should the Irish change their attitude toward the

Negro, Ward predicted, it would lift "one of the most serious obstacles to the cause of the Negro." He ended the chapter on Ireland with a plea from Robert Burns, the Scots poet: "That Man to Man, the world o'er / Shall brothers be for a' that."[46]

Ward was not the first Black American visitor to Ireland to be surprised by, and comment on, the levels of poverty he saw. Douglass, Wells Brown, and Charles Lenox Remond all commented on it. Douglass's observations touched on a common theme. Men and women, he wrote, "married, and single, old and young, lie down together, in much the same degradation as the American slaves. I see much here," he continued, "to remind me of my former condition, and I confess I should be ashamed to lift up my voice against American slavery, but that I know the cause of humanity is one the world over." He too made no mention of the devastation caused by the famine. But like Ward, these other visitors all had an eye on relations between Irish immigrants and African Americans and sought ways to improve them. Ward knew from bitter experience that many in the mob that attacked his community in 1834 were Irish immigrants. Yet he made no direct mention of it in his discussion of Irish poverty.[47]

Ward also devoted chapters of his autobiography to a discussion of the Welsh and Scots. The Welsh, he argued, were limited by the tenacity with which they held onto their language, but their devotion to evangelical Protestantism almost guaranteed their development and progress. He had great admiration for Scots abolitionists, even those who slighted him. The Scots were a people marked by "high-toned religious sentiment" and a deep commitment to education. When they took these traits to the colonies, they brought to bear "the impress of their character," producing "the best fruits of energy and intelligence." But they were also instrumental in the maintenance of slavery in the colonies. "The record of them, and the names of their perpetrators, would be the largest, blackest roll and record of infamy that ever disgraced the Scottish name or blighted Scottish character." As slaveholders in the United States, they too had treated "their children of African blood as half-castes, and denied them social equality with whites . . . making them a silly, supercilious, unmanly, half-race, unfit for any social position, alike uncomfortable among whites or blacks." Yet there was a silver lining of sorts: Scots slaveholders who fathered children with slave women, as a rule, did not "*trade* in the persons of their own children." It would be interesting to know on what evidence Ward based that observation.[48]

A cursory look at Ward's autobiography could lead one to believe that he met and broke bread with every lord and lady in the land. He dedicated the book to the Duchess of Sutherland, his "honoured patroness, and the generous friend of the Negro people of all lands." She and her family had shown Ward "many undeserved kindnesses." But beyond his presence at Elizabeth Greenfield's musical recital, hosted by the duchess, there is little evidence that Ward was in regular contact with her. Other members of the aristocracy, however, play a prominent part in the stories he told of his experiences in Britain, no one more so than Lord Shaftesbury. Ward was also deeply impressed by the support he and the cause received from evangelical Protestants. That support was reflected in the composition of the committee that supervised his lecture tour in support of fugitive slaves in Canada. It was made up of members of the aristocracy, evangelical ministers, businessmen, and lawyers. It should come as no surprise that Ward would lavish praise on these people. They gave of their time, support, and money. But he was also gratified by the support he received from the working class. The way the "poor people" of the Sussex seaside town of Seaford, for example, took to the cause by contributing what little they could spare "from the wages of daily toil" was more than he could have expected. Such support from "England's sturdy working toilers," he predicted, would awaken widespread interest in the Canadian cause. Ward also managed to win support from the "poor toilers" in other areas of the country. This was not something new to him. For years, he had worked, and sometimes succeeded, to bring the White working class into the abolitionist movement in the United States. When A. C. Luther, a "working man" from Syracuse, wrote Ward praising his newspaper's promotion of social and political equality, Ward responded with equal warmth. Luther was a kindred spirit, one of that large class of "our fellow citizens who must work hard for a living and receive but one third of his earnings in cash, and the rest in 'store pay' or 'orders.'" How mechanics such as Luther could become anything else than "mere houseless, homeless serfs, while young and strong, and paupers when old and infirm" Ward could not fathom. The bosses of Syracuse were doing all they could to reduce the workingmen of the city to the condition of those in London, Birmingham, Dublin, and New Orleans.[49]

Elisa Tamarkin expresses surprise at the disposition of Black visitors toward Britain, noting their "extravagant fixation on aspects of British culture far removed from, and far surpassing, the political imperative of abolition itself." The rhetoric of anti-slavery, she writes, "mixes haphazardly with a profound engrossment in 'old England,'" resulting in what she calls "Anglophilia." She identifies Ward as one of its purveyors. His *Autobiography,* she writes, with its "fatiguing accounts," suffers from "an inscrutable detailism." That is a legitimate criticism, but it is expressed in a tone that is haughty, dismissive, and patronizing. Moreover, Tamarkin fails to engage with the history of anti-slavery transatlantic cooperation. Visits to Britain provided a temporary free space away from the daily grind of struggling against American oppression. When, for instance, William G. Allen declared his love for the "English people" because of the "entire absence of prejudice against color," one has to keep in mind that he and his wife-to-be had just escaped a lynch mob in Fulton, New York. Tamarkin treats Ward's book in isolation, with little regard to the context in which it was written or how it reflected Ward's long struggle against slavery and Negro-hate. Ward did lavish praise on the English, but he was also critical when he thought it warranted. In fact, he devoted a short chapter, "Pro-Slavery Men in England," to pointing the finger at the editor of the *London Times* for his criticism of *Uncle Tom's Cabin* and for ridiculing and misrepresenting the Negro. Ward spent a good deal of the chapter on those who claimed to be supporters of the cause but who were dismissive of efforts to improve the lot of the Negro. At a meeting to discuss "Negro Education" soon after his arrival, Ward was stunned by the comments of Judge Thomas Chandler Haliburton, who expressed his opposition to a proposal to revive the idea of opening the Berkeley College in Bermuda. The college was first proposed in 1725 by Governor Berkeley to train "native" boys to evangelize their people. The boys were to be kidnapped on the mainland and brought to the island, trained, and later sent back as missionaries. Haliburton, author of the Sam Slick books, which denigrated Blacks, ridiculed the idea of a college for Negroes. The idea, he said, was "entirely out of the question." Ordinary schools he could support, but colleges were meant to train gentlemen. To call such a school a college was to pander to the "conceit of the coloured people, who would soon be aspiring to the hands of the daughters of the whites" and demanding equality. Ward devoted six pages of the autobiography as well as countless lectures to refuting such ideas. His criticism of the British inability or unwillingness to challenge the United States over the imprisonment of Black seamen in Southern ports also flies in the face of Tamarkin's analysis. There are other examples one could cite. More important, those who knew Ward best would be surprised by Tamarkin's line of argument. He was not one to shy away from criticizing those he found wanting—and that included many in Britain.[50]

Ward returned to his rooms at the Radley Hotel in London at the end of his Irish tour, with little to do and in the midst of what he openly admitted was the "most embarrassing, private business." During a dinner, his host James Massie, the Congregationalist minister, suggested Ward write an account of his visit to Britain as a sort of memorial to his work. Ward started writing at the end of August and within two months had a four-hundred-page manuscript ready for his publisher, John Snow. It was a remarkable achievement given that it was written, as Ward recalled, without the benefit of his personal papers. It was also a testament to Ward's ability to undertake sustained and taxing activity. It was how he managed to produce weekly copies of the *Impartial Citizen* while on the road lecturing and collecting subscriptions. One reviewer compared Ward's application to that of Erasmus, the Dutch philosopher, who, it is said, sometimes wrote while he rode. Surprisingly, the *Anti-Slavery Reporter*, organ of the BFASS, largely ignored it, although it did reprint a rather flattering commentary from the *Christian Weekly News* that predicted this "volume of deep and romantic interest" would attract a wide readership. It is not clear that it did. We have no idea how many copies were printed or how well they sold. The *Friend* thought it a credit to its author, but less "toadyism," it felt, would have made it more acceptable. While Ward's expression of gratitude for the support he received was admirable, "the abounding acknowledgements of the author to his friends" were wearisome. It would be a curious statistic, the review concluded, to determine "how often the term 'I am honoured,' by this or that gentleman or lady, appears in the volume."[51]

The book was generally well received, but its reception reflected divisions in the anti-slavery movement. The *Anti-Slavery Advocate*, organ of the Garrisonian wing of the movement in Britain, provided an extensive review. It coincided with the views of Parker Pillsbury who, in a note to a colleague in Boston, observed that the word "Esquire" broke out in the book like "the measles or chicken pox." Ward completely ignored the AASS, Pillsbury griped, and only mentioned Garrison once—and that without "Mr. in front and Esquire behind." On the other hand, Ward lumped so much praise on Gerrit Smith that if the man from Peterboro should swallow, it was akin to Jonah swallowing the whale. Ward praised and pampered the nobility who had plucked him up following Stowe's visit, and as a result he had as his reward what amounted to the gift of a plantation in Jamaica. If only our "hero," the reviewer in the *Advocate* wrote sarcastically, "had been as fair as he had been sable," adding that "we do not see how the way in which he spent much of his time could be fairly called efforts for the abolition of slavery." What it should be called, he did not say. The reviewer then directed his attention to the lords and ladies Ward mentions. Ward had used his race to worm himself into the good graces of the nobility. "Black, portly, fluent, *reverend,* and clever—a lion unmistakably African—he found his way into circles where a white man, with much greater claims to the respect and gratitude of mankind, could hardly have gained access." "Mingled with much valuable matter," the reviewer opined, "we have much that indicates the complacent, highly-professing character of the writer."

Having impugned Ward's motives, the reviewer finally got around to what mattered: the meaning of anti-slavery. The reviewer identified what made Ward's book different from conventional slave narratives. There were many other narratives containing more "romantic and exciting events," but no other abounds in so "many passages of substantial value in illustration of the condition of the free colored race." Ward's account, he observed, "includes a wide circuit" that recognizes every Negro who works to improve his lot. To some extent Ward was right, but he too broadly included those who "do nothing and care nothing" for the cause. True anti-slavery labor, the reviewer countered, is performed effectively only by "those whose lives are spent in lecturing, building conventions, distributing tracts, editing journals, or in some way endeavouring, actively and disinterestedly, to influence public opinion in an anti-slavery direction." (Reading this, Ward must have wondered what the reviewer thought he had been doing the last fifteen years.) The true abolitionists were those "who have borne the chief burden and heat of the day," the reviewer insisted, not those he dismissed as "Christian abolitionists." He found some sections of the book commendable, but he felt the need to protest against passages that "deprecate by marked silence or direct implication, the refutation of the most independent friends of the slave." Such silences the reviewer dismissed as unacceptable, but he found them even more "inexcusable in an intelligent Negro." Nonetheless, he concluded, "no oppressed people ever owed a deeper debt of gratitude to its champions, than does the race to which Mr. Ward belongs."[52]

The reviewer in the *Christian Witness* said he read the book with "the massive image of the writer still in our eyes, and his thundering intonation rolling over the ear." He suggested three ways to look at the book. The first was at the author. During his tour, Ward was tested in the pulpit, on the platform, and in social circles "to an extent . . . no man of colour ever before underwent," proving himself "superior to most, and inferior to none." Second, what did Ward hope to achieve? The book was meant to be a "memorial of a visit." Coupling that with his "life and labours" in America, the book possessed "an instructive and pleasing completeness." The third looked at the record of "the various spheres" in which Ward labored. The book chronicled the "dreadful" wrongs and sorrows, all of which Ward recounted with "equanimity." In doing so, the author was "temperate almost to excess." He thought Ward could have done more for his people had he betrayed "a little more sympathy, or at least expressed himself with a little more warmth." In this case, the reviewer thought, "Warmth is a virtue." Ward's contribution to spreading the word against slavery had been invaluable. The way he handled his experience on the ship from New York City showed Ward to be "a wiser and better man than most of those who despised him, and, in particular, than the miserable Yankees who would not eat with him." It did not seem to occur to the reviewer that the ship was British owned, which was Ward's point. The account of his travels around Britain was one of "universal kindness on the part of the people, and corresponding gratitude on the part of Mr. Ward." Unlike others, this reviewer found the mention of "some names" acceptable. It was simply, he concluded, a reflection of the "representatives of their several classes."[53]

Long before the reviews appeared, Ward was on his way to Jamaica. He had scuttled plans to return to his family in Toronto. His frequently expressed hope to return to his family and to work with his hoe and "preach the gospel as opportunity may offer" seemed almost fanciful. Emily and friends had been expecting his return since the spring of 1854. Frederick Douglass pleaded with him to return. Following Ward's presentation to the Cheltenham Literary Society, Douglass wrote that Ward had "one thing more to do after that able paper and that is to come back to these United States to confront with his logic, learning, and genius, the malicious prejudice which presses his people very grievously just now." Douglass would renew his plea over the next few months. He knew Ward's value to the struggle. Yet, as Ward told friends, demands on him in Britain had only grown since his arrival. But by the autumn of 1855, those demands had been met and there was nothing to keep him in London. Emily was unimpressed by his explanations of why he had not returned. She and the family had been barely making ends meet. The Toronto Society did extend a helping hand. It paid a Mr. O'Dea £15 6s. 7d. to cover rent arrears as well as £39 10s. 10d. for Ward's "rent and taxes." Yet it was never enough to meet the family's needs. Emily despaired. Samuel had not returned, she told Gerrit Smith, because he could not "meet the demands of his creditors." He was bankrupt. As a result, the family was left to fend for itself in "a land of strange people and on the verge of ruin." Creditors were about to seize "all that we have on earth." Emily pleaded for assistance. She and members of the family who were willing to work could move to the country where, she thought, their chances were better. She also asked Smith to write Samuel at the Radley Hotel and ask him to return.[54]

If Ward ever had plans to return to Toronto to face his creditors, he abandoned them when he took out a loan of £140 with William Baynham, a London tradesman. It appears Baynham and his family were planning to migrate to Canada and had approached the Reverend James Carlisle of Woolwich and James Crook, a cheese factor of Slough, Buckinghamshire, for advice. Both Carlisle and Crook were at the Radley Hotel when Baynham agreed to make Ward the loan. According to Baynham, Ward persuaded him to sell off his business and move to Toronto. Evidently, Ward told Baynham he held property in Toronto worth £5,000. Baynham, his wife, and six children would leave first. Ward would follow on a faster steamer to be there when the Baynhams arrived. When Baynham got to Ward's home, he discovered that Ward was still in London and Emily did not know when to expect him. He also found Ward's family "very much neglected" and living in straitened circumstances. To his surprise, he discovered that Ward was "not worth one cent." What furniture the family possessed had been seized to cover arrears in the rent. The family, Baynham wrote Carlisle, was in a "very pitiful condition." Baynham appealed to the Anti-Slavery Society, which promised to contact its counterparts in London. It appears the society gave Baynham temporary relief. Thomas Henning, secretary of the Toronto Society, wrote Chamerovzow asking who had given Ward the land in Jamaica and whether the donor would be willing to repay Baynham's losses. Henning also wanted to know if Ward had been in the habit of claiming he was a man of property. He makes this teasing comment without any explanation: "We have other evidence to produce to the same effect." It is unclear what Henning meant. Chamerovzow contacted a number of people, including John Candler, in an effort to locate Ward. But Ward was already in Kingston and no one seemed to know how to contact him.[55]

We have only one side of the story, but all the evidence points to the fact that by the second year of his stay in England, Ward was deep in debt. Fees from his lectures were never enough to meet his personal needs, to say nothing of sending money to Emily and the children. It also appears that he was seriously considering moving to Jamaica even before Candler's gift of land. He spoke of dividing his time between Toronto and Kingston, but that option was never fully thought out. He was marking time in London, with nothing to do beyond the periodic lecture, when friends suggested he write his autobiography. That, at least, had the benefit of concentrating his mind and energies. But it did nothing to address his pressing financial needs. This was not the first time Ward had fallen into debt from which he could not extricate himself. It was the situation in Boston all over again. Then his extensive lecture tour of the West had helped him to repay some of what he owed. What finally solved the problem in 1851 was his escape to Canada.

Ward's stay in Britain was something of a liberating experience, a time away from the pressing demands of the struggles against slavery and Negro-hate. He was warmly welcomed wherever he went. He participated in meetings of all the major philanthropic societies, whose leaders, he wrote, were a "band who have no equals in the world or superiors in any age." There was so much to be learned from a country where civilization was at its "summit—society in consequence presenting every attraction, and every form of social improvement and instruction." He came to see the country as a "book, ancient, medieval, and modern," from which much could be learned. The English had emancipated their slaves and welcomed those struggling against slavery—it was no wonder that Black Americans such as Ward looked to the English as their "friend." Wherever he went, Ward reported, he, and the cause he represented, was treated with "the kindest consideration." This "poor backwoodsman," as he was fond of calling himself, made his way easily. He, in turn, left his mark on those he met. With the exception of a handful of Garrisonian abolitionists, Ward's talents and contributions to the cause were acknowledged widely. It was, however, never enough to guarantee a living. If there was once hope in a Toronto exile, Jamaica now seemed to offer even greater opportunities.[56]

CHAPTER 5

———

Turning His Back on North America

W ARD HANDED HIS MANUSCRIPT to his publisher, John Snow, in early November 1855 and promptly left for Jamaica. Few knew of his destination. Emily had pleaded with him to return to Toronto. Ward chose instead to follow the path of many other Black Americans who, since Jamaica's emancipation in 1834, saw its promise of freedom as an alternative to American slavery and Negro-hate. With emancipation, Jamaica joined Haiti as the southern arm of an international movement that sought to win freedom for slaves throughout the Atlantic world. Some emigrants went as missionaries; others were sojourners; fugitive slaves sought refuge; and yet others looked for new opportunities. Isaiah De Grasse, a schoolmate of Ward's in New York City, may have been one of the first to move to Jamaica after 1834. He had grown disillusioned with the Episcopal Church's refusal to admit him to its seminary, where he had hoped to train to become a missionary. De Grasse was so light-skinned he could pass for White, but his choice to attend St. Phillip's, the city's Black Episcopal congregation, raised suspicion among the church's hierarchy about his race. De Grasse died, at age twenty-seven, of yellow fever soon after his arrival in 1841. The most consequential African American missionary was Ward's cousin Henry Highland Garnet, who in the summer of 1852, during his tour of Britain, applied to and was accepted as a missionary by the United Presbyterian Church of Scotland. Garnet left for his post in Sterling, Westmorland, weeks before Ward's arrival in Liverpool. These were trying times for the church, which found it difficult to man its missionary stations on the island. A series of smallpox and measles epidemics had wreaked havoc in the country. Despite the death of his infant son soon after the family's arrival in Kingston, Garnet wrote approvingly of what he saw once he settled in Sterling, on the west side of the island. He and his wife, Julia, opened schools for boys and girls. Garnet encouraged Black Americans to move to the island. Yet in the end, his frustration that this "beautiful and fruitful country" had been ruined "morally and commercially," coupled with the penury of a missionary's life, led Garnet to sever his ties with the United Presbyterian Church and return to the United States in early 1856, not long after Ward's arrival in Kingston.[1]

Robert Douglass Jr., the painter and daguerreotypist, spent a number of years in the Caribbean, first in 1837 in Haiti, where he was the official artist of President Boyer, and then in the late 1840s in Jamaica, where he was commissioned to paint scenes of missionary stations. Douglass may have crossed paths with J. W. C. Pennington, the fugitive slave and Presbyterian minister, who visited the island for four months in 1846, prompted by the need to put some distance between himself and his master, who had threatened to retake him. Pennington sent home sympathetic reports of the conditions of the freed people. "I have visited these people in the cane-field—men, women and children; I have seen them on the road, going to the market; I have seen them working on their own estates; I have gone into the coffee-fields; and into the sugar works; and I am quite prepared to say *that they are by no means a lazy people. The women and the children do more work than any class of men in America. I do not except the Irish laborers on the public works.*" Pennington's was a telling rebuke to the skeptics who questioned the legitimacy and potential of the emancipation project. On his return to the United States, Pennington encouraged African Americans to migrate to the island where, he told audiences, "their natures as men and their characters and station among men, would be duly appreciated and accorded to them." Although no Black organization publicly endorsed his proposal, Pennington continued to promote emigration to the island during his tour of Britain four years later. Fugitive slaves in Canada, he told audiences, should be encouraged to go to the West Indies, where they could cultivate cotton, rice, and other staples. As he had written from Kingston earlier, he was convinced that there was "too little acquaintance between us and these brethren." None of these efforts resulted in any appreciable migration of Black Americans to the island.[2]

Like Pennington and Garnet, the other two "Maryland lads," as Parker Pillsbury dismissed them, Ward had been promoting the cultivation of tropical staples in Jamaica during the latter stages of his tour of Britain. He was going to Jamaica, however, not to encourage the cultivation of free-labor products but because he had no other option. To return to Toronto would be to open himself to possible prosecution for the money he owed William Baynham and, even more personally and emotionally damaging, the sneers of his former colleagues. John Candler's gift of fifty acres of land in St. George parish—and the promise of acquiring more at cost—provided Ward with an option that he seized readily. Once in Jamaica, Candler suggested, Ward should contact his solicitor, William Wemyss Anderson, who would arrange to have the property transferred. Anderson, a Scot, had settled in Jamaica around the time of emancipation and had become a major force in liberal causes. He was particularly interested in attracting African American settlers to the island. He made at least two trips to the United States, the first in 1849, in an effort to interest Black Americans in Jamaica. He published two pamphlets promoting the island as an emigration destination, hoping to attract a new labor force to replace the freedmen who had abandoned the estates and plantations following emancipation. It is very likely Anderson had met and discussed the prospects of Black American emigration with Pennington during his visit in 1846. In fact, when Anderson toured northeastern cities in 1851, Pennington was his host in New York City.[3]

While the efforts to attract Black American emigration had failed to generate much interest, the island nonetheless remained a beacon of freedom for slaves from the Eastern Seaboard slave states. Months before Ward's arrival, John Anderson was removed from an American ship anchored in Savanna-la-Mar. Anderson had gone on board the ship in Baltimore posing as a free Black and claiming he was a cook. The captain, Samuel Rogers, hired him, only to discover before the ship had left the Chesapeake Bay that Anderson could not cook. Wary of being accused of harboring a runaway, Rogers decided to clap Anderson in irons and continue on his course to Jamaica. His plan was to return Anderson to Baltimore. Soon after the ship dropped anchor in Savanna-la-Mar, a crowd of three hundred, many of them women, gathered on the wharf. A number rowed out to the ship, removed Anderson, and took him before a magistrate. The U.S. consul in Kingston, Robert Monroe Harrison, came to the defense of Captain Rogers, claiming the action of the crowd was a direct assault on American property. Harrison had been in the region since 1838 and adamantly opposed emancipation as an experiment with dire social, economic, and political consequences. He was also convinced that, in an effort to destroy slavery in the United States, the British frequently dispatched abolitionist emissaries from Jamaica to America such as William W. Anderson, whom he dismissed as a "petty fogging Lawyer." Harrison could not prevent John Anderson's appearance before the magistrate. In a telling exchange over the meaning of freedom and the significance of free soil, the magistrate asked Anderson why he had come to Jamaica. He answered: "I have been kept in bondage and hearing that this was a free country I tried to get here."[4]

There is no evidence that Ward was aware of what had happened on the other side of the island. He was focused on this new phase of his life. Ward's dream, it appears, had been fulfilled. If there is a thread that runs through his autobiography, it is the yearning for land he could call his own. It was on the family's small plot in New Jersey that William had introduced his son to the mysteries of farming. There, father and son bonded. There, Ward recalled, "I followed my father up and down his garden, with fond childish delight; the plants, shrubs, flowers, etc., I looked upon as of his creation." After moving to Canada, he told Henry Bibb, "God sparing me, I shall go upon a farm in April, and, I hope, by the use of my hoe, to supply the wants of my family, and, occasionally, by my pen, to fill a very small corner of your paper." Although it never became the center of his existence, the farming life—or, more specifically, tilling the soil with his hoe and producing his own food—became a metaphor for a life well lived. It was unlikely, however, that Ward could fulfill his dream, for he arrived at a time when the colony was in deep distress. Cholera and smallpox epidemics had wracked the island in the early years of the decade. These were followed by periods of drought. The British government's free-trade policies had worsened conditions in what was already an antiquated agricultural economy. Sugar estates and coffee plantations in many parts of the island lay in ruins. Wages were depressed and irregular. Small settlers were clamoring for land. At a time of dire unemployment, planters lobbied the government to expand immigration subsidies to bring in indentured laborers from India. All the while, Swithin Wilmot writes, political elites "feuded over office and status" and neglected to provide relief for the neediest. Back in Toronto, Mary Ann Shadd reported hearing from a mutual friend that Ward was living on a fifty-acre farm, three-quarters of a mile outside Kingston, and that he planned to return to Canada in the spring for his family. That must have come as news to Emily.[5]

There is no evidence that Ward moved to St. George parish or that he ever took possession of the Candler lands. In fact, by 1856 he was living on James Street, Kingston, and had bought the Chamberlaine pen on Hope Road in lower St. Andrew, less than two miles from the city limits, on which he kept a cow or two, as so many of his neighbors did. A life-long Congregationalist, Ward joined what was reported to be the largest Baptist congregation in the world on East Queen Street. He also began preaching sometime in 1856, the first time he had done so, in a sustained way, since leaving his church in Cortlandville, New York, five years earlier. The city left much to be desired. Two years later, he wrote to a Central New York editor that the city of approximately thirty thousand had only forty miles of road, all in poor condition, making travel physically taxing. Inadequate draining meant frequent flooding, especially in the rainy season. The mail was carried by mule. Communication across the island was poor. There was not a single stagecoach in the colony. The island's sixteen miles of railroad ended abruptly in the bush. There was only one telegraph line and that was between the capital, Spanish Town, and Kingston. Trade across the island was carried out almost exclusively by small coastal vessels. Ward concluded, rather somberly, "We depend upon the United States for almost everything."[6]

The East Queen Street Church seemed to be in a state of constant turmoil. Samuel Oughton, a British missionary, had been its leader since 1839. His first year was a difficult one. Charges were leveled against him for defamation of character when he accused a member of the congregation of taking "indecent liberties" with a Black woman. The disputes affected his health. There were divisions in the church in 1843 that led to the expulsion of some and the departure of others. One of his congregants accused him of "assault and false imprisonment." Two years later, there was another crisis when a group of Native Baptists—that is, Baptists led by Black ministers not affiliated with either the British or Jamaican Baptist unions—attempted to seize church property. In 1854, violence erupted over who controlled church property and the composition of the church's trustees. Oughton opposed the move to take over the church and went to court but failed to win a ruling. He then called on the governor to send out the military to protect the church. The governor refused but showed his support for the minister by going to the church and persuading the crowd, estimated in excess of eight thousand, to disperse peacefully. The question of who controlled the property, however, remained unresolved. Tensions continued. According to Oughton, early in 1855, opponents seized most of the church and appointed their own minister, limiting Oughton to a small section of the property. The authorities again refused to eject the occupiers. Again, Oughton went to court. His appeal was granted, but the decision led to a riot. When the disturbance continued for a second day, the Riot Act was read and fifty-three were arrested. Oughton had no doubt the most recent dispute was led by the "notorious Mr. Ward." Since coming to Jamaica, Oughton wrote, Ward had been baptized by a Native Baptist minister and had become "their minister."[7]

As a result of the most recent crisis, a congregation of nearly 3,000 had been reduced to roughly 250. Worshipers, whom Ough-

ton dismissed as "spiritual vagabonds," chose to join other congregations or to form their own. Ward became minister at the
newly formed New East Queen Street Church, which met on
Hanover Street around the corner from the old church. It was not
long before Ward had to confront crises over his authority. Ward
had first suspended and, after a church trial, excommunicated
John William Dick, a shoemaker and head of the church's Christian Religious Society. It is not clear what the nature of the complaints against Dick were, but he did not go quietly. He printed
and published a pamphlet accusing Ward of immorality with
members of the congregation. Ward took the matter to the leadership of the congregation, and on their advice and that of others,
decided to sue Dick for publishing "several false, malicious and
defaming libels" and depriving Ward of his "good name, fame,
credit and reputation." It would have been much better had Ward
let sleeping dogs lie. In going to court, he provided Dick with another platform on which to air, once again, all the sordid details
he had leveled against Ward in his pamphlet.

The case came to trial in October 1857 before Chief Justice
Bryan Edwards, grandson of the well-known historian of the same
name. In his testimony, Dick accused Ward of carrying on relations, by letter and otherwise, with six female members of his
congregation. All the incidents had occurred between October
1856 and January 1857 at either Ward's homes on James and Fleet
Street or at a house on his pen. It is clear from Dick's accounts that
he followed or had someone tail Ward. Mary Ann Rowley, wife of
John Rowley, was seen going to or leaving Ward's Chamberlaine
pen "early and other times of the evening where they remained
for hours." Ward also visited her at her home. Dick showed the
court letters Ward had written to Mrs. Rowley, the content of
which, we can assume, confirmed Dick's accusation. How he got
the letters, he did not say. Sarah Darby was a regular visitor to the

pen "morning, noon and night" while her husband, Robert, was away in Panama. They had been seen lying on a bed and kissing with the lights off. How they were visible in the dark Dick did not say, nor did the court ask. She had also spent one night at the pen. Such actions, Dick insisted, were "unnatural and unchristian." The married Ann Austin, Dick testified, slept at the pen on more than one occasion. The widowed Jane Ryan went regularly to the pen on Monday evenings. Eleanor Vickers, wife of Edward Vickers, a prominent Black politician (ironically, Ward would later move to Vickersville, Vickers's country residence, east of Kingston), was seen going to the pen on one occasion before dawn. She also visited Ward at his Kingston home where, Dick testified, Ward was seen with his "arms around her." Finally, the unmarried Jane Rogers occasionally met Ward on Mondays and Wednesdays. On one occasion, he visited her at her home between 7 p.m. and 4 a.m. In explaining his decision to make these assignations public, Dick insisted that Ward's behavior was unbecoming a Christian minister. There needed to be a public investigation so that "the people, and especially those of the lower classes who make up the majority of Baptist congregations, may be deterred from being led away from the paths of virtuous and well-ordered life in a Christian country." Dick maintained he had acted in the best interest of the public. The jury dismissed the case against Dick. The accusations, however, seemed to have had little effect on Ward's ability to function as leader of the chapel.[8]

Nothing in Ward's background could have prepared him for the hurly-burly life of a Baptist minister in Kingston. Life in his two previous pastorates, in South Butler and Cortlandville, New York, must have appeared tame by comparison. Yet he continued as pastor of the congregation until his move to Vickersville, eleven miles east of Kingston, in what is known as the Eleven Miles District, in late 1860 or early 1861. There was also nothing in Ward's background to suggest he was a philanderer. He did frequently comment on the beauty and grace of the women he met during his frequent lecture tours that took him away from home for extended periods, but these never strayed far from the boundaries of mid-nineteenth-century middle-class decorum. In Dover, New Hampshire, for instance, he reported he was entertained at the home of Edward Brackett, a barber, and his "amiable wife and daughter." As he told his readers, he was no "flatterer of women," but those who knew him would understand when he said that the two ladies were "among the best specimens of female excellence" it had been his good fortune to meet on the tour. He then felt compelled to offer what appears to be something of a defense; both women, he reported, reminded him more of his wife and eldest daughter than any other persons he had seen since he left home. From a married man, he concluded, this was, without violating norms of decency, the "highest possible compliment." Emily was, as he said many times, his *vade mecum*, his guide and counsel, who frequently accompanied him on tour. One suspects, though, that she was also there to protect Ward against temptation.[9]

In the months before his suit against Dick, rumors did the rounds among friends in the United States that Ward had been convicted of forgery and had been sent to the notorious prison on Van Diemen's Land in present-day Tasmania. Old friends, however, gave the rumors little credence. They knew, as one said, that Ward "bore a good reputation for honesty, although he was always deeply involved in debt." Frederick Douglass's "belief in the man did not permit [him] to entertain for a moment the idea he could be guilty of such a crime." Emily also made it known there was no foundation to the rumor. The rumor, however, persisted, driven by Ward's opponents in the struggle over the East Queen Street Church, who knew he had left London under a cloud. Ward had not only defrauded William Baynham of £400,

Oughton later wrote, he had also "cheated his creditors in England and Jamaica." Now, he was also "convicted by a jury (to which he had ventured to appeal by an action for the vindication of his character) of being guilty of the gross and polluting crimes that had been attributable to him and is now the object of contempt and disgust."[10]

Had Emily and the family been there, one suspects that Ward's life would have taken a different course. But they were stuck in Toronto, trying to survive on what small jobs they could muster and the aid of friends. Even after the Anti-Slavery Society of Canada had paid off their rent arrears and other outstanding debts, the family was still unable to meet the cost of getting to Kingston. It was not until the fall of 1858 that Emily and Ringgold could afford to travel to Jamaica. One daughter, possibly Alice, would join them later. It was, to say the least, a great relief for Ward to have the family together again after all this time.

Life in the church may have been hectic, but Ward was a lonely man and their arrival eased his sense of isolation. In May 1859, he received two copies of the *Franklin Visitor*, a small weekly published in Delaware County, New York, by G. W. Reynolds. What otherwise would have been considered a relatively normal event became for Ward a measure of his isolation from friends he cherished. He wrote Reynolds in response, "You are the first and only American editor who has thus exhibited a kind remembrance of me since I came to this island in November 1855." Implied was his disappointed expectation that old friends such as Douglass and Gerrit Smith would have reached out to him. That they did not tells us how far Ward had fallen out of favor as well as how quickly old friends had distanced themselves from him.[11]

In response to Reynolds's gesture, Ward promised to write a series of articles on the three racial groups in Jamaica: the Whites, whom he called Anglo-Saxons, the Coloreds, and the Blacks. Only the first two articles covering the history of Whites in the islands have survived—assuming, of course, that Ward ever completed the trilogy. The articles were written at a particularly troubling time for the colony. Faced with worsening economic conditions, settlers were clamoring for more land. Estate laborers were demanding higher wages. These pleas went largely unaddressed by the planter class and their representatives in the Assembly, who saw their economic future in the importation of alternative sources of labor. While the island's laws, Ward observed, made "no distinction as to color," custom had established a three-tiered racial system. Prior to emancipation, Whites held all the power. The Coloreds did receive some education and a few inherited some property from their White fathers, making them eligible for the "full enjoyment of equal rights, privileges, and powers, with the whites." Blacks, on the other hand, were denied "all education, and almost all means of moral and intellectual enlightenment." They were unprepared for emancipation. Since emancipation, next to nothing had been done by "our sapient Legislators" to improve educational opportunities.

Ward then turned his attention to the Whites, who numbered roughly five thousand. They continually carped about the government having taken away their property by the emancipation act, ignoring the fact that they had received a portion of the £20 million compensation fund. They cried consistently that they'd been ruined. Many had abandoned their estates or sold out and retired to England, leaving "the island . . . poorer by so much as they abstracted from it." One would have to search far and wide to find a "set of farmers who verily played the fool as our Jamaican planters of the old regime." They complained of being ruined about as often as "your fire-eaters have dissolved the Union and your 'doughfaces' saved it." This cry of ruination was a ruse designed to find alternative sources of labor, especially the "heathen semi-slaves from India, to work at sixpence per day." The farms in Jamaica were more productive than were those in England, and labor was cheaper. Yet, despite their cries of woe, these absentee landowners refused to sell to Black farmers. They were averse to work; "a hoe handle, a plow handle must never enter their precious hands." Like the rich man in Luke 16, the planter must "dress in purple and fine linen, and fare sumptuously every day," while Lazarus, the poor Negro, worked cheaply to supply him the riches he needed to live like "a lord, and not like a farmer." If the methods of farming used in Oswego and Delaware Counties, New York, were introduced to Jamaica, Ward was confident the "wilderness would blossom as the rose [and] Jamaica would be what God made it to be—a paradise." Like Southern slaveholders and slaveholders everywhere, the Whites had "acquired habits of effeminacy" in body, mind, and morals, demonstrating the "saddest specimens of weakness and degeneracy." As in the South, "enervation, imbecility, and an absence of all enterprise—indeed, an unfitness to breathe the very air of freedom—is the result of slavery upon the dominant class." Much that was needed to build a vibrant economy could be found locally, from the plants to make enough paper to supply the world to deposits needed to produce lime. Yet paper was imported and there was not a limekiln in the country. "We are farmers. But we import pork, lard, butter, hams, cheese—save the mark!—Indian corn!!! So, it was in the days of slavery—so it is now." Ward ended with a scathing denunciation of the poor condition of the island's infrastructure, especially in its largest city.[12]

Ward's was an unrestrained indictment of White power since emancipation. It echoed, in many aspects, James Phillippo's earlier criticisms of what he called "the most oppressive and impolitic expedients" deployed by the old order to maintain control over the freed people. Ward had read the book while in England as he started thinking seriously about going to Jamaica. Ward's condemnations echoed those made by Black workers, peasants, and Baptist missionaries. Contemporaneously, Edward Underhill, secretary of the Baptist Missionary Society, confirmed that conditions were worsening. During a five-month tour of the island, beginning in 1859, he visited every one of the seventy-seven Baptist churches on the island, consulted with their pastors, and addressed huge audiences at dozens of meetings. The island's problems, he concluded, were due largely to the planters, blinkered as they were by self-interest. Their refusal to pursue enlightened policies had been the ruin of Jamaica.[13]

Conditions would grow progressively worse in the years after Underhill's visit. Provisions were scarce and wages were low—when they were paid. Alternating droughts and heavy rains made conditions worse by destroying provision grounds. The outbreak of the American Civil War added to the misery, for the island had long relied for many of its basic needs, as Ward observed, on American suppliers. By 1865, the price of cotton had doubled and that of fish trebled. Cornmeal had gone up 75 percent, flour 83 percent. Heavy taxes compounded the hardship. As Assemblyman Andrew H. Lewis put it, the poor "were taxed on their bread, their salt, their lucifers, their clothes, and everything else they used." It did not help that, in 1862, the Colonial Office sent Edward Eyre as a temporary replacement for Governor Charles Darling, who had returned home on leave. Eyre was singularly unsuited, both in temperament and in style, for the job. He took umbrage easily—not a trait needed at a time of economic and political uncertainty. Almost from the moment of his landing in the island, Douglas Hall writes, Eyre "became involved in political troubles." Not long after his arrival, he found himself in political hot water, accused of a misuse of funds.[14]

The issue of land was at the center of rising political tensions.

Those who had none, Thomas Holt has argued, "wanted a plot independent of the estate's control"; those who already had some "wanted more." Black settlers seized abandoned estates, convinced they were entitled to the land. Prodded by Baptist missionaries, Edward Underhill wrote the secretary for the colonies, Edward Cardwell, in January 1865 about the worsening conditions on the island. The "people . . . are starving," Underhill warned. Larceny was on the increase, brought on by a two-year drought and the lack of employment at a time when large parts of the island were uncultivated. Not only were members of the "coloured population" denied political rights, they were burdened by unjust taxations to finance expensive immigration schemes. Underhill made a number of recommendations, including calling for an inquiry into the actions of the Assembly, encouraging the cultivation of goods for export by freeholders through the establishment of producer cooperatives, and promoting investment aimed at increasing employment. Cardwell forwarded Underhill's letter to Eyre for his response. Eyre, in turn, sent it to local authorities, soliciting their views about conditions in their area. Eyre needed to look no further than the address he received from thousands of peasants in St. David following a tour of the eastern parishes. Labor, they told him, was seasonal and poorly paid. Land was hard to come by, and the cost of food and clothing was prohibitive. Cattle from estates overran provision grounds. To add to their misery, those too "lazy to work" stole their crops. Eyre was unmoved. He lectured them on the cultivation of Victorian social habits, including attending to their "daily dress" and educating their children in "religion, industry, and respectability."[15]

Frustrated by the lack of a response to their pleas, the poor people of St. Ann parish sent a memorial to the queen in April 1865 complaining about the lack of work and the low prices their crops fetched. Their provision grounds were exhausted due to overuse, and they were forced to rent land at exorbitant prices. In many instances, they reported, cattle trampled their crops because of the lack of fences. They appealed to the queen to rent them Crown land so they could put their "hands and hearts to work," cultivating coffee, corn, canes, cotton, tobacco, and other produce. They planned to form a company for that purpose "if our Gracious Lady Victoria our Queen will also appoint an agent to receive such produce as we may cultivate."

The reply from the Colonial Office was a marvel of colonial insensitivity. The petitioners were told that their prosperity, like that of all other working people, depended on "their working for wages, not uncertainly, or capriciously, but steadily and continuously, at the times when their labour is wanted, and for so long as it is wanted." Doing so would make the plantations more productive and allow the estate owners to pay higher wages for "the same hours of work that are received by the best field labourers" in Britain. Because "the cost of the necessities of life is much less in Jamaica . . . they would be enabled, by adding prudence to industry, to lay by an ample provision for seasons of drought and dearth." Their "industry and prudence"—not schemes "suggested to them" by others—were the only means to improve their condition. Eyre was so pleased with the "Queen's Response" he had fifty thousand copies printed for circulation.[16]

In the weeks and months following the St. Ann memorial to the Queen, "Underhill" meetings in many parts of the island adopted petitions requesting relief. Not a few of these provided a "radical critique of the government and the ruling class of Jamaica." At a Kingston meeting, for example, the Reverend Edwin Palmer, a Black Baptist minister, complained that the poverty among the people was made worse by the planters who robbed them of their wages and a government that did nothing to improve their condition. Merchants in Kingston "employed none but white or coloured men in their stores." But, he warned, the time would "soon come when they would be compelled to do it." This should have sounded familiar to Ward, who for years had leveled similar criticisms against White American employers, including many abolitionists. Yet these meetings and their criticism of the government and employers seemed to unnerve Ward. It may have been because of the meetings' call "upon all the descendants of Africa . . . to form themselves into Societies . . . and co-operate for the purpose of setting forth their grievances, especially now, when our philanthropic friends in England are leading the way." Although in the past, Ward had defended the call for African Americans to meet in racially exclusive conventions, he had always been deeply committed to cross-racial alliances to attack slavery and Negro-hate. That was the promise, in his mind, of the Liberty Party. These meetings clearly had a different intent.[17]

Ward had also developed an antipathy to George William Gordon, one of the principal figures in the struggle. Born a slave, Gordon was freed by his father, a wealthy planter and attorney. Gordon later opened a produce store in Kingston that was so successful he was able to acquire land all over the island. He first served in the Assembly from 1844 to 1849, generally voting with planters. Raised an Anglican, Gordon became increasingly attracted to Baptist beliefs. In 1861, he was baptized in a Baptist ceremony by James Phillippo, the Baptist missionary. By the late 1850s, he had also become increasingly identified with the Native Baptists. One of his lieutenants, Paul Bogle, was minister of a Native Baptist church in Stony Gut, in the parish of St. Thomas-in-the-East. By 1863, Gordon was a major political force. He was a member of the Assembly as well as a magistrate in St. Thomas-in-the-East and other parishes. He ran afoul of Eyre in both political arenas. Eyre had him removed from all parish magistracies, ostensibly for slandering the rector of St. Thomas-in-the-East. Eyre,

Gordon told his colleagues in the Assembly, lacked "administrative capacity," and was devoid of the "natural endowments" that would qualify him to be governor of the colony. If he were not soon removed, Gordon predicted, much to the consternation of his colleagues, the country would "be thrown into a state of confusion." Eyre was "dangerous to the peace of the country, and a stop should at once be put to his most dogmatic, partial, and illegal doings." To Ward, who had first met Gordon in 1854 while they were both in England, this sounded like a call to insurrection. Ward had issued similar calls that many considered insurrectionary during the crisis over the Fugitive Slave Law. As Ward later observed, Gordon's views had a tendency to "unsettle the peasantry," to interfere in "relations of master and employee, landlord and tenant." He was "a man of a good deal of revengefulness" who had developed a dislike for Ward because of an article Ward had written critical of Gordon's activities. The dislike was mutual.[18]

Samuel Clarke, a Black carpenter and vestryman and an ally of Gordon, invited Ward to participate in a meeting he called at Easington Courthouse in St. David parish on June 24, 1865. Clarke had a long history of mobilizing Black voters and by the time of the meeting was one of the most consequential political figures in the parish. Planters, he told small settlers, believed that Blacks were "made purposely to do nothing but make sugar and rum for them." He opposed the importation of indentured labor and the taxes imposed on the Black laboring population to finance it. It was Clarke who had presented Eyre with the address following the governor's visit to St. David the previous year. Ward initially agreed to attend the meeting but later withdrew because, he told the Jamaica Commission, he did not "believe in the object for which the meeting was called. It was called to express belief in the starvation of the people, and that was not true."

He, however, sent a letter to the meeting calling on members not to be discouraged. It was a rousing call to action, something of a manifesto that laid out Ward's vision for the future. Jamaica, he told those gathered, depended on them, "the smaller yeomanry." The coffee and sugar they produced comprised the bulk of the island's exports. The produce of the large estates was in their hands, as were the "minor productions." The population would starve were it not for their provision grounds. If they allowed any cause to palsy their hands, he asked, what was to become of Jamaica? You, he told them, are the "self-helping tillers of the soil" who do the work. Capitalists were vital to any country, but if a nation had to do "without either, it could better afford to spare the mere man of money than the man of labour." He then returned to the theme of his letter to the *Franklin Visitor*. In a country such as Jamaica, where landowners had neither capital nor muscle, they who "put up a piteous wail of ruin thrice in every decade, [and who] feel obliged to honour money until their credit is exhausted wherever they are known," were as "useless to a young poor community like ours as drones in a bee-hive." The workingmen of Jamaica, on the other hand, sent up "no cry of ruin across the Atlantic," nor did they depend on uncompensated indentured labor to do their work. They did not live beyond their means by residing in "lordly castles at princely expenses." As a result, they were able to "grow bread" for their families and produce "a surplus for the markets" as well as contributing their "full share to the exportable products of the Island." You, he told the meeting, "are rooted to the soil." What, then, would become of their country if they yielded to despair? He called on them to increase what they produced, to enlarge their fields, and if, perchance, they had "time and labour to spare" and were needed on estates, they should take advantage of "cash employment." Be not discouraged, he pleaded. They had another important duty to perform as free men. They had to educate the next generation. They must also do all they could to improve themselves. These had long been the twin pillars of Ward's notions of self-improvement. If they stood together and performed the duties "incumbent on [them] as a class," he had no doubt they would be able to withstand all with which they had to contend. Some in the Assembly, he acknowledged, were determined to burden them with onerous taxes and then abuse them, knowing that they could not defend themselves. But, he pleaded once more, be not discouraged. Ward called on the meeting to appoint a "central corresponding committee" to meet with "small planters" throughout the island as the best way to protect their "interests, rights, and position." Thirty thousand "independent farmers," working in unison, could not be ignored. For a quarter of a century, the "tillers of the soil" had been taxed to raise loans for "a feeble, pampered, helpless class." But thirty thousand "sturdy yeomen, who have raised themselves, under God, from nothing to your present position in thirty years, ought not to be discouraged by the lowering of a few clouds of adversity in this good year of grace." Quoting Psalms 37:3, he assured them that God had not forsaken them. He had promised a "seed time and harvest." He then turned to Psalms 67:5–6, concluding, "Let all the people praise Thee, O God; yea, let all the people praise Thee, then shall the earth yield her increase, and even our God shall bless us." Ward signed off "Your adopted countryman."[19]

The meeting voted on a series of ten resolutions that addressed the needs and hopes of small settlers and estate laborers. There was unprecedented distress in the parish brought on by drought, scarcity of food, a lack of work, and heavy taxation. Laborers on estates were poorly paid, and herds of estate cattle frequently destroyed the provision grounds of small farmers. The island's press, what the meeting's members called the "Guardian of slavery," was opposed to the aspirations of the "laboring classes."

The courts were corrupt. There was "a law for the rich and a law for the poor." The Assembly, "filled with hankering favourites," looked after its own interests. The meeting called for the establishment of an "island agricultural loan bank" that would address the need for capital by small settlers. Without naming him, the meeting condemned the custos (or mayor) of St. David, W. P. Georges, "one of our bitterest enemies," who destroyed "negro houses," broke "negro tombs," and blocked the roads leading to "their provision grounds." As Ward had suggested, the meeting appointed a "Central Corresponding Committee" to exchange ideas with "yeomen throughout the Island on subjects of agriculture and other branches of native industry." Ward was named to a deputation to present the resolutions to Eyre and to request that they be sent to the secretary for the colonies. Ward, however, refused to be part of the delegation. He later regretted the "sort of interview" the deputation had with the governor and the remarks made at it.

Another member of the delegation was the Black American poet J. W. Menard, who had settled in St. David in early 1864. Hired by Abraham Lincoln's Emigration Office, Menard was sent to British Honduras to investigate a proposed settlement of Black Americans under the auspices of the British Honduras Company. When the British government withdrew its support for the project, Menard moved to Jamaica, where he was hired as a bookkeeper on a sugar estate, wrote for local newspapers, and started a literary society.[20]

Although he refused to attend the meeting, Ward was convinced that his letter, which he reported occupied the attention of the participants, had a positive influence on the deliberations. After reading the resolutions, and before the deputation met with the governor, Ward persuaded its members to drop the seventh resolution condemning the custos of St. David. W. P. Georges, the custos, wrote to Eyre condemning Samuel Clarke and the other organizers of the meeting who, he said, "delight in political excitement." He admitted that the drought had been severe, but insisted that its effects had been grossly exaggerated, as were the protests against higher taxes, the rise in unemployment, the lowering of wages, the destruction of provision grounds, and the complaints of favoritism in the local courts. For those willing to work, Georges insisted, there were jobs available paying fair wages for fair work. Clarke and the others were tilting at windmills. The "industrious portion of the inhabitants and small freeholders" were not fooled by their antics and therefore had chosen to stay away from the meeting.[21]

Weeks later, George William Gordon applied to the custos of Morant Bay, Baron Von Ketelhodt, for permission to use the courthouse for a public meeting. The custos refused, but Gordon held the meeting outdoors in the courthouse square. A German and naturalized British subject, Von Ketelhodt came into extensive property in Jamaica through his English wife. Eyre had appointed him to the position in 1862. Two years later, he and others brought a successful court action against Gordon's election as churchwarden, citing the fact that Gordon was no longer an Anglican. He and Gordon also sparred about Gordon's election to the vestry, which the custos opposed. The placard announcing the meeting read, "Poor People! Starving people! Naked People, etc. You who have no sugar estates to work on, nor can find other employment, we call on you to come forth. Even if you are naked, come forth and protest against the unjust representations made against you by Mr. Governor Eyre and his bands of custodes. You don't require custodes to tell your woes; but you want men free of Government influence—you want honest men." The meeting covered many of the same issues as those aired at Easington. Von Ketelhodt was denounced for his "illegal and oppressive conduct towards the rights of the constituency of this parish and the island generally." Denying the meeting the use of the courthouse was censured as unconstitutional.[22]

An open-air meeting at Vere days later, at which Gordon was the main speaker, seems to have bothered Ward even more than the Easington meeting. Gordon did not say much that was out of character. He denounced Eyre as a "bad man" and complained about the lack of justice and the poverty of the people. After reading Gordon's Vere speech, Ward met with Stephen Cooke, the clerk of peace of St. Thomas-in-the-East; Henry Mais, a White Creole and ally of Von Ketelhodt; and A. G. Fyfe, stipendiary magistrate of St. David and a member of the Assembly. They concluded that the only way to counter Gordon's "evil influence" was to organize "counter-meetings" to teach the people "loyalty and good order." Ward would be the main speaker. Ward wrote Von Ketelhodt for permission to use the courthouse to address the peasantry, "without," as he said rather disingenuously, "any respect to politics." The custos readily acceded to the request, eager to present an alternative voice to Gordon's. The meeting was held on September 9, 1865, which so happened to be court and market day. A large crowd attended, made up, Ward remembered, of both the gentry and peasantry. He later recalled that his speech was well received by "the peasantry" and "very well received by the gentry" which suggests there was some dissent. Ward later heard rumors that George McIntosh, one of Gordon's lieutenants, had done "his utmost to raise a riot against" him during the meeting by marshaling men to injure him.[23]

What Ward feared most occurred one month after his meeting at Morant Bay. The petty sessions court met on market day, Saturday, October 7, to hear a case brought against Lewis Miller for assault on a woman. The presiding judge ruled against the accused and imposed a fine of 4 shillings as well as ordering him to pay costs of 12s. 6d. At this point, James Geoghegan, a spectator, shouted that the lad should pay the costs but not the fine. The judge called for the arrest of Geoghegan. When the police attempted to take hold of him, they were attacked and beaten back by spectators.

On the following Monday, October 9, the court issued a summons for the arrest of Paul Bogle. Bogle had been born into slavery around 1820. A baker by trade, he was one of the small settlers who had established freeholds in Stony Gut in the early 1840s. A Native Baptist preacher, Bogle was an ally of Gordon and a major figure among the free people of the parish. He had been one of the speakers at the outdoor meeting at Morant Bay on August 12 when Von Ketelhodt was accused of corruption, and he had headed the delegation that subsequently traveled to Spanish Town to deliver a petition to the governor, who refused to meet with them. The trouble began when surveyors were sent to three estates in the area that were to be subdivided to pay off debts. Peasants had occupied and cultivated the abandoned estates for several years. A group of angry peasants, including Miller, attacked the surveyors. Eight Black police officers sent to Stony Gut to enforce the warrant were beaten and forced to swear to "cleave to the black" and to "join their colour." It was rumored that Bogle planned to lead an attack on the vestry meeting scheduled for the 11th. Concerned, Von Ketelhodt asked Eyre to send troops to protect the town. That same evening Bogle and nineteen members of his church sent a petition to Eyre insisting that the incident on the 7th had been caused by overzealous police. They called for protection, insisting they were loyal subjects. If protection was refused, they warned, "we will be compelled to put our shoulder to the wheel." They had been imposed upon for a period of twenty-seven years despite "due obeisance to the laws of our Queen and country." Such imposition, they declared, had to stop.

On Wednesday, October 11, the custos and a small contingent of militia could not prevent Bogle and his followers from entering the square outside the courthouse. Von Ketelhodt began to read the Riot Act from the courthouse steps. Before he could finish, the crowd started throwing stones. The custos ordered the troops to open fire. Several in the crowd were hit. Angered, the crowd stormed the courthouse. The custos and the militia retreated into the courthouse, which was set on fire. Several were killed trying to escape the flames, including Von Ketelhodt, the Reverend Victor Herschell, the Anglican curate of Bath, and sixteen others; thirty-one were wounded. Bogle's followers occupied the town. The next day, they marched on Bath, attacking and burning plantations along the Plantain Garden River. Eyre declared martial law and dispatched one hundred Black troops from the First West India Regiment by the HMS *Wolverine* to Morant Bay. The troops fanned out in search of the rebels, aided by Maroons. Suspects were shot where they were apprehended. Others were tried by drumhead courts and executed. Some were found guilty by court-martial, even though no evidence was provided. Homes were set on fire and other property destroyed. Many, men and women, were flogged on suspicion of being involved in the rebellion. The period of martial law lasted a month, during which one thousand prisoners were brought to Morant Bay. Two hundred of them were executed and another two hundred flogged. Others were tortured to extract confessions. Paul Bogle was caught and hanged on October 25. Of those hanged in Morant Bay, seven were women. Gordon was arrested in Kingston on October 20 and taken by ship to Morant Bay, where he was tried by court-martial for "high treason and sedition" without the benefit of counsel. He was found guilty and hanged from the beams of the burned courthouse. Seventeen others were put to death the same morning.[24]

The rebellion seems to have taken Ward by surprise. There was, he acknowledged, social unrest in the months between June and September. Samuel Clarke and others had been "disturbing things and seeking to get control of everything in their hands." They stirred up "confusion" between themselves and Georges, with whom Clarke was at constant loggerheads. They were determined to get rid of all the schoolteachers and asked Ward if he would take over one of the schools, but he refused. He also objected to the hiring of John Willis Menard, who had recently settled in the parish. Ward admitted he was "quite intimate" with Clarke, who wanted to go to England to plead their case. Ward insisted there was no case to plead and that all the English people wanted was for them to behave themselves. Although the rebels never came close to Ward's home in Vickersville, Clarke did visit on October 16 as he tried to escape the troops. Ward was working in his garden when his son informed him that Clarke was at their house. According to Ward, Clarke was afraid one of his enemies would betray him to the soldiers. During breakfast with the family, Ward was struck by how far the normally "bold and cheerful" Clarke had "sunk in despondency." Ward tried to get Clarke to divulge what he knew of the rebellion, but he seemed reluctant to say much. He claimed to be penitent, but Ward was unconvinced. As far as Ward was concerned, to be sincerely penitent one had to confess fully, and, try as he might, Ward could not bring Clarke into what he called "close quarters." That was enough to convince Ward that Clarke was a "rebel of high position." Clarke was arrested in Kingston and taken to Morant Bay, where he was executed following a court-martial. Ward never faltered in his belief that Clarke was involved in the plot. There is, however, little direct evidence tying Clarke to the rebellion.[25]

Word of the rebellion reached London in early November.

Weeks later, reports filled in the details of the authority's harsh reactions. Immediately, Louis Chamerovzow and the British and Foreign Anti-Slavery Society besieged the Colonial Office with calls for an investigation. Other prominent figures such as the author Thomas Hughes as well as philanthropic societies joined the call. Eyre had his defenders, but the clamor to recall the governor and initiate an inquiry proved irresistible. These individuals and groups came together in early December to form the Jamaica Committee, many of whose leaders had been involved in the public campaign to win support for the Union in the American Civil War. The secretary of state announced the formation of a Royal Committee, headed by Sir Henry Storks, governor of Malta, to investigate both the rebellion and the repression. Storks was also to replace Eyre as interim governor.[26]

Eyre was convinced he had done all he could to protect one of the empire's most valuable colonies. He was also determined to safeguard his good name. At the end of October, he circulated a letter to prominent Jamaicans, including Ward, seeking evidence to support the validity of his actions. Eyre asked recipients to address three questions: what were the origins of the rebellion; was it local or island-wide; and was it suppressed savagely? Ward prepared a lengthy answer. In fact, he had already begun composing a pamphlet examining the origins of the rebellion even before Eyre's letter arrived. He prefaced his remarks with words that echoed those of Eyre's justifying his reactions. He expressed deep regret that Eyre's actions to suppress the rebellion "should have brought so much censure and actual persecution." Ward had no doubt that the governor's measures had saved the "island to the Crown" and protected the lives and property of many threatened by "imminent certain destruction." He prayed that God would sustain Eyre in his trials and lead him to "as brilliant a conquest over your assailants as he has given you over the disturbers of

Jamaica's peace." Ward need not have said more; he was firmly committed to Eyre's interpretation of events. Before addressing Eyre's three questions, however, he felt it necessary to revisit his association with Samuel Clarke. He and the others were "disturbing things and seeking to get control of everything into their own hands." He recalled Clarke's association with Gordon and his lieutenants, their open-air meeting at Morant Bay, and McIntosh's opposition to Ward. That opposition had led Clarke to withdraw his invitation to Ward to speak at a meeting in Mt. Libanus in mid-September. Mt. Libanus, in the Blue Mountain District of St. Thomas-in-the-East, ten miles north of Morant Bay, was home to many of Bogle's supporters. Ward reported that Clarke later told him it was fortunate he did not attend for the people there were deeply committed to the rebellion. That, and the conversation at Ward's home while Clarke was trying to evade capture, confirmed that his old acquaintance was "a rebel of high position."

Ward then turned to an assessment of the aims of the rebels. They aimed to "spread their fiendish designs east, west and north of Montego Bay," to "murder, plunder and destroy." They were united in their determination to "spread desolation and death." The arrival of the military on October 12, the "early occupation of the district by the troops" and Maroons, and the "benefit of the stern energy with which those troops hunted, shot and hung the conspirators" saved the day. Ward had no doubt that the "master spirit" of the rebellion was George William Gordon. Every "active Rebel" in Morant Bay was a "partisan" of Gordon's. Every one of his opponents was a target of the rebels. That is why Von Ketelhodt and Charles Anthony Price, a Black builder and member of the vestry whose home stood next to the courthouse, were killed. "Not one solitary act was at any time committed inconsistent with . . . the design of a general massacre, a distribution of property among the Rebel chiefs and their followers, and the elevation of Mr. G. W. Gordon to the seat of supreme authority." No one was spared who opposed these designs.

Ward next addressed Eyre's three questions. The rebellion had its origin in the "*seditious* and *treasonable teachings of George William Gordon*," who in lectures, pamphlets, and rallies and with the aid of agents set out to "unsettle the minds of the peasantry," teaching them to "disregard and undervalue the authorities of the land and persons in respectable positions." Gordon, the "most indefatigable apostle of mischief," led an "army of ignorant and unthinking negroes." The rise of Gordon, and his ability to attract a cadre of capable lieutenants, should have come as no surprise, given conditions on the island. "A man of like status, in circumstances equally favourable, and with a heart equally depraved, would have wrought quite as much mischief in any other part of the empire." Ward declared he had never given much credence to the claims of Underhill's letter and so did what he could to undermine them. Those who had long planned to subvert the system were the ones who had exploited the letter for political purposes. The claims of starvation were unfounded, Ward later claimed, given the "condition and appearance of those who attended the Underhill meetings. Their horses, their clothes, their freeholds, and the produce of their lands, all gave the lie direct, to the starvation talk."

Ward had no doubt that Gordon had plans for an island-wide uprising. He had spoken against the governor and other leaders. As he said, he intended to use "muskets and rebellion and blood." The government had ample evidence there was to be a general uprising on Christmas Day. The demeanor of the peasantry and the "lower classes in Kingston" justified fears of a widespread attack. That, and the fact that within forty-eight hours of the first attack on Morant Bay, the rebels had "carried desolation and destruction" over a vast area was ample proof that plans were in place for a general uprising. In light of these facts, the claims that Eyre's reprisals were severe were unfounded. Fond of claiming he was a "humble" man who was reluctant to comment on the actions of men of superior rank, Ward nonetheless offered an analysis that was neither humble nor modest. "Martial law lasted but 30 short days." Most of the island, outside of the actively rebellious districts, was not disturbed by the repressive measures. The safety of the whole island—its property, order, and life—was endangered. The lives of "the very best of the population" were savagely destroyed. "Scenes more horrible than the sacrifices of Dahomey had been exhibited." In fact, the "foundations of civilized society had been uprooted and overturned. Cool deliberate diabolism had vested itself with the hottest fire of sanguinary excitement on purpose to perpetuate deeds of the most infernal ferocity; and when the Government put forth its strong arm, the more than savage foe was flushed and gloating with partial triumph and exulting in hope of more complete victory."

Ward would temper his views, if only a little, in his pamphlet *Reflections upon the Gordon Rebellion,* published in February 1866, a month after his letter to Eyre. There, he insisted he was "neither a Judge, a general, a magistrate, nor anything else," nor could he "speak positively, or with authority," for he knew too well that "the opinion of a poor working man, is esteemed as of no value." That did not stop him from concluding, however, that "*justice, protection, restoration,* and not vengeance, directed and limited all the *aims* and acts of the Government." What was done was necessary to conserve the island and "will bear most favourable comparison with like measures resorted to in the emergencies wheresoever they are recorded on the historic page." Ward must have had in mind British responses to the Indian Mutiny eight years

earlier. In fact, he tended to employ many of the same justifica-
tions for the colonial authorities' actions in Jamaica, echoing the
arguments of Eyre's defenders in Britain.[27]

After an overview of events between October 7 and 10 in Morant Bay, which comprised the pamphlet's first two pages, Ward
drew, almost word for word, from that portion of his letter to Eyre
in which he responded to the governor's questions. He added,
however, a fourth query. How, he wondered, would the rebellion
"affect the character of negroes, as to their loyalty"?—a question,
he thought, that had been largely ignored in discussions of the
rebellion. It was common knowledge, he observed, that "the negro
is not judged of by the same rule that is applied to other men."
All the Irish were not stigmatized by the actions of the Fenians,
nor were all Americans by the actions of the Confederacy. Not so
in the case of the Negro, all of whom were blamed for the actions
of "any portion who do wrong." It was almost futile to protest
against this view "for the simple reason that some people will not
see any good in the negro, while an equally blind class will not see
in him anything bad." Ward had leveled similar criticisms, years
earlier, against the effects of slavery and Negro-hate in the United
States as well as against the tendency of abolitionists, eager to
promote the freedom of slaves and the welfare of free Blacks, to
ignore the shortcomings of Negroes for political reasons. Neither
approach, Ward had long maintained, did the Negro much good.
Ward leveled his gaze on both sides of the debate over the rebellion and its suppression. Neither side had provided a nuanced
interpretation of events. He offered to provide one.

Ward laid out a number of specific observations about the rebellion in his interpretation of the position of Negroes in a racist
colonial society that had just experienced a wrenching rebellion.
The uprising, he insisted, could not be laid at the door of the
"respectable and best educated" Negroes, for they had remained

loyal. So too had the majority of the peasantry and yeomanry. Black soldiers and Maroons had done their part to put down the rebellion. Employers therefore could take comfort in the knowledge that "the employed are loyal and true." Who, then, was responsible for the rebellion? Ward had a ready answer: it was the work of a "mulatto" and a few of his "white associates." Because of their "ductility," many Negroes were drawn in "as subordinates and made cat's paws." The blame for fomenting the rebellion rested squarely with Gordon, a mulatto, and not upon a few such semi-savage Negroes as Paul Bogle. Yet, he concluded, the authority's response was commensurate with the crime. "I see . . . no sense and less law," he concluded, "in the fault found with the repressive measures . . . or as to the numbers executed." Those who committed crimes were the ones who were brought to justice. What Ward failed to see—or would not acknowledge—was that, by the time of his writing, most observers were convinced that Eyre had overreacted and that many, including Clarke, had nothing to do with the organization of the rebellion.[28]

Ward had long believed that, in the struggle for freedom and racial equality, leadership mattered. He had used the pages of his newspapers, on occasion, to castigate Black leaders for leading the people astray both by what they did and by their statements. He had encountered many "leaders" who, like Gordon, had refused to act in the best interests of Black people. His antipathy for Gordon, whose racial background he rarely failed to mention, was out of character. Ward had worked closely with mulattos in the United States. He and Jermain Loguen were inseparable until they parted ways following the demise of the *Impartial Citizen*. He and Frederick Douglass had their differences, but theirs was a working relationship based on mutual respect and admiration. He was fond of teasing Douglass by reminding his friend that he was the product of an interracial relationship while Ward was untouched by the White racial brush. Yet they worked together to silence racists and promote the cause of emancipation and racial equality. Their tandem performance at the American Anti-Slavery Society's annual meeting in New York City in May 1850 was a case in point. Douglass was first to attack the racist bile spewed by Dr. Grant and Isaiah Rynders; Ward followed to add the finishing touches. In the United States, where they were a racial minority, Blacks—and particularly Black leadership—could ill afford the luxury of recognizing color niceties. Their task was daunting enough without promoting such divisions. In Jamaica, on the other hand, the Colored class was well established even before emancipation. There the three-tiered racial order mattered. Gordon was clearly a beneficiary of that order and, as far as Ward was concerned, used his position for both personal and political aggrandizement. It did not help that Gordon had shown Ward little respect, cutting him, as Ward put it, on a number of occasions. It was sheer hubris, Ward believed, that led Gordon to think he could reorder Jamaican society. In Ward's view, the Morant Bay rebellion was the work of a depraved, self-serving, and misguided leader who duped his followers into believing he offered a better future.

Ward made a number of suggestions about ways to prevent a recurrence of the rebellion. Landlords must take a "deeper," paternalistic interest in their people and "acquire over them the influence which to landlords belong[s]." Increase the size and effectiveness of the police force and constabulary by employing men of "higher grade" and increasing their pay. If they wished to root out Native Baptists, missionaries should stop living in "indolent splendour" in England and instead "visit the dark districts and carry the gospel to the benighted portions of our lovely isle." Black people should cease following "bad mulatto" leaders into acts of disloyalty that could only lead "to the gallows, and to perdition." Should these recommendations be followed, Ward predicted the results would be a "quiet . . . loyal, and peaceable" land. As he had done in a few of his best-known lectures, Ward turned to Chronicles 4:40 to express his sense of hope for a new day for his people: "And they found fat pastures and good, and the land was wide and quiet and peaceable; for they of Ham had dwelt there of old." There was a future for his adopted country, one in which the Black man could live to his full potential free from racial hatred.[29]

Ward appeared before the Royal Commission on February 27, the twenty-ninth day of its hearings. He was queried about certain aspects of the crisis. In response, he retraced his knowledge of and reactions to the rebellion. But he also spent time discussing what he believed was a society that had undergone significant social changes—and not all for the best—since his arrival in late 1855. With the exception of the "educated rising generation," he was struck by increasing levels of "insolence" among the peasantry and laboring class, particularly since the Religious Revival of 1860–61. They had become "rough and insulting." When he first arrived, he could intervene in disputes and help to resolve them. That was no longer the case. He believed the change was the result, in part, of an absence of "systematic education." The government allocated a mere £3,000 annually to education. School provisions were minimal, and teachers generally lacked training. Teachers who graduated from the normal school were paid poorly—if they could even find a job. It did not help that the peasantry and laboring classes showed no interest in educating their children. He agreed with the suggestion from one of the commissioners that the government should introduce compulsory education. It would help to address what he believed was a lack of moral training at home. He tried to instill some of this training, he reported, at the school he and one of his daughters, possibly the teenage Alice, ran from his home. As he had experienced in his first teaching job on Long Island, thirty years earlier, Ward struggled to persuade parents to enroll their children in his school. There were about forty students attending. They were taught a mix of traditional subjects, including reading of the Scriptures.

Three-quarters of the way through his testimony, Ward was confronted with an issue he would rather not have revisited. John Horne Payne, the Jamaica Committee's second representative on the commission, asked him a series of questions that aimed to undermine Ward's credibility. Was he the "celebrated gentleman" who had escaped slavery and visited England? Ward responded brusquely that he was not "the" celebrated gentleman, nor was he "the" man who had escaped slavery; he was one of many who had. Had he been received by the Duchess of Sutherland? Ward simply replied that he had been. Then came the point of Payne's line of questioning: "Did you bring an action some time ago against a man of the name of Dick?" Ward answered he had. Was it an action of libel, Payne continued. The next question drove home Payne's objective: "What was the nature of the libel?" It was, Ward responded, an "attack on his moral character." Probing further, Payne forced Ward to explain the circumstances leading up to the suit. Ward did so, without providing any of the details. Payne persisted: was the subject of the libel, he asked, immorality with members of Ward's congregation? Ward calmly admitted that it was, although he insisted the action did "not amount" to libel, but that was "what it hinted at, and I took it as it was meant." Payne had made his point: the minister who had condemned the leaders of the rebellion and those who followed them was himself morally bankrupt. Yet Ward held his ground, admitting to the charge while avoiding revealing the sordid details uncovered at the trial.

Sensing that the proceedings were losing focus, another member of the commission intervened with a question that returned to the issue of education. Yet the questions soon reverted to issues of morality. Were the majority of the people with whom Ward came into contact married; were their "children legitimate or illegitimate?" That, Ward responded, as only he could, was "a very queer question for Jamaica." Only one-half of the children in his school, he pointed out, were born to parents who were married. The parents of the others lived together as man and wife, although they were not married. Ward was quick to point out these sorts of arrangements were not limited to the "lower class." The same applied to the "merchants, the planters, the overseers, and almost everybody." The society as a whole, Ward implied, if he did not say so directly, was morally bankrupt. Ward's testimony ended with a return to a discussion of his involvement with Clarke and the Easington meeting.[30]

Ward was one of 730 witnesses examined by the commission over fifty-one days. The commission completed its 1,162-page report in early April 1866. The chief causes of the outbreak, it concluded, were, as Thomas Holt phrased it, "the desire for land and the lack of confidence in the system of justice." While the outbreak was localized, the commission members agreed with Eyre that it had the potential to become an island-wide affair. Given this fact, they praised the governor's "skill, promptitude and vigour" in dealing with the danger. However, they condemned Eyre's decision to extend the period of martial law beyond the time required to address the crisis. Gordon's trial, they concluded, was illegal and the punishments meted out to accused rebels were excessive, "barbarous," and cruel. The sentences of death were "unnecessarily frequent," floggings "were reckless," and the burning of homes was "wanton and cruel." The level of death, punishment, and destruction was staggering. Militiamen had killed seven in Morant Bay. Three hundred and fifty-eight were executed after court-martial. Eighty-five were shot or hanged without trial. More than six hundred were flogged. The authorities burned one thousand homes. Ward left no responses to the commission's conclusions.[31]

Eyre returned to England in August 1866 to face charges brought by the Jamaica Committee. His supporters, including such luminaries as Thomas Carlyle, John Ruskin, Charles Kingsley, and Charles Dickens, countered with the Eyre Defence Committee. The *Times* spoke for many of Eyre's defenders: "It seems impossible to eradicate the original savageness of the African blood. . . . Wherever he attains to a certain degree of independence there is the fear that he will resume the barbarous life and the fierce habits of his African ancestors." Had Ward read the editorial he would have winced in discomfort, for that was precisely the sort of broad denunciation of the race he had fought against in his writings on events leading up to the rebellion and his testimony before the royal commission. It was also a struggle he had waged all his adult life. Thousands in Britain signed their names to petitions supporting Eyre. Earlier, twenty-five hundred in Jamaica, including Ward, had signed an address in support of Eyre prior to his departure, expressing "utter detestation and abhorrence of the recent atrocities and massacres committed by the lower orders at the instigation of demagogues and fanatics." Emily had added her name to a separate address from the "Ladies of Jamaica" thanking Eyre for saving "us, our families and our houses from outrage, desolation and ruin." Interestingly, neither of the Ward children signed the addresses. Eyre left Jamaica with these tokens of support to face the Jamaica Committee's efforts to bring him to justice. The court cases would drag on over the next two years before the former governor was acquitted by a

London court. Ten years later, the Disraeli government granted Eyre a second-class pension.[32]

Ward was, as he proudly told the royal commission, a simple farmer who also ran a school. If he had anticipated rewards for his support of the governor and his condemnation of the rebels, he was to be sadly disappointed. He largely disappeared from the island's records. In 1867, he was listed as one of thirteen members of the Parochial Road Commission of the new parish of St. Thomas. According to Tim Watson, he seems to have held the same post in 1869. By that time, the family had moved to Yallahs along the coast of St. Thomas closer to Morant Bay.[33]

Even before Eyre's acquittal, Ward and his family had stepped off the pages of history. Vincent Harding writes that Ward dropped "out of sight into the hills of Jamaica at the height of his manhood powers." Many, with some justification, thought those powers were greatly diminished. It is not clear when or where he died; he simply vanished from the scene. One wonders if he recalled a conversation he had with his gravely ill father, who told him, "Let repenting, believing, everything else, be sought at a proper time; let dying alone be done at dying time." The Christian should have "his preparation for his departure made, and completed in Christ, before death, so as when death should come, he should have nothing to do BUT TO DIE." There were no obituaries in the United States, Canada, Britain, or Jamaica. Years later, Frederick Douglass remembered his old friend and sometime protagonist as witty and gifted, a superior orator and thinker, a man whose intellect "went to the glory of [his] race," a giant among men who was sadly lost to the cause when he moved to Jamaica.[34]

Conclusion

THE QUESTION LINGERS: how to explain a life begun in the obscurity of Maryland slavery and ended, equally obscurely, somewhere in Jamaica? More to the point, how does one explain the arc of Ward's political life, begun with a frontal assault on slavery and Negro-hate in 1840 only to end in 1865 in support of the horrific suppression of a colonial rebellion?

Ward, like most of his contemporaries, was an apostle of Black self-elevation. The Negro and all other oppressed people, Ward and others insisted, had to lift themselves up by their own exertions, or, as Ward put it, they must "cultivate self-respect, dignity of demeanor, refinement of manners, intelligence, morality, and religion." A depressed people, he was fond of saying, "cannot be elevated by any other than themselves." They must learn to read so as to acquaint themselves with "the intelligence of the day." They must cultivate "polished manners and refined sensibilities." They must take the lead in the removal of the oppression they faced. There was no other option. This did not apply only to the Negro. It helps to explain Ward's harsh criticism of the beggars he encountered on his visit to Ireland in 1855. Others might help to lift these burdens by lending encouragement, but more than that they could not do. There was an elitist mid-Victorian element to this approach, but Ward's solution was one to which most of his contemporaries subscribed.

Ward's father had led the way, teaching his son to read and later making sure he attended possibly the best public school open to Black boys in New York City. As a young man, Ward did everything he could to build and expand on those foundations. He read widely, especially in the classics, and sought the assistance of tutors. He was nothing if not ambitious. Aware of his abilities, Ward searched for a place to make his mark. He was teacher, preacher, lecturer, and editor. He also tried his hand at law and medicine. Yet his efforts could not guarantee success in an oppressive system. In the end, all his efforts went unrewarded, for he was, as he himself acknowledged, "neither lawyer, doctor, teacher, divine, nor lecturer." Throughout it all, he left the impression that farming was his natural calling, to till the soil and use the hoe his ultimate ambition. Farming, in a way, became a refuge from the humbling experiences a talented Black man faced trying to make ends meet in a racially hostile country. Looking back on his first thirty-eight years, he laid the blame for his failures on a lack of patience and perseverance as well as misfortune and racial animus. He left young readers with a piece of sage advice: "Find your own appropriate place of duty," he told them. "When you have found it, by all means keep it; if ever tempted to depart from it, return to it as speedily as possible." Ward never found his "place of duty," and that may be the tragedy of his life. He simply came up short.[1]

He tried his hand at teaching in Long Island, Newark, and Poughkeepsie, then turned away from it in 1840, only to return to it in Jamaica in 1865. It did not suffice financially—or at least not enough to keep himself and his family adequately housed and fed.

He was plagued by constant debt that strained his ability to supply his personal needs and those of his family. As far as I can tell,
he owned one modest home in the United States, in South Butler, that he was forced to relinquish in 1842 to meet outstanding
debts. The effort to repay those debts turned him into a wanderer.
He must have lectured and preached in every county in New York.
The pressure of work affected his health. He was frequently ill,
which periodically forced him to abandon the lecture circuit. On
occasion, Gerrit Smith came to the rescue with small gifts and
loans, but these were never enough to meet his needs.

Leaving America seemed a reasonable option. In this respect,
he was not alone. His schoolmate Alexander Crummell also suffered long periods of poverty as he struggled to build a congregation. He finally escaped to England, where he graduated from
Cambridge University before migrating to Liberia. Ward seems
to have had better luck in Jamaica. He preached, farmed, ran a
school with one of his daughters, and owned property. Later in
life, Crummell would return to the United States. Ward never did.
Of all his major contemporaries, he was the only one who did not.
Years after Ward had moved to Jamaica, his cousin Henry Highland Garnet addressed African Americans' unwillingness to acknowledge and support their talented countrymen. Douglass may
have called on Ward and others to return and contribute to the
struggle, but Garnet put the problem differently. One of the finest
and ablest orators of the present age, Ward was "never sustained
by his people." He never "received the wages of a good cook or of
a respectable coachman. Hampered, discouraged and embarrassed,
Ward was driven to take shelter in a strange land. Had his people
stood by him, he would have stood by them." That, in a nutshell,
was the arc of his life, from an enslaved child in Maryland to an
exiled and largely forgotten African American in Jamaica.[2]

Ward's individual and racial strivings went hand in glove with his sustained assault on the temples of slavery and Negro-hate. The Black man had to improve himself to attack the system that kept him down. Ward could be devastatingly critical of those he thought were working against the race's best interests, and that included African Americans who, by their votes, sustained political parties that supported slavery. Only the Liberty Party, he insisted, offered a superior alternative to the Whigs and Democrats. It was the one true anti-slavery political party. Yet there were African Americans who consistently voted against their best interests. They voted for those who trampled the rights of Negroes "under foot, because at some time Mr. so-and-so has given us a dollar, or a day's work, or an old coal while he would revolt at the idea of recognizing our equal manhood, and our inalienable rights." Throughout the 1840s, Black New Yorkers fought over the contending merits of the political parties. Ward was front and center in most of those disputes. They were always edgy, sometimes bitter, and Ward gave as good as he got. He remained the party's stalwart until his departure for Canada. For eleven years, he devoted his time and energy to the party. He was, as one opponent put it derisively, the party's "big gun," called out to do battle everywhere he was needed. He was a formidable opponent. A reporter remembered a debate between Ward and the Reverend Luther Myrick, a Presbyterian minister and a leading figure in the Liberty Party. Myrick, the reporter acknowledged, was an "able man," but he fell into the "hands of a strong man when he came in contact with Samuel Ringgold Ward, with whom it will not do for every man to grapple, though young in years." Another correspondent heard Ward speak at a Liberty Party meeting in Livingston County, New York, and left impressed. "His strokes," he recalled, "are sudden and startling as a clap of thunder—they come like the . . . blast of the tempest."[3]

Ward was never shy about crossing swords with those with

whom he worked. One gets the impression he relished the give-and-take of debates. Sometimes the disagreements were expressed gently, as when he criticized Garnet for his positive remarks about Liberia following its independence. The former colony of the American Colonization Society, Liberia had long been considered a third rail in African American and abolitionist circles. Ward carried on a vigorous and meaningful intellectual exchange with Douglass, debating him about contending methods of attacking slavery. Yet he could be scathing and, some thought, unnecessarily vituperative. When the Committee of Thirteen issued a welcome to the Hungarian exile Lajos Kossuth to New York City, Ward was beside himself. Formed to protect the community in the wake of the Fugitive Slave Law, the committee calculated that the presence of the prominent foreigner would add visibility to the struggle against slavery. Welcoming a man who "knows little and cares less about the black people on this continent" struck Ward as a gesture "wanting in self-respect." Why, he wanted to know, would his people "run after such a man?" Ward had a history of testy exchanges with many of the prominent figures in the city's Black community who made up the leadership of the committee.[4]

Ward asserted that African Americans who belonged to denominations that did not take a stand against slavery were helping the enemies of the race. It pained him that, with but four exceptions, all the Colored churches in New York were in "ecclesiastical connexion with the veriest haters and revilers of our race." By maintaining these connections, Blacks sanctioned "proslavery religion, and invite its votaries to commit against us their deeds of darkness." Black churches should sever connections with these denominations. Yet he was critical of the proliferation of small, unsustainable Black churches that he believed were a drag on the race's aspirations. Small and poor, they survived by begging. This was true even in large cities with substantial Black populations. Why, he wondered, could they not come together to form larger units or even cooperate with liberal White congregations? Rather than preaching the word of God and exploring biblical tenets, the untrained ministers who led these churches spent most of their time whipping their congregations into a frenzy. Like Frederick Douglass, he worried these ministers encouraged their congregations to shout rather than think. Although he preached frequently in Black churches and acknowledged they were vital community centers in the struggle, he never pastored one. In his churches in both South Butler and Cortlandville, Ward and his family were the only Black members of the congregation. He was convinced that both congregations had set an example of interracial fellowship that others should follow. They had taken the lead to invite a Black man to become their pastor. Theirs was an act of defiance against the racial order, and that, Ward believed, had the potential to break down racial barriers. Yet they remained White, not interracial, congregations. Ward was never able to attract Black members to his churches. His first and only Black congregations were those in Kingston and Vickersville, Jamaica. His Kingston congregation was beset by the kinds of internecine squabbles he had preached against in America. We know nothing of his other church. There was little peace in the temple.[5]

With the exception of his mentor Gerrit Smith, Ward was equally critical of Whites with whom he worked in the anti-slavery movement. They tended to be patronizing, he thought, toward their Black colleagues. They loved the Colored man, he observed, "at a distance." While he admitted the movement had done a great deal to promote the cause of emancipation, too many of those involved gave "encouragement to prejudice against color, at the polls, in the social circles, and in the church." In politics, they supported laws that disenfranchised Blacks, and the parties that upheld and sanctioned those laws. When in the company of African Americans, they found it "difficult to see the colored man, though they have spectacles on their noses." They had little to say about segregation in churches. Ward was impatient with pleas to go slowly, to not destroy what together Whites and Blacks had built. If they wished to effect meaningful change, Whites, Ward believed, had to empathize with the plight African Americans faced, to see the world, as Gerrit Smith had done, through Black eyes. "Had you worn a colored skin from October 1817 to June 1840, as I have, in this pseudo-republic," he told White colleagues, "you would have seen through a very different medium." The lack of empathy constrained the movement. As a result, "professed friends" were largely unsympathetic to their demands. Blacks must therefore act for themselves. There were two types of abolitionists. One thought Blacks were "not to be encouraged to be anything more than a sort of halfway set of equals," while the other desired and claimed "for us a full recognition of our equal and inalienable rights." Ward left no doubt with which group he associated. Such fierce criticism discomforted many in the movement. As John Scoble, the former secretary of the British and Foreign Anti-Slavery Society, wrote colleagues on the eve of Ward's departure for England, despite his many gifts and obvious talents, he worried about Ward's "tendency towards a belligerent spirit."[6]

Scoble spoke for many in the movement, Black and White, who were concerned about what they saw as Ward's radical tendencies. William J. Wilson, a regular correspondent to *Frederick Douglass' Paper*, worried that Ward did not always have "proper command over his inner self." Wilson chose not to elaborate. There was no doubt Ward was one of the most effective and gifted orators, but he sometimes discomforted allies with his criticism of their and the movement's shortcomings. Opponents in Jamaica also felt the sting of his criticism. Yet Ward knew how to flatter

White colleagues he admired, especially those who treated him as an equal, and none more so than Gerrit Smith. Sharing the platform at his second meeting in Toronto with Dr. Michael Willis, president of the Anti-Slavery Society of Canada, and a Professor Essen, Ward seemed awestruck. "To be on a platform with men of such positions, talents and erudition, so distinguished and so justly beloved, made me feel about the size of Tom Thumb." Feeling small, even in such distinguished company, was uncharacteristic, for Ward was always aware of his worth and talents. He employed flattery knowingly; he never used it randomly. When he showered praise on those who supported his mission to Britain, it was done with an end in mind: to raise money to aid fugitive slaves in Canada and to help the cause of emancipation in the United States. Yet one gets the distinct impression that the flattery Ward showered on his British hosts was different, both in kind and in substance, than his praise of Whites in the United States.[7]

By the start of his tour to Britain, Ward had come to see himself as a British "subject" entitled to the rights and privileges of the queen's other subjects. In his first weeks in Canada, he had made it clear to all who would listen that he was no longer American. In his move to Canada, he had left all things American behind. America, he told Douglass, with all its racial baggage, was his and he could keep it. There was work to be done in Canada to improve the lot of the Negro, but at least its laws made no racial distinctions. Ward was willing to ignore the fact that the law was not always applied evenly and that racial discrimination surely existed there, as he himself experienced during his first week in his new home. Yet his relocation to Toronto had a profound and almost immediate effect on his views of his statehood. He was now Canadian and, as such, a subject of the British Empire. Jeffrey Kerr-Ritchie has argued, I think correctly, that Ward came to see himself as an "imperial subject." He would live the rest of his life in Canada, Britain, and Jamaica. His relocation, Kerr-Ritchie argues, and his "espousal of equal rights under the law for all colonial subjects" were the measures of Ward's "transformation into an imperial subject."[8]

Yet that helps only partially to explain Ward's position on the Morant Bay Rebellion. He did all he could to stem the tide of the movement, which he considered misguided. Ward remained deeply committed to the notion that the working poor, the peasants and small farmers who had, by their energy and determination, made something of themselves by becoming the backbone of the Jamaican economy, were uninterested in any political upheaval. Those who embraced such a violent course were susceptible to the blandishments of the self-appointed leadership of men such as William Gordon. In this Ward was consistent. His critique of the planter class in Jamaica was as devastating as anything he had leveled against American slaveholders. Neither did the colonial state escape criticism for its failure to provide for its subjects. It was, he insisted, the small farmers and estate laborers who had been responsible for keeping the economy afloat since the end of slavery, yet their requests for assistance from the colonial state were rejected. Nonetheless, Ward held firm to the idea that there was no reason why, with the right organization, they could not ensure their prosperity and that of the colony. Do not be discouraged, he told anyone who would listen. His suggested resolution, however, seems oblivious to the fact that London and its local representatives consistently rejected, out of hand, all efforts by Jamaican estate workers and small farmers to acquire the one thing they needed: land. Ward the farmer should have been more empathetic.

NOTES

Preface

1. Frederick Douglass, *The Life and Times of Frederick Douglass* (1892; repr., New York, 1962), 277; Tim Watson, *Caribbean Culture and British Fiction in the Atlantic World, 1780–1870* (London, 2008), 104.

2. C. Peter Ripley et al., eds., *The Black Abolitionist Papers*, vol. 1, *The British Isles, 1830–1865* (Chapel Hill, 1985), 335–36; I have used the Johnson Publishing Company's reissue of Samuel Ringgold Ward, *Autobiography of a Fugitive Negro: His Anti-Slavery Labors in the United States, Canada, & England* (1855; repr., Chicago, 1970), 17071.

3. James McCune Smith, introduction to *A Memorial Discourse by the Rev Henry Highland Garnet Delivered in the Hall of the House of Representatives, Washington City, D.C. on Sabbath, February 12, 1865, with an Introduction by James McCune Smith, M.D.* (Philadelphia, 1865), 23.

CHAPTER 1. Taking Leave

1. Samuel Ward to Gerrit Smith, South Butler, April 18, 1842, Gerrit Smith Papers, Syracuse University; Samuel Ringgold Ward, *Autobiography of a Fugitive Negro: His Anti-Slavery Labors in the United States, Canada, & England* (1855; repr., Chicago, 1970), 3; Ebner M. Pettit, *Sketches of the History of the Underground Railroad* (Fredonia, NY, 1879), 80–88; *Frederick Douglass Paper*, November 29, 1853.

2. Barbara Jeanne Fields, *Slavery and Freedom on the Middle Ground: Maryland during the Nineteenth Century* (New Haven, 1985), 13, 24.

3. *Autobiography*, 6, 17.

4. R. R. Wright, *The Bishops of the African Methodist Episcopal Church* (n.p., 1963), 350–54.

5. C. Peter Ripley et al., eds., *The Black Abolitionist Papers*, vol. 4, *The United States, 1847–1858* (Chapel Hill, 1991), 234; *A Memorial Discourse by Rev Henry Highland Garnet Delivered in the Hall of the House of Representatives, Washington City, D.C. on Sabbath, February 12, 1865, with an Introduction by James McCune Smith, M.D.* (Philadelphia, 1865), 18–20.

6. On Black communities in southern New Jersey, see Maria Boyton, "Springtown, New Jersey: Explorations in the History and Culture of a Black Rural Settlement" (PhD diss., University of Pennsylvania, 1986), 81; James J. Gigantino, *The Ragged Road to Abolition: Slavery and Freedom in New Jersey, 1775–1865* (Philadelphia, 2015), 216; Christopher P. Barton, "Antebellum African American Settlements in Southern New Jersey," *The African Diaspora Archaeology Network* (December 2009): 3–4, 10.

7. *Autobiography*, 8, 17, 20.

8. Graham Russell Gao Hodges, *David Ruggles: A Radical Black Abolitionist and the Underground Railroad in New York City* (Chapel Hill, 2010), 38; Daniel Perlman, "Organizations of the Free Negroes in New York City, 1800–1860," *Journal of Negro History* 56, no. 3 (July 1971): 184–87; Leslie M. Harris, *In the Shadow of Slavery: African Americans in New York City, 1616–1863* (Chicago, 2003), 124–28; Carla Peterson, *Black Gotham: A Family History of African Americans in Nineteenth Century New York City* (New Haven, 2011), 63, 72, 99; Jane H. Pease and William H. Pease, *Bound with Them in Chains: A Biographical History of the Antislavery Movement* (Westport, CT, 1972), 141; James McCune Smith, introduction to *A Memorial Discourse by the Rev Henry Highland Garnet Delivered in the Hall of the House of Representatives, Washington City, D.C. on Sabbath, February 12, 1865, with an Introduction by James McCune Smith, M.D.* (Philadelphia, 1865).

9. Charles C. Andrews, *History of the New York African Free School* (New York, 1830), 15, 18, 59–61; *Aliened American*, April 9, 1853, Black Abolitionist Papers (microfilm), BAP 14051.

10. *A Memorial Discourse*, 25–26; Wilson Jerimiah Moses, *Alexander Crummell: A Study of Civilization and Discontent* (New York, 1989), 16–17; *Autobiography*, 19.

11. Dorothy B. Porter, "David Ruggles, an Apostle of Human Rights," *Journal of Negro History* 28, no. 1 (January 1943): 23–28; Hodges, *David Ruggles*, 46; *Autobiography*, 22.

12. On Pennington's experiences, see R. J. M. Blackett, *Beating against the Barriers: Biographical Essays in Nineteenth-Century Afro-American History* (Baton Rouge, 1986), 10; *Autobiography*, 22.

13. Harris, *In the Shadow of Slavery*, 192–98; Leslie M. Alexander, *African or American? Black Identity and Political Activism in New York City, 1784–1861* (Urbana, IL, 2008), 85–86; Linda K. Kerber, "Abolitionists and Amalgamators: The New

York City Race Riots of 1834," *New York History* 48, no. 1 (January 1967): 30–31; Lewis Tappan, *The Life of Arthur Tappan* (New York, 1870), 206–14; Graham Russell Hodges, *Root & Branch: African Americans in New York and East Jersey, 1613–1863* (Chapel Hill, 1999), 227–28. On William Howard Day's recollections, see Blackett, *Beating against the Barriers*, 288–89.

14. *Autobiography*, 36–37. On the Kidnapping Club, see Jonathan Daniel Wells, *The Kidnapping Club: Wall Street, Slavery, and Resistance on the Eve of the Civil War* (New York, 2020), 73.

15. Benjamin Quarles, *Black Abolitionists* (New York, 1969), 28–29; C. Peter Ripley et al., eds., *The Black Abolitionist Papers*, vol. 3, *The United States, 1830–1846* (Chapel Hill, 1991), 132–35; *Emancipator*, May 27, 1834; *Weekly Advocate*, February 18, 1837; *Colored American*, August 11, 1838; *Autobiography*, 22–23.

16. *Colored American*, September 28, 1839.

17. *Autobiography*, 38.

18. *Emancipator*, September 12, 1839. On Burnley and his efforts to attract emigrants to the island following the end of the Apprenticeship Scheme in 1838, see Selwyn R. Cudjoe, *The Slave Master of Trinidad: William Hardin Burnley and the Nineteenth Century Atlantic World* (Amherst, MA, 2018), 148–49.

19. *Autobiography*, 38, 41.

CHAPTER 2. Finding His Voice

1. William Wells Brown, *The Black Man: His Antecedents, His Genius and His Achievements* (New York, 1863), 284; *North Star*, February 9, 1849; Hugh C. Humphreys, *"Agitate! Agitate! Agitate!" The Great Fugitive Slave Law Convention and Its Rare Daguerreotype* (Oneida, NY, 1994), 5; John Stauffer, *The Black Hearts of Men: Radical Abolitionists and the Transformation of Race* (Cambridge, MA, 2002), 141.

2. *Fifth Annual Report of the American Anti-Slavery Society, May 8, 1838* (New York, 1838), 35.

3. Samuel Ringgold Ward, *Autobiography of a Fugitive Negro: His Anti-Slavery Labors in the United States, Canada, & England* (1855; repr., Chicago, 1970), 42–43; *Impartial Citizen*, November 2, 1850, in Black Abolitionist Papers (microfilm), BAP 11028; Ward to Smith, Cortlandville, December 24, 1849, Gerrit Smith Papers, Syracuse University; Stauffer, *The Black Hearts of Men*, 39, 68.

4. For Wright, see Jane H. Pease and William H. Pease, *Bound with Them in Chains: A Biographical History of the Antislavery Movement* (Westport, CT, 1972), 218–244. On Leavitt, see Hugh Davis, *Joshua Leavitt: Evangelical Abolitionist* (Baton Rouge, 1990), 168; Stauffer, *The Black Hearts of Men*, 11; C. Peter Ripley et al., eds., *The Black Abolitionist Papers*, vol. 4, *The United States, 1847–1858* (Chapel Hill, 1991), 50.

5. *New York Tribune,* August 27, 1853; *Colored American,* October 9, 1841; *Friends of Man,* May 18, 1841; *Autobiography,* 60.

6. *Autobiography,* 59–64, 70–71.

7. S. R. Ward to J. A. Murray, Geneva, November 3, 1841, Ward to C. Hall, South Butler, April 10, 1843, Ward to Murray, South Butler, February 20, 1843, American Home Missionary Society Papers, Amistad Research Center, Tulane University, in BAP, 15264, 15271, 15272.

8. Ward to Murray, Geneva, November 10, 1843, American Home Missionary Society Papers, in BAP 15401; *The Friend of Man,* February 9, 1841.

9. Ward to Murray, South Butler, May 25, 1843, American Home Missionary Society Papers, in BAP 15273. On the Black population in the county, see Milton C. Sernett, *North Star Country: Upstate New York and the Crusade for African American Freedom* (Syracuse, 2002), 281–82.

10. Ward to Murray, South Butler, February 20, 1843, and August 18, 1843, American Home Missionary Society Papers, in BAP, 15271, 15278.

11. S. R. Ward to Gerrit Smith, South Butler, April 18, 1842, Smith Papers; *Autobiography,* 11, 23.

12. *Autobiography,* 24; *Impartial Citizen,* March 6, April 24, 1850; *New York Tribune,* May 10, 1850; Ripley et al., *The Black Abolitionist Papers,* 4:400–401.

13. *Emancipator,* October 18, 1838; Sernett, *North Star Country,* 104–5; Reinhard O. Johnson, *The Liberty Party, 1840–1848: Antislavery Third Party Politics in the United States* (Baton Rouge, 2009), 11.

14. Betty Fladeland, *James Gillespie Birney: Slaveholder to Abolitionist* (Ithaca, NY, 1955), 182; *Friend of Man,* August 12, 1840.

15. Sernett, *North Star Country,* 115; Johnson, *The Liberty Party,* 19–20, 27; Alan Morton Kraut, "The Liberty Men of New York: Political Abolitionism in New York State, 1840–1848" (PhD diss., Cornell University, 1975), 71.

16. Howard H. Bell, *A Survey of the Negro Convention Movement, 1830–1861* (New York, 1969), 43.

17. Alan M. Kraut and Phyllis F. Field, "Politics versus Principles: The Partisan Response to 'Bible Politics' in New York State," *Civil War History* 25, no. 2 (June 1979): 103–7; Van Gosse, *The First Reconstruction: Black Politics in America from the Revolution to the Civil War* (Chapel Hill, 2021), 421–32.

18. *Religious Record,* July 19, 1849. My thanks to Angie Murphy for this reference.

19. *Impartial Citizen,* March 6, 1850, in BAP 10546; *Autobiography,* 24. My thanks to Sophie Clough and Tabatha Scoville of the Cortland Historical Society for information on the Wards' children.

20. *Impartial Citizen,* January 2, 1850, in BAP 10378; *Liberator,* October 20,

1848; *Autobiography*, 259–60; Benjamin Quarles, *Black Abolitionists* (New York, 1969), 98.

21. *Impartial Citizen*, February 13, 1850, in BAP 10514.

22. *Onondaga Standard*, July 4, 1849; *Religious Recorder*, December 13, 1849; *Autobiography*, 243.

23. *Albany Patriot*, December 16, 1846, in BAP 14757.

24. Johnson, *The Liberty Party*, 65, 72, 85, 149.

25. Oliver Dyer, *Phonographic Report of the Proceedings of the National Free Soil Convention at Buffalo, New York, August 9th and 10th, 1848* (New York, 1848), 6, 8, 21, 27; Johnson, *The Liberty Party*, 85; *Charter Oak*, August 31, 1848; Gosse, *The First Reconstruction*, 449.

26. In the *Amistad* incident, Africans being moved from one port in Cuba to another as part of the Atlantic slave trade rebelled on the ship *Amistad*, killing the captain and others. They ordered the remaining crew to take them back to Africa. The navigator deceived the Africans by tacking along the Atlantic coast; the ship was picked up off Long Island. The issue of whether the Africans should be returned to the Cubans who claimed them or freed became a cause célèbre. Marcus Rediker, *The* Amistad *Rebellion: An Atlantic Odyssey of Slavery and Freedom* (New York, 2012).

27. *North Star*, September 1, 1848. On Dix, see Eric Foner, *Politics and Ideology in the Age of the Civil War* (New York, 1980), 83.

28. *North Star*, September 1, 15, 1848. (Further quotations from Douglass in the next few paragraphs are also taken from this source.) Gosse argues that Douglass "demolished Ward with short sharp explanations of why black men should back the Free Soilers." *The First Reconstruction*, 439–40.

29. Frederick J. Blue, *The Free Soilers: Third Party Politics, 1848–1854* (Urbana, IL, 1973), 118–21; Howard H. Bell, "The Negro Convention, 1848," *Ohio Historical Quarterly* 67 (1958): 357–59; Ward to Gerrit Smith, Cortlandville, August 14, 1848, Smith Papers, in BAP 9140.

30. *Cortland Democrat*, September 9, 1848, in BAP 9207; Ripley et al., *The Black Abolitionist Papers*, 4:27–29, 93–95; *Cortland County Whig*, October 5, 1848, in BAP 9232; *Impartial Citizen*, February 6, 1850.

31. *Impartial Citizen*, September 26, 1849, May 8, 1850; *Onondaga Standard*, September 12, 1849.

32. *North Star* (extra), May 30, 1850.

33. *North Star*, June 27, 1850.

34. *Impartial Citizen*, May 5, June 12, 1850.

35. *North Star*, May 4, 23, 25, 1849. See also Robert K. Burke, *Samuel Ringgold Ward: Christian Abolitionist* (New York, 1995), 36.

36. John Blassingame et al., eds., *The Frederick Douglass Papers*, series 1, vol. 2, *1847–1854* (New Haven, 1982), 235–43; David W. Blight, *Frederick Douglass: Prophet of Freedom* (New York, 2018), 202–4; *Toronto Globe*, May 5, 14, June 1, 1850; *New York Herald,* May 8, 1850; *Independent*, n.d., reprinted in *Montreal Witness,* May 20, 1850, in BAP 10726; Tyler Anbinder, "Isaiah Rynders and the Ironies of Popular Democracy in Antebellum New York," in *Contested Democracy: Freedom, Race, and Power in American History,* edited by Manisha Sinha and Penny Von Eschen (New York, 2007), 32–41; *Philadelphia Ledger*, August 19, 1850. My thanks to Angie Murphy for a copy of the *Ledger* article.

37. *New York Tribune,* May 10, 1850; American and Foreign Anti-Slavery Society, *Tenth Annual Report* (New York, 1849), 15.

38. *Impartial Citizen*, March 14, 1849.

39. Sylvia G. Faibisoff and Abigale S. Kelly, "A Biography of Newspapers in Fourteen New York State Counties," *New York History* 54, no. 1 (January 1973): 94; *North Star*, December 15, 1848, January 5, 1849; *Impartial Citizen*, November 14, 1849, January 2, February 6, 1850.

40. *Impartial Citizen,* October 10, 1849, in BAP 10093.

41. *Impartial Citizen,* September 5, 1849, in BAP 10008, June 12, 1850, in BAP 10758, and September 19, 1849.

42. *Impartial Citizen,* April 11, 1849, in BAP 9692, June 27, 1849, in BAP 9820; *Impartial Citizen,* October 26, 1850, November 21, 1849, in BAP 11007, 10166; *Autobiography*, 40.

43. *Autobiography*, 40.

44. *Impartial Citizen,* September 26, October 24, 1849, March 27, November 2, 1850.

45. Ripley et al., *The Black Abolitionist Papers*, 4:48–51; *Liberator*, April 5, 1850. On the *Creole* case, see Jeffrey Kerr-Ritchie, *Rebellious Passage: The Creole Revolt and America's Coastal Slave Trade* (New York, 2019).

46. *Impartial Citizen,* March 27, April 3, 10, 17, September 14, 1850.

47. *Impartial Citizen,* April 17, September 14, 21, 1850, in BAP 10606, 10867, 10874.

48. *North Star*, September 14, 1849, in BAP 10046.

49. *Impartial Citizen,* October 5, November 2, 1850; *Autobiography*, 77–80. On the Harrisburg incident, see R. J. M. Blackett, *Making Freedom: The Underground Railroad and the Politics of Slavery* (Chapel Hill, 2013), 32–35. See also Derrick R. Spires, *The Practice of Citizenship: Black Politics and Print Culture in the Early United States* (Philadelphia, 2019), 220–21.

50. *Syracuse Standard,* October 7, 1850. My thanks to Angie Murphy for a

copy of the report. Angela F. Murphy, *The Jerry Rescue: The Fugitive Slave Law, Northern Rights, and the American Sectional Crisis* (New York, 2016), 89.

51. *Impartial Citizen*, November 2, 1850, in BAP 11028.

52. *New York Tribune*, July 17, 1850; Ward to Smith, Springfield, Mass., April 30, 1850, Ward to Smith, Boston, July 11, 1850, Smith Papers; *Voice of the Fugitive*, November 5, 1851, in BAP 11993.

53. *Voice of the Fugitive*, July 1, 27, September 9, 1852, in BAP 12865, 12934, 13046. On Smith's land grants, see Stauffer, *The Black Hearts of Men*, 139; *Cortland County Whig*, October 22, 1845, in BAP 1544; *Autobiography*, 43.

54. *Voice of the Fugitive*, July 29, 1852, in BAP 12934. I have not been able to locate transcripts of the case.

55. *Saturday Visiter*, August 16, 1851; *Pittsburgh Gazette*, August 3, 1851; *Autobiography*, 83; *New York Tribune*, August 16, 1851; *Onondaga Standard*, April 10, 1851; James Collins to Gerrit Smith, Chicago, July 25, 1851, Smith Papers.

56. Thomas P. Slaughter, *Bloody Dawn: The Christiana Riot and Racial Violence in the Antebellum North* (New York, 1991), 53, 66, 77; *Autobiography*, 83–84.

57. Ward to Gerrit Smith, South Butler, April 18, 1842, Smith Papers; *Autobiography*, 84.

58. *Impartial Citizen*, April 11, 1849, in BAP 9690.

59. *Autobiography*, 84–89; *The Rev. J. W. Loguen as a Slave and as a Freeman: A Narrative of Real Life* (Syracuse, 1859), 401–15; Murphy, *The Jerry Rescue*, 114–22; Daniel Webster, *The Writings and Speeches of Daniel Webster* (Boston, 1903), 13:419–20.

60. *Voice of the Fugitive*, November 5, 1851, in BAP 11993; Scrapbook 2, A. G. Beman Papers, Beinecke Library, Yale University.

CHAPTER 3. Going into Exile

1. *Pittsburgh Journal*, n.d., quoted in *Pennsylvania Freeman*, October 3, 1850; R. J. M. Blackett, *The Captive's Quest for Freedom: Fugitive Slaves, the 1850 Fugitive Slave Law, and the Politics of Slavery* (New York, 2018), 46–47; John Blassingame et al., eds., *The Frederick Douglass Papers: Speeches, Debates, and Interviews*, series 1, vol. 2, 1847–1854 (New Haven, 1982), 245; Samuel Ringgold Ward, *Autobiography of a Fugitive Negro: His Anti-Slavery Labors in the United States, Canada, & England* (1855; repr., Chicago, 1970), 90; *Voice of the Fugitive*, November 5, 1851, in Black Abolitionist Papers (microfilm), BAP 11993; *First Annual Report: Presented to the Anti-Slavery Society of Canada, March 24th 1852* (Toronto, 1852), 15, 17; Jason H. Silverman, "The American Fugitive Slave in Canada: Myths and Realities," *Southern Studies* (Fall 1980): 215.

2. Ward to G. Whipple, Montreal, October 13, 1851, and Ward to Whipple, Toronto, October 24, 1851, both in AMA Collection, Amistad Research Center, New Orleans, in BAP 30399 and 11981.

3. *Voice of the Fugitive*, November 5, 1851, in BAP 11993; *Frederick Douglass Paper*, December 11, 1851, in BAP 12095; *Autobiography*, 104.

4. *Brown's Toronto Directory, 1856* (Toronto, n.d.); C. Peter Ripley et al., eds., *The Black Abolitionist Papers*, vol. 2, *Canada, 1830–1865* (Chapel Hill, 1986), 318; Robin W. Winks, *The Blacks in Canada: A History* (New Haven, 1971), 180, 253–55.

5. *Voice of the Fugitive*, November 5, 1851, February 26, 1852, in BAP 11993, 12456; *Frederick Douglass Paper*, December 11, 1851, in BAP 12095; *Autobiography*, 95–96; C. Peter Ripley et al., eds., *The Black Abolitionist Papers*, vol. 1, *The British Isles, 1830–1865* (Chapel Hill, 1985), 336–37.

6. *Colored American*, February 6, 20, March 13, 1841. See Jane H. Pease and William H. Pease, *Bound with Them in Chains: A Biographical History of the Antislavery Movement* (Westport, CT, 1972), 115–39, for an essay on Wilson. Jason Howard Silverman, "Unwelcome Guests: American Fugitive Slaves in Canada" (PhD diss., University of Kentucky, 1981), 62–63.

7. *Voice of the Fugitive*, December 17, 1851, February 12, 1852, in BAP 12108, 12413; *Frederick Douglass Paper*, December 12, 1851, in BAP 12095.

8. *Voice of the Fugitive*, May 21, 1851, in Ripley et al., *The Black Abolitionist Papers*, 2:136–37.

9. *Voice of the Fugitive*, February 12, September 9, October 21, November 4, 1852, in BAP 12413, 13042, 13140, and 13201; Victor Ullman, *Martin R. Delany: The Beginning of Black Nationalism* (Boston, 1971), 183–89.

10. *Voice of the Fugitive*, October 21, November 4, 1852, in BAP 12413, 13042, 13140, 13201; Alexander Lovell Murray, "Canada and the Anglo-American Anti-Slavery Movement: A Study in International Philanthropy" (PhD diss., University of Pennsylvania, 1960), 337.

11. *Frederick Douglass Paper*, February 19, 1852, in BAP 12448.

12. *Frederick Douglass Paper*, June 30, 1854; *Autobiography*, 46–53; *Impartial Citizen*, August 15, October 17, November 21, 1849, in BAP 9933, 10111, 10171.

13. *Impartial Citizen*, March 27, April 3, 10, May 22, 1850, in BAP 10728, 10565, 10579, 10593; *Autobiography*, 150–51.

14. *Frederick Douglass Paper*, December 11, 1851, February 12, 1852, in BAP 12095, 12409; *Voice of the Fugitive*, December 17, 1851, March 11, 1852, in BAP 12108, 12492; C. Peter Ripley et al., eds., *The Black Abolitionist Papers*, vol. 4, *The United States, 1847–1858* (Chapel Hill, 1991), 32–33. On Shadd, see Jane Rhodes, *Mary Ann Shadd Cary: The Black Press and Protest in the Nineteenth Century* (Bloomington, IN, 1998).

15. *Autobiography,* 29–33, 46–53, 97; *Friend of Man,* May 18, 1841; *Impartial Citizen,* January 30, 1850, in BAP 10448; John R. McKivigan, *The War against Proslavery Religion: Abolitionism and the Northern Churches, 1830–1865* (Ithaca, NY, 1984), 17.

16. *Voice of the Fugitive,* November 5, 1851, in BAP 12005.

17. *First Annual Report,* 10; Winks, *The Blacks in Canada,* 253; Fred Landon, "The Anti-Slavery Society of Canada," *Journal of Negro History* 4, no. 1 (January 1919): 33–35; Murray, "Canada and the Anglo-American Anti-Slavery Movement," 204, 341; Blassingame et al., *The Frederick Douglass Papers,* series 1, vol. 2, 327–30.

18. *Frederick Douglass Paper,* December 11, 1851, February 19, 1852; *First Annual Report,* 15; *Frederick Douglass Paper,* December 11, 1851, in BAP 12095; *Voice of the Fugitive,* November 19, December 17, 1851, in BAP 12033, 12106; Murray, "Canada and the Anglo-American Anti-Slavery Movement," 341.

19. Ripley et al., *The Black Abolitionist Papers,* 2:256–60; *Voice of the Fugitive,* February 26, August 28, 1852, in BAP 12456, 13005; Rhodes, *Mary Ann Shadd Cary,* 60; Murray, "Canada and the Anglo-American Anti-Slavery Movement," 217–18; *Autobiography,* 99–106.

20. *Second Annual Report Presented to the Anti-Slavery Society of Canada by the Executive Committee, March 23rd, 1853* (Toronto, 1853), 8–9; Silverman, "Unwelcome Guests," 66–67; Rhodes, *Mary Ann Shadd Cary,* 42–43; Ripley et al., *The Black Abolitionist Papers,* 2:147.

21. *Voice of the Fugitive,* February 26, November 4, 1852, in BAP 12456, 13206; Winks, *The Blacks in Canada,* 205–6; *Autobiography,* 150–51; Ripley et al., *The Black Abolitionist Papers,* 2:245–51.

22. Reinhard O. Johnson, *The Liberty Party, 1840–1848: Antislavery Third Party Politics in the United States* (Baton Rouge, 2009): 148–49; Rhodes, *Mary Ann Shadd Cary,* 65–66; Murray, "Canada and the Anglo-American Anti-Slavery Movement," 421–24.

23. Ward to Gerrit Smith, Cortlandville, August 14, 1848, Gerrit Smith Papers, Syracuse University; *Pennsylvania Freeman,* January 6, 1853, in BAP 13839; Ripley et al., *The Black Abolitionist Papers,* 2:256–60.

24. *Provincial Freeman,* March 24, 1853, in BAP 13991.

25. Murray, "Canada and the Anglo-American Anti-Slavery Movement," 429.

26. Murray, "Canada and the Anglo-American Anti-Slavery Movement," 229–30, 429; *Frederick Douglass Paper,* April 22, 29, 1853.

27. *Frederick Douglass Paper,* March 18, 1853, in BAP 13983; *Provincial Freeman,* March 24, 1853, in BAP 13990; Winks, *The Blacks in Canada,* 395–96.

28. *New York Tribune,* quoted in *Frederick Douglass Paper,* May 13, 1853.

29. *Aliened American,* April 9, 1853, in BAP 14051.

CHAPTER 4. Going on a Mission

1. C. Peter Ripley et al., eds., *The Black Abolitionist Papers*, vol. 4, *United States, 1847–1858* (Chapel Hill, 1991), 142–44; Leslie M. Harris, *In the Shadow of Slavery: African Americans in New York City, 1626–1863* (Chicago, 2003), 239; Philip S. Foner, *Organized Labor and the Black Worker, 1619–1973* (New York, 1974), 11; *Anti-Slavery Bugle*, July 27, 1850, in Black Abolitionist Papers (microfilm), BAP 17953.

2. Alexander Lovell Murray, "Canada and the Anglo-American Anti-Slavery Movement: A Study in International Philanthropy" (PhD diss., University of Pennsylvania, 1960), 232; Samuel Ringgold Ward, *Autobiography of a Fugitive Negro: His Anti-Slavery Labors in the United States, Canada & England* (1855; repr., Chicago, 1970), 241.

3. R. J. M. Blackett, *Building an Antislavery Wall: Black Americans in the Atlantic Abolitionist Movement, 1830–1860* (Baton Rouge, 1983), 136–37; Wilson Jerimiah Moses, *Alexander Crummell: A Study of Civilization and Discontent* (New York, 1989), 55–57.

4. John Scoble to the Executive Committee, New York, April 7, 1853, Anti-Slavery Papers, University of Oxford; Murray, "Canada and the Anglo-American Anti-Slavery Movement," 230–31; *Autobiography*, 171. On Scoble in Canada, see Robin W. Winks, *The Blacks in Canada: A History* (New Haven, 1971), 201–2; Philip S. Foner, *The Life and Writings of Frederick Douglass*, vol. 1, *The Early Years* (New York, 1950), 143–44.

5. *British Banner*, September 28, 1853; *Religious Recorder*, June 12, 1851; *Autobiography*, 5–6, 273.

6. Tappan Diary, entry April 6, 19, 1853, Tappan Papers, Library of Congress.

7. *Autobiography*, 161.

8. *Autobiography*, 159–64.

9. On Douglass's experience, see David W. Blight, *Frederick Douglass: Prophet of Freedom* (New York, 2018); on Brown's daughters, Ezra Greenspan, *William Wells Brown: An African American Life* (New York, 2014).

10. *Autobiography*, 164–65. On Thackeray's first tour of the United States, see M. D. McInnis, *Slaves Waiting for Sale: Abolitionist Art and the American Slave Trade* (Chicago, 2011), 17–22.

11. *Autobiography*, 165–69.

12. C. Peter Ripley et al., eds., *The Black Abolitionist Papers*, vol. 1, *The British Isles, 1830–1865* (Chapel Hill, 1985), 335–36; *Autobiography*, 170–75.

13. Betty Fladeland, *Men and Brothers: Anglo-American Antislavery Cooperation* (Urbana, IL, 1972), 351–52; *Liberator*, June 3, 1853; *Autobiography*, 263.

14. Ripley et al., *The Black Abolitionist Papers*, 1:340–41; Greenspan, *William Wells Brown*, 289–90; William Edward Farrison, *William Wells Brown: Author and Reformer* (Chicago, 1969), 213; *Liberator*, June 3, 1853.

15. *Nonconformist*, May 18, 1853, in BAP 14151. See the Congregational Union's *Year Books* for 1853, 1854, and 1855 (all published in London).

16. *British Banner*, July 6, 1853; *Temperance Chronicle*, July 1853.

17. Harriet Beecher Stowe, *Sunny Memories of Foreign Lands* (Boston, 1854), 1:105; *Halifax Courier*, March 17, 1855.

18. *Autobiography*, 173.

19. *Anti-Slavery Reporter*, July 1, 1853; Ripley et al., *The Black Abolitionist Papers*, 1:362–65; *Nonconformist*, June 29, 1853, in BAP 14262; *Autobiography*, 171–73; Murray, "Canada and the Anglo-American Anti-Slavery Movement," 393.

20. *Cheltenham Free Press*, September 26, November 26, 1853; *Frederick Douglass Paper*, November 18, 1853, in BAP 14612; *Patriot*, October 3, 1853, in BAP 14523; *Birmingham Mercury*, October 22, 1853; *Montrose, Arbroth, and Brechin Review*, December 23, 1853; *Dundee, Perth, and Cuper Advertiser*, December 20, 1853; *Anti-Slavery Reporter*, December 1, 1853; *British Banner*, July 6, 1853, February 12, 1854; Thomas Raffles to Peter Bolton, Liverpool, November 1, 1853, Anti-Slavery Papers, Oxford University; *Autobiography*, 174, 225–27, 234–36; C. Duncan Rice, *The Scots Abolitionists, 1833–1861* (Baton Rouge, 1981), 148.

21. *Cheltenham Free Press*, November 26, 1853; *Autobiography*, 186, 269–71.

22. *Glasgow Examiner*, November 12, 1853.

23. John Blassingame et al., eds., *The Frederick Douglass Papers*, series 1, vol. 1, 1841–46 (New Haven, 1979), 269–70.

24. *British Banner*, reprinted in *Liberator*, September 16, 1853, in BAP 14502; *Autobiography*, 227.

25. *Anti-Slavery Reporter*, May 1854; *British Banner*, February 22, 1854; *Provincial Freeman*, March 25, April 15, 1854, in BAP 14959, 15032; *Liberator*, September 16, 1853, in BAP 14502.

26. Ripley et al., *The Black Abolitionist Papers*, 1:392.

27. *Nonconformist*, May 17, 1854; *British Banner*, May 10, 24, 1854; *British Banner*, May 10, 1854; *Missionary Record*, May 1853.

28. *British Banner*, May 17, 1854.

29. Robert T. Lewit, "Indian Missions and Antislavery Sentiment: A Conflict of Evangelical and Humanitarian Ideas," *Mississippi Valley Historical Review* 1 (1963): 42; *British Banner*, May 17, 1854; *Anti-Slavery Reporter*, December 1, 1854; *Autobiography*, 171, 179, 198, 208, 217.

30. *Frederick Douglass Paper*, June 26, 1854, in BAP 15308; Fladeland, *Men and Brothers*, 320–21; Louis Chamerovzow, ed., *Slave Life in Georgia: A Narrative of the*

Life, Sufferings, and Escape of John Brown, a Fugitive Slave Now in England (London, 1855), 31–44; Philip M. Hamer, "British Consuls and the Negro Seamen Acts, 1850–1860," *Journal of Southern History* 1, no. 2 (May 1935): 138–68.

31. *Manchester Examiner and Times*, August 2, 1854, in BAP 15478; *Anti-Slavery Advocate*, September 1, 1854, in BAP 15626; *Anti-Slavery Reporter*, January 1, 1855; *Boston and Louth Gazette and Lincolnshire Advertiser*, December 13, 1854.

32. *Bradford Observer*, June 1, 1854; *Provincial Freeman*, July 1, 1854, in BAP 15344; *Report of the Proceedings of the Anti-Slavery Conference and Public Meeting Held in Manchester on August 1, 1854* (London, 1854), 21; *Liberator*, August 25, 1854; *Anti-Slavery Reporter*, September 1, 1854. For the dispute with Barker, see Clare Taylor, *British and American Abolitionists* (Edinburgh, 1975), 409. The best work on Barker remains Betty Fladeland, *Abolitionists and Working-Class Problems in the Age of Industrialization* (Baton Rouge, 1984), 132–70.

33. *North Wales Chronicle*, August 19, 1854; *Caernarvon and Denbigh Herald*, August 19, 1854; *The Welshman*, August 25, 1854; *Autobiography*, 260–67; Daniel G. Williams, *Black Skin, Blue Books: African Americans and Wales, 1845–1945* (Cardiff, 2012), 38. Daniel Williams kindly shared with me reports in two Welsh-language newspapers of a meeting at the Welsh Calvinist Chapel in London, just after Ward's return from Wales, to raise money for the conversion of Jews in Jerusalem. Ward was one of the two main speakers. My thanks also to Wyn James.

34. *Impartial Citizen*, January 30, October 5, 1850; Ripley et al., *The Black Abolitionist Papers*, 1:393; *Frederick Douglass Paper*, June 23, 1854, in BAP 15308.

35. Douglas Cameron Riach, "Ireland and the Crusade against Slavery, 1830–1860" (PhD diss., University of Edinburgh, 1975), 396; *Anti-Slavery Reporter*, September 1, 1854; *Provincial Freeman*, September 23, 1854, in BAP 15734.

36. Douglas Hall, *Free Jamaica, 1838–1865: An Economic History* (New Haven, 1959), 126–27; *Anti-Slavery Reporter*, June 1, 1854; *British Banner*, May 24, 1854; *Provincial Freeman*, July 1, 1854, in BAP 15348; *Autobiography*, 209; *Voice of the Fugitive*, September 24, 1851; *Bristol Post*, September 1, 1862. Bourne had established the Jamaica Cotton Company, which ran an experimental program in three eastern parishes on Jamaica. Floyd J. Miller, *The Search for a Black Nationality: Black Colonization and Emigration, 1787–1863* (Urbana, IL, 1975), 111–13.

37. *Boston and Louth Guardian and Lincolnshire Advertiser*, December 13, 1854; *Chelmsford Chronicle*, December 15, 1854; *Autobiography*, 272–73; West Indies, *Extracts from the Journal of John Candler Whilst Travelling in Jamaica, Part I* (London, 1841), 19–22; Hall, *Free Jamaica*, 34; Fladeland, *Men and Brothers*, 251, 347–48; Annie Heloise Abel and Frank J. Klingberg, eds., *A Side-light on Anglo-American Relations, 1839–1858* (1927; repr., New York, 1970), 4–5, 212, 338; Catherine Hall, *Civilising*

Subjects: Metropole and Colony in the English Imagination, 1830–1867 (Chicago, 2002), 353–54.

38. John Blassingame et al., eds., *The Frederick Douglass Papers*, vol. 2, *1847–54* (New Haven, 1982), 499–512.

39. *National Anti-Slavery Standard*, July 2, 1840; *Frederick Douglass Paper*, February 23, 1855, in BAP 16401; Ripley et al., *The Black Abolitionist Papers*, 1:412–14; Taylor, *British and American Abolitionists*, 412. On Pillsbury, see Stacey M. Robertson, *Parker Pillsbury: Radical Abolitionist, Male Feminist* (Ithaca, 2000).

40. *Autobiography*, 186–97.

41. *Frederick Douglass Paper*, April 20, 1854.

42. Philip S. Foner, *The Life and Writings of Frederick Douglass* (New York, 1950), 2:359–62.

43. *Autobiography*, 272–73; *Provincial Freeman*, June 6, July 8, 1854; *National Anti-Slavery Standard*, July 22, 1854.

44. *Autobiography*, 247–48; *Sligo Chronicle*, June 9, 1855. See also Christine Kenealy's chapter on Ward in her *Black Abolitionists in Ireland* (London, 2020).

45. *Autobiography*, 248–49; *Limerick Herald*, June 9, 1855. Ward first mentions Martin in *Autobiography*, 6.

46. *Autobiography*, 251–59; Jeffrey R. Kerr-Ritchie, "Samuel Ward and the Making of an Imperial Subject," *Slavery & Abolition* 33, no. 2 (2012).

47. Quoted in Riach, "Ireland and the Crusade against Slavery," 440; William S. McFeely, *Frederick Douglass* (New York, 1991), 126–27; *Autobiography*, 237–38. Kenealy, *Black Abolitionists in Ireland*, is much more critical of Ward's views on the Irish than I am. She insists they suggest a "deep-rooted prejudice," a "narrowness and elitism" that shows his humanity was selective.

48. *Autobiography*, 238.

49. *Patriot*, October 3, 1853, in BAP 14523; *Impartial Citizen*, July 11, 1849, in BAP 9854. See also Ward's lengthy editorial "The Despised Poor" in *Impartial Citizen*, February 28, 1849.

50. Elisa Tamarkin, "Black Anglophilia; or, The Sociability of Antislavery," *American Literary History* 14, no. 3 (Autumn 2002): 445–50; *Anti-Slavery Reporter*, July 1, 1853; *Autobiography*, 180–85; *Liberator*, July 22, 1853, in BAP 14358. See also Ward's criticism of Richard Cobden's views on the slave trade in *British Banner*, June 21, 1854, in BAP 15301.

51. *Autobiography*, xiii–xiv; *Friend*, January 1856; *Christian Weekly News*, n.d., in *Anti-Slavery Reporter*, February 1, 1856.

52. Pillsbury to S. May Jr., Manchester, December 7, 1855, Anti-Slavery Papers, Boston Public Library; *Anti-Slavery Advocate*, February 1, 1856.

53. *Christian Witness* 13, no. 147 (March 1856).

54. *Frederick Douglass Paper*, January 6, 1854; Ripley et al., *The Black Abolitionist Papers*, 1:336; Emily Ward to Gerrit Smith, Toronto, September 14, 1855, Gerrit Smith Papers, Syracuse University; *Sixth Annual Report of the Anti-Slavery Society of Canada Presented at the Annual Meeting Held on the 29th April 1857* (Toronto, 1857), 14; Murray, "Canada and the Anglo-American Anti-Slavery Movement," 274–77.

55. William Baynham to Rev. Carlisle, Toronto, December 10, 1855, Thomas Henning to Dear Sir, Toronto, December 10, 1855, John Candler to Chamerovzow, Chelmsford, November 20, 1855, Anti-Slavery Papers, University of Oxford; Murray, "Canada and the Anglo-American Anti-Slavery Movement," 274–77.

56. *Autobiography*, 175, 205–6, 268–69.

CHAPTER 5. Turning His Back on North America

1. On De Grasse, see Craig D. Townsend, *Faith in Their Own Color: Black Episcopalians in Antebellum New York City* (New York, 2005), 64–68. For Garnet's appointment, see the series of letters from Andrew Somerville, 1851–56, in the United Presbyterian Church Papers, National Library of Scotland, Edinburgh; *The Slave*, July and November 1852; *Missionary Record*, May 1854.

2. On Douglass, see Julie Winch, *Philadelphia's Black Elite: Activism, Accommodation, and the Struggle for Autonomy, 1787–1848* (Philadelphia, 1988), 49–50; *Union Missionary*, June 1846; *National Anti-Slavery Standard*, May 14, 1846, April 20, 1848; *Anti-Slavery Reporter*, August 1, 1850. On Pennington, see *Kelso Chronicle*, January 3, 1851. See also R. J. M. Blackett, *Beating against the Barriers: Biographical Essays in Nineteenth-Century Afro-American History* (Baton Rouge, 1989), 33–34.

3. Samuel Ringgold Ward, *Autobiography of a Fugitive Negro: His Anti-Slavery Labors in the United States, Canada, & England* (1855; repr., Chicago, 1970), 272–73; William Wemyss Anderson, *Jamaica and the Americas* (New York, 1851); William Wemyss Anderson, *A Description of the History of the Island of Jamaica* (Kingston, 1851). Gale Kenny concludes that "fewer than two thousand" black Americans went to Jamaica in the years after 1838. Gale L. Kenny, "Manliness and Manifest Destiny: Jamaica and African American Emigration in the 1850s," *Journal of the Civil War Era* 2, no. 2 (June 2012): 154–56.

4. For coverage of the Anderson case, see R. J. M. Blackett, *Making Freedom: The Underground Railroad and the Politics of Slavery* (Chapel Hill, 2013), 22–31; Edward B. Rugemer, "Robert Monroe Harrison, British Abolition, Southern Anglophobia and Texas Annexation," *Slavery & Abolition* 28, no. 2 (August 2007): 172.

5. *Autobiography*, 20; *Voice of the Fugitive*, February 12, 1852, in BAP 12413; Swithin Wilmot, "The Road to Morant Bay: Politics in Free Jamaica, 1838–1865,"

Journal of Caribbean History 50, no. 1 (2016): 2; *Provincial Freeman*, March 1, 1856, in Black Abolitionist Papers (microfilm), BAP 17602.

6. Ward's letter to the editor of the *Franklin Visitor*, reprinted in the *Weekly Anglo-African*, August 27, 1859, in BAP 20920. Ward surely underestimated the size of the population and overestimated the miles of railroad.

7. Catherine Hall, *Civilising Subjects: Metropole and Colony in the English Imagination, 1830–1867* (Chicago, 2002), 246–48; Robert J. Stewart, *Religion and Society in Post-Emancipation Jamaica* (Knoxville, TN, 1992), 93–94; Ronald K. Burke, *Samuel Ringgold Ward: Christian Abolitionist* (New York, 1995), 58; Jeffrey Kerr-Ritchie, *Rites of August First: Emancipation Day in the Black Atlantic World* (Baton Rouge, 2007), 199; [Samuel Oughton], *Jamaica: Who Is to Blame? By a Thirty Year Resident* (London, 1866), 69–70.

8. On the reduced size of the congregation, see Tim Watson, *Caribbean Culture and British Fiction in the Atlantic World, 1780–1870* (New York, 2008), 137; Great Britain, *Parliamentary Papers (House of Commons), 1866 (no. 3595)*, vol. 51, *Papers Relative to the Affairs of Jamaica*, 558; Ward v. John William Dick, Heard at Home Circuit Court, Kingston, JA 1A/5/1/04, p. 198, Home Circuit Court Indictment Register for Kingston and St. Andrew, 1856–62, Jamaica Archives. My thanks to Jonathan Dalby for pointing me to the court transcript.

9. *Impartial Citizen*, September 5, 1849, May 8, 1850.

10. *Syracuse Standard*, March 2, 6, 28, 1857; *New York Tribune*, April 15, 1857. Frederick Douglass's comments, printed in *Onondaga Standard*, March 23, 1857; Oughton, *Jamaica*, 69–70.

11. On Emily and Ringgold's departure for Kingston, see the letter from Garnet and J. W. Duffin to Gerrit Smith in C. Peter Ripley et al., eds., *The Black Abolitionist Papers*, vol. 4, *The United States, 1847–1858* (Chapel Hill, 1991), 399; *Weekly Anglo-African*, August 20, 1859, in BAP 20865.

12. The article was reprinted in two installments in the *Weekly Anglo-African*, August 20, 27, 1859, in BAP 20865, 20920.

13. James M. Phillippo, *Jamaica: Its Past and Present State* (London, 1843), 186.

14. Hall, *Civilising Subjects*, 226–27; Thomas C. Holt, *The Problem of Freedom: Race, Labor, and Politics in Jamaica and Britain, 1832–1938* (Kingston, 1992), 264–65, 274; Douglas Hall, *Free Jamaica, 1838–1865: An Economic History* (New Haven, 1959), 242.

15. Underhill's letter is reprinted in Oughton, *Jamaica*, 18–19; Holt, *The Problem of Freedom*, 270–73.

16. Gad Heuman, *"The Killing Time": The Morant Bay Rebellion in Jamaica* (London, 1994), 48–49; Eric Williams, *British Historians and the West Indies* (London, 1966), 116; Holt, *The Problem of Freedom*, 278.

17. Heuman, *"The Killing Time,"* 52.

18. Gad Heuman, *Between Black and White: Race, Politics, and the Free Coloreds in Jamaica, 1792–1865* (Westport, CT, 1981), 61, 176; Williams, *British Historians and the West Indies,* 113–14; Wilmot, "The Road to Morant Bay," 7–8; Great Britain, *Parliamentary Papers (House of Commons), 1866,* 556.

19. Swithin Wilmot, "The Politics of Samuel Clarke: Black Political Martyr in Jamaica, 1851–1865," *Jamaican Historical Review* 19 (1996): 18, 27; Watson, *Caribbean Culture and British Fiction,* 140; Great Britain, *Parliamentary Papers (House of Commons), 1866,* 230–31.

20. See a copy of the resolutions in Great Britain, *Parliamentary Papers (House of Commons), 1866,* 228–29. On Menard, see Tim Watson, "The Caribbean Career of John Willis Menard," *Journal of Caribbean History* 50, no. 2 (2016): 171, 176, 190–91; and Philip W. Magness and Sebastian Page, *Colonization after Emancipation: Lincoln and the Movement for Black Resettlement* (Columbia, MO, 2011), 100–101.

21. The final set of resolutions adopted at the meeting and Georges's letter are in Great Britain, *Parliamentary Papers (House of Commons), 1866,* 229–32.

22. Wilmot, "The Road to Morant Bay," 8, 13; Williams, *British Historians and the West Indies,* 116–17; Heuman, *"The Killing Time,"* 58.

23. Heuman, *"The Killing Time,"* 58–59; Great Britain, *Parliamentary Papers (House of Commons), 1866,* 555–56.

24. Heuman, *"The Killing Time,"* 3–14, 131–43, 147–50; Stewart, *Religion and Society in Post-Emancipation Jamaica,* 153–54; Wilmot, "The Road to Morant Bay," 11.

25. Great Britain, *Parliamentary Papers (House of Commons), 1866, Report of the Jamaica Royal Commission,* 556–58; Wilmot, "The Politics of Samuel Clarke," 28.

26. Bernard Semmel, *Jamaican Blood and Victorian Conscience* (Westport, CT, 1962), 15–28; Bridget Brereton, *Law, Justice and Empire: The Colonial Career of John Gorrie, 1829–1892* (Kingston, 1997), 36.

27. Great Britain, *Parliamentary Papers: Papers Laid before the Royal Commission of Inquiry by Governor Eyre* (1866), 264–66.

28. Wilmot, "The Politics of Samuel Clarke."

29. Samuel R. Ward, *Reflections upon the Gordon Rebellion* (n.p., 1866), 6–8. See *Cheltenham Free Press,* November 26, 1853, for his use of Chronicles 4:40. See also Watson, *Caribbean Culture and British Fiction,* 126–27.

30. Great Britain, *Parliamentary Papers (House of Commons), 1866, Report of the Jamaica Royal Commission,* 554–59.

31. Holt, *The Problem of Freedom,* 304; Heuman, *"The Killing Time,"* 170; Brereton, *Law, Justice and Empire,* 34, 45.

32. *The Times,* quoted in Brereton, *Law, Justice and Empire,* 53; Semmel, *Ja-*

maican Blood and Victorian Conscience, 142–76; *Address to His Excellency Edward John Eyre, Esquire, etc. etc., 1865, 1866* (Kingston, 1866), 63; Watson, *Caribbean Culture and British Fiction,* 114.

33. *Jamaica Gleaner,* May 25, 1867; Watson, *Caribbean Culture and British Fiction,* 153.

34. Vincent Harding, foreword to Ward, *Autobiography,* vii; Frederick Douglass, *The Life and Times of Frederick Douglass* (1892; repr., New York, 1962), 277.

Conclusion

1. Samuel Ringgold Ward, *Autobiography of a Fugitive Negro: His Anti-Slavery Labors in the United States, Canada, & England* (1855; repr., Chicago, 1970), 25.

2. *Impartial Citizen,* March 14, 1849, in Black Abolitionist Papers (microfilm), BAP 9582; *Weekly Anglo African,* January 26, 1861, in BAP 23397; *Autobiography,* 25.

3. *Colored American,* September 19, 1840, in BAP 13411; *Emancipator,* September 2, 1844.

4. *Frederick Douglass Paper,* February 12, 1852, in BAP 12409.

5. *Impartial Citizen,* March 14, 1849, in BAP 9582.

6. *National Anti-Slavery Standard,* July 2, 1840, in BAP 4736; C. Peter Ripley et al., eds., *The Black Abolitionist Papers,* vol. 3, *The United States, 1830–1846* (Chapel Hill, 1991), 340–41; C. Peter Ripley et al., eds., *The Black Abolitionist Papers,* vol. 1, *The British Isles, 1830–1865* (Chapel Hill, 1985), 391; John Scoble to the Executive Committee, New York, April 7, 1853, Anti-Slavery Papers, University of Oxford.

7. *Voice of the Fugitive,* December 17, 1851, in BAP 12106.

8. Jeffrey Kerr-Ritchie, *Freedom Seekers: Essays on Comparative Emancipation* (Baton Rouge, 2013), 87–93; Jeffrey Kerr-Ritchie, "Samuel Ward and the Making of an Imperial Subject," *Slavery & Abolition* 33, no. 2 (2012).

INDEX